Edexcel GCSE

Mathematics B
Modular
Foundation

Student Book
Unit 3

Series Director: Keith Pledger
Series Editor: Graham Cumming

Authors:
Chris Baston
Julie Bolter
Gareth Cole
Gill Dyer
Michael Flowers
Karen Hughes
Peter Jolly
Joan Knott
Jean Linsky
Graham Newman
Rob Pepper
Joe Petran
Keith Pledger
Rob Summerson
Kevin Tanner
Brian Western

A PEARSON COMPANY

Published by Pearson Education Limited, a company incorporated in England and Wales, having its registered office at Edinburgh Gate, Harlow, Essex, CM20 2JE. Registered company number: 872828

Edexcel is a registered trademark of Edexcel Limited

Text © Chris Baston, Julie Bolter, Gareth Cole, Gill Dyer, Michael Flowers, Karen Hughes, Peter Jolly, Joan Knott, Jean Linsky, Graham Newman, Rob Pepper, Joe Petran, Keith Pledger, Rob Summerson, Kevin Tanner, Brian Western and Pearson Education Limited 2010

The rights of Chris Baston, Julie Bolter, Gareth Cole, Gill Dyer, Michael Flowers, Karen Hughes, Peter Jolly, Joan Knott, Jean Linsky, Graham Newman, Rob Pepper, Joe Petran, Keith Pledger, Rob Summerson, Kevin Tanner and Brian Western to be identified as the authors of this Work have been asserted by them in accordance with the Copyright, Designs and Patent Act, 1988.

First published 2010

12 11 10
10 9 8 7 6 5 4 3 2

British Library Cataloguing in Publication Data

A catalogue record for this book is available from the British Library
ISBN 978 1 84690 806 4

Typeset by Tech-Set Ltd, Gateshead
Picture research by Rebecca Sodergren
Printed in Great Britain at Scotprint, Haddington

Acknowledgements
The publisher would like to thank the following for their kind permission to reproduce their photographs:
(Key: b-bottom; c-centre; l-left; r-right; t-top)

4Corners Images: Schmid Reinhard 135tr; **Alamy Images:** Asia Images Group Pte Ltd 69, Chris Rout 134cr, Sinibomb Images 133; **Corbis:** Artiga Photo 135tc; **Getty Images:** Digital Vision 180l, Hisham Ibrahim 134bl, Oscar Mattsson 134c, Martin Rose 48, Terry Vine 121; **iStockphoto:** 134r, Anthony Collins 183b, Joe Gough 183c, HannamariaH 135bc, Wayne Howard 182, laughingmango 183t, Mammamaart 134cl, Susan McKenzie 135br, mm88 134bc, Katherine Moffitt 134tc, muharrem öner 135tl, redmal 62, Brian sullivan 134br, Natalia Vasina Vladimirovna 134tr, josef volavka 13; **Oxfam:** 40; **Pearson Education Ltd:** Corbis 134tl; **Peter Bull:** 100; **Photolibrary.com:** Brand X 22, Angelo Cavalli 161, Amish Patel 90; **Rex Features:** Alisdair Macdonald 135bl; **Science Photo Library Ltd:** Adam Hart-Davis 1; **Shutterstock:** Martin Kemp 180

All other images © Pearson Education

Disclaimer
This material has been published on behalf of Edexcel and offers high-quality support for the delivery of Edexcel qualifications.
This does not mean that the material is essential to achieve any Edexcel qualification, nor does it mean that it is the only suitable material available to support any Edexcel qualification. Edexcel material will not be used verbatim in setting any Edexcel examination or assessment. Any resource lists produced by Edexcel shall include this and other appropriate resources.

Copies of official specifications for all Edexcel qualifications may be found on the Edexcel website: www.edexcel.com

Contents

About this book

All set to make the grade!

Edexcel GCSE Mathematics is specially written to help you get your best grade in the exams.
Remember this is a calculator unit.

Section objectives show what you'll be learning.

Recap with a skills check at the start of a section – make sure you're up to speed.

Crystal-clear worked examples – step-by-step guides to answering questions correctly, with helpful hints and reminders.

Loads of practice to help you feel secure before you move on.

Graded questions – so you know what you're achieving.

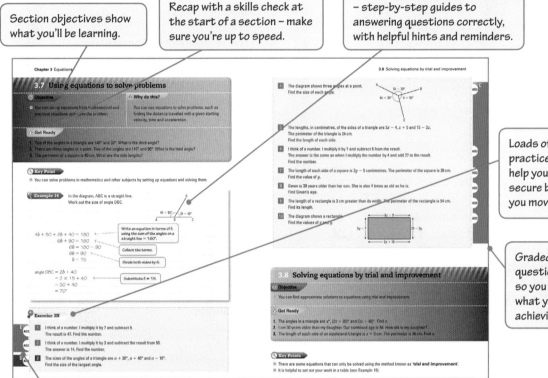

Full coverage of the new-style assessment objective questions – A02 and A03.

'Focus on A02/3' pages demystify the new assessment objectives.

A fully worked example of an A02/3 question… …makes other A02/3 questions on the same topic easy to tackle.

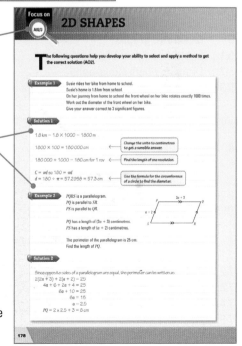

And:

- A pre-check at the start of each chapter helps you recall what you know.

- Functional elements highlighted – within ordinary exercises and on dedicated pages – so you can spend focused time polishing these skills.

- End-of-chapter graded review exercises consolidate your learning and include past exam paper questions indicated by the month and year.

About ActiveTeach

Use **ActiveTeach** to view and present the course on screen with exciting interactive content.

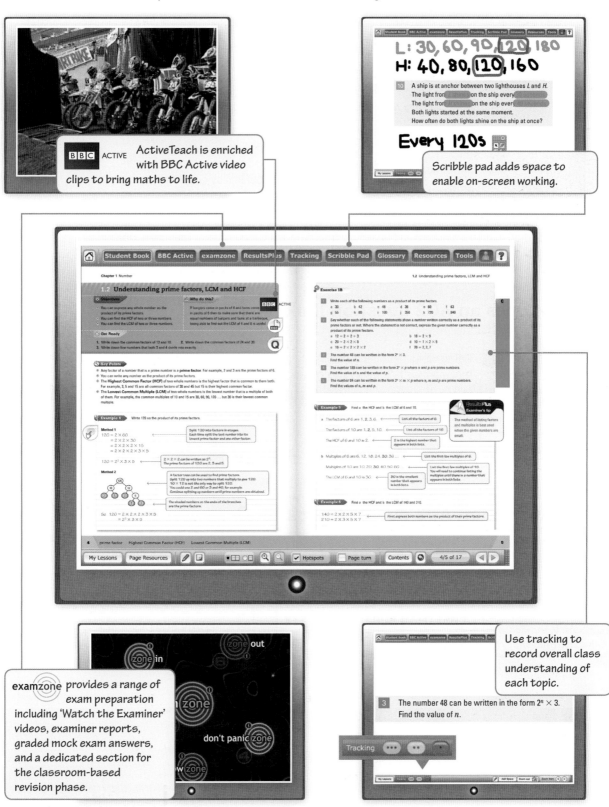

ActiveTeach is enriched with BBC Active video clips to bring maths to life.

Scribble pad adds space to enable on-screen working.

examzone provides a range of exam preparation including 'Watch the Examiner' videos, examiner reports, graded mock exam answers, and a dedicated section for the classroom-based revision phase.

Use tracking to record overall class understanding of each topic.

About Assessment Objectives

Assessment Objectives define the types of question that are set in the exam.

Assessment Objective	What it is	What this means	Range % of marks in the exam
A01	**Recall** and use knowledge of the prescribed content.	Standard questions testing your knowledge of each topic.	45-55
A02	**Select** and apply mathematical methods in a range of contexts.	Deciding what method you need to use to get to the correct solution to a contextualised problem.	25-35
A03	**Interpret** and analyse problems and generate strategies to solve them.	Solving problems by deciding how and explaining why.	15-25

The proportion of marks available in the exam varies with each Assessment Objective. Don't miss out, make sure you know how to do AO2 and AO3 questions!

What does an AO2 question look like?

D AO2

This just needs you to
(a) read and understand the question and
(b) decide how to get the correct answer.

16 Katie wants to buy a car.
She decides to borrow £3500 from her father. She adds interest of 3.5% to the loan and this total is the amount she must repay her father. How much will Katie pay back to her father in total?

What does an AO3 question look like?

D AO3

Here you need to read and analyse the question. Then use your mathematical knowledge to solve this problem.

17 Rashida wishes to invest £2000 in a building society account for one year. The Internet offers two suggestions. Which of these two investments gives Rashida the greatest return?

CHESTMAN BUILDING SOCIETY	DUNSTAN BUILDING SOCIETY
£3.50 per month Plus **1% bonus** at the end of the year	**4%** per annum. Paid yearly by cheque

Focus on
A02/3

We give you extra help with AO2 and AO3 on pages 176–179.

vi

About functional elements

What does a question with functional maths look like?

Functional maths is about being able to apply maths in everyday, real-life situations.

GCSE Tier	Range % of marks in the exam
Foundation	30-40
Higher	20-30

The proportion of functional maths marks in the GCSE exam depends on which tier you are taking. Don't miss out, make sure you know how to do functional maths questions!

In the exercises...

D A03 **20** The Wildlife Trust are doing a survey into the number of field mice on a farm of size 240 acres. They look at one field of size 6 acres. In this field they count 35 field mice.

a Estimate how many field mice there are on the whole farm.

b Why might this be an unreliable estimate?

> You need to read and understand the question. Follow your plan.
>
> Think what maths you need and plan the order in which you'll work.
>
> Check your calculations and make a comment if required.

...and on our special functional maths pages: 180–183!

Quality of written communication

There will be marks in the exam for showing your working 'properly' and explaining clearly. In the exam paper, such questions will be marked with a star (*). You need to:

◉ use the correct mathematical notation and vocabulary, to show that you can communicate effectively

◉ organise the relevant information logically.

ResultsPlus

ResultsPlus features combine exam performance data with examiner insight to give you more information on how to succeed. ResultsPlus tips in the **student books** show students how to avoid errors in solutions to questions.

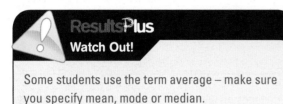

ResultsPlus
Watch Out!

Some students use the term average – make sure you specify mean, mode or median.

This warns you about common mistakes and misconceptions that examiners frequently see students make.

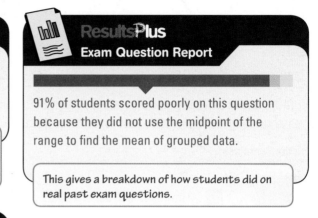

ResultsPlus
Exam Question Report

91% of students scored poorly on this question because they did not use the midpoint of the range to find the mean of grouped data.

This gives a breakdown of how students did on real past exam questions.

ResultsPlus
Examiner's Tip

Make sure the angles add up to 360°.

This gives exam advice, useful checks, and methods to remember key facts.

ResultsPlus in the **ActiveTeach** provides interactive practice for AO2 and AO3 questions…

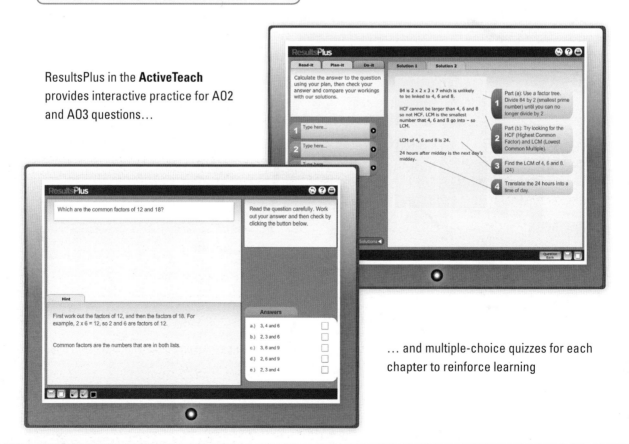

… and multiple-choice quizzes for each chapter to reinforce learning

1 USING A CALCULATOR

Charles Babbage was a 19th century inventor who was frustrated by the errors found in mathematical and astronomical tables calculated by hand. He designed the 'Difference Engine', a machine that would do the calculations correctly. Many people thought the task impossible and he died before he was able to complete it. 150 years later a team at the Science Museum in London finally built the machine.

◉ Objectives

In this chapter you will:
- ◉ work out reciprocals, powers, square roots and cube roots using a calculator
- ◉ use a calculator to work out complex calculations.

◈ Before you start

You need to be able to:
- ◉ write a fraction as a decimal
- ◉ work out powers, including squares and cubes
- ◉ work out square roots and cube roots
- ◉ round to one decimal place
- ◉ use the correct order of operations when carrying out a calculation.

1.1 Finding reciprocals

◎ **Objective**

○ You can work out the reciprocal of a number.

❓ **Why do this?**

Reciprocals are used in engineering and applied maths.

Get Ready

Work out

1. $1 \div 4$ **2.** $1 \div 0.4$ **3.** $1 \div 25$

Key Points

◎ The **reciprocal** of a number is 1 divided by the number.

The reciprocal of 2 is $\frac{1}{2}$ (or 0.5). The reciprocal of 3 is $\frac{1}{3}$ (or $0.\dot{3}$).

◎ To find the reciprocal of a fraction, turn it upside down.

The reciprocal of $\frac{3}{4}$ is $\frac{4}{3}$ (or $1\frac{1}{3}$). The reciprocal of $\frac{1}{3}$ is $\frac{3}{1}$ (or 3).

◎ To work out reciprocals you can use the reciprocal key on a calculator.

It is usually shown by $\boxed{1/x}$ or $\boxed{x^{-1}}$

◎ Any number multiplied by its reciprocal gives the answer 1.

◎ Zero has no reciprocal, because you cannot divide a number by zero.

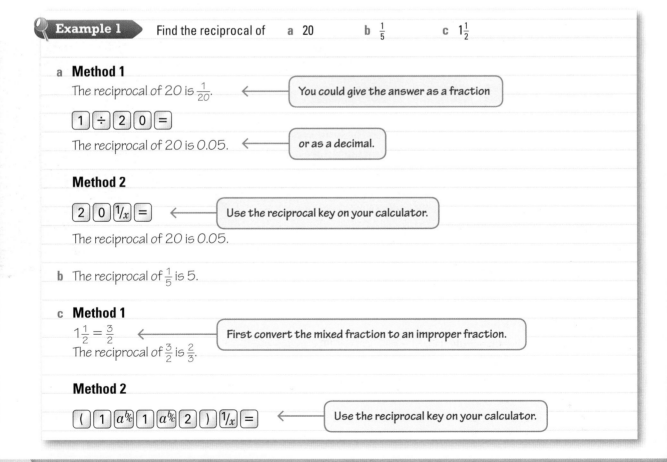

Example 1   Find the reciprocal of   **a** 20   **b** $\frac{1}{5}$ **c** $1\frac{1}{2}$

a Method 1

The reciprocal of 20 is $\frac{1}{20}$. ← You could give the answer as a fraction

$\boxed{1}\boxed{\div}\boxed{2}\boxed{0}\boxed{=}$

The reciprocal of 20 is 0.05. ← or as a decimal.

Method 2

$\boxed{2}\boxed{0}\boxed{1/x}\boxed{=}$ ← Use the reciprocal key on your calculator.

The reciprocal of 20 is 0.05.

b The reciprocal of $\frac{1}{5}$ is 5.

c Method 1

$1\frac{1}{2} = \frac{3}{2}$ ← First convert the mixed fraction to an improper fraction.

The reciprocal of $\frac{3}{2}$ is $\frac{2}{3}$.

Method 2

$\boxed{(}\boxed{1}\boxed{a^b/c}\boxed{1}\boxed{a^b/c}\boxed{2}\boxed{)}\boxed{1/x}\boxed{=}$ ← Use the reciprocal key on your calculator.

✷ Exercise 1A

Questions in this chapter are targeted at the grades indicated.

1 Find the reciprocals of these numbers.
    a 10   **b** 4   **c** 8   **d** 5   **e** 9

2 Find the reciprocals of these fractions.
    a $\frac{1}{3}$ **b** $\frac{1}{4}$ **c** $\frac{2}{3}$ **d** $\frac{5}{6}$ **e** $\frac{3}{10}$
    f $\frac{4}{3}$ **g** $\frac{7}{5}$ **h** $2\frac{2}{3}$ **i** $3\frac{1}{2}$ **j** $1\frac{1}{6}$

3 Use your calculator to find the reciprocals of these numbers.
    a 2.5   **b** 50   **c** 16   **d** 80   **e** 0.2
    f 0.5   **g** 0.05   **h** 0.125   **i** 0.04   **j** 0.01

4 The reciprocal of 1000 is 0.001. What is the reciprocal of 0.001?

5 **a** Find the reciprocal of 40.   **b** Multiply 40 by its reciprocal.

6 **a** Find the reciprocal of 100.   **b** Multiply 100 by its reciprocal.

7 Find the reciprocal of 25.

8 Find the reciprocal of 0.8.

1.2 Interpreting a calculator display

◎ Objective

● You can interpret the answer on a calculator display.

◈ Why do this?

If you are checking a shopping bill you need to be able to interpret the calculator display correctly.

◈ Get Ready

1. Work out the total cost of 4 magazines costing £1.67 each.
2. £375 is shared equally between 5 people. How much does each person get?
3. Work out the total cost of a notebook costing £2.79 and 3 pens costing 65p each.

🔍 Key Points

● You need to take care when writing down the answer from a calculator display.
If you are working in pounds, the calculator display 3.4 means £3.40.
Answers that are in pounds and pence should always be written with two figures after the decimal point.
● You must make sure that your answer makes sense in the context of the question.
Sometimes the answer to a problem must be a whole number and if the calculator display shows a decimal you will need to think carefully about whether to round it up or round it down.

Example 2 In a factory, bottles of drink are packed into boxes. Each box holds 8 bottles.
How many of these boxes can be completely filled using 670 bottles?

$6\ 7\ 0\ \div\ 8\ =$

This gives 83.75. ← To the nearest whole number 83.75 rounds to 84 but 84 boxes cannot be completely filled.

So 83 boxes can be completely filled.

Examiner's Tip

Always write down the calculation that you are doing.

 Example 3 It takes 22 minutes to fill a water tank.
How many tanks can be filled completely in 10 hours?

10 hours = 10 × 60 = 600 minutes ← Convert the hours into minutes so that both measurements are in minutes.

$6\ 0\ 0\ \div\ 2\ 2\ =$

27.2727…
So 27 tanks can be completely filled.

Exercise 1B

E

1 The total cost of five adult cinema tickets is £44.50. Work out the cost of one adult cinema ticket.

2 Ryan buys four bars of chocolate costing £1.45 each and one packet of sweets costing £1.30.
Work out the total cost.

3 Hannah buys two magazines costing £3.85 each.
Work out how much change she should get from £10.

4 A garden centre sells plants for £1.90 each. Lee buys 14 plants. Work out the total cost.

5 Tom's company pays him 45p for each mile that he drives his car.
Work out how much money Tom's company pays him when he drives 126 miles.

6 Petrol costs 115.9 pence per litre. Richard buys 38 litres of petrol. How much should Richard pay?

7 Colin needs 160 tiles for a room.
Tiles are sold in boxes. There are 12 tiles in each box.
Work out the least number of boxes of tiles that Colin needs.

8 458 students and teachers are going on a coach trip.
Each coach holds 54 passengers.
Work out the smallest number of coaches needed.

9   A beaker holds 225 m*l* of orange squash.
How many of these beakers can be completely filled using 2000 m*l* of orange squash?

10   It takes 35 seconds to fill a bucket. How many buckets can be completely filled in 20 minutes?

11   The battery life of a calculator is 420 hours. Work out the battery life in days and hours.

12   A pen costs 38p. Sam has £5. He buys as many pens as he can.
Work out how much change Sam should get from £5.

* **13**   Raja sees this new monthly plan for a mobile phone.
Raja's current plan gives him 200 minutes and unlimited
texts for £25 per month. He wants to find out if he should
switch to the new monthly plan.
In September, Raja used 140 minutes and 230 texts.
In October, he used 145 minutes and 190 texts.
In November, he used 135 minutes and 260 texts.
Should Raja switch to the new monthly plan? Explain your answer.

A02
A03

YOU PAY per month	YOU GET per month
£15	**FREE** - 100 minutes **FREE** - 200 texts

Extra minutes: 20p each Extra texts: 12p each

1.3   Working out powers and roots

Objectives

○ You can work out powers using a calculator.
○ You can work out square roots and cube roots using a calculator.

Why do this?

Scientists, financial analysts and economists make use of powers and roots.

Get Ready

1. Work out 6^2.   **2.** Work out 2^3.   **3.** Work out $\sqrt{25}$.

Key Points

◉ With a scientific calculator you can work out squares using the $\boxed{x^2}$ key.
(You met square numbers in Unit 2 Section 2.3.)

◉ Some scientific calculators have an $\boxed{x^3}$ key for working out cubes.

To work out 3.5^2, key in $\boxed{3}$ $\boxed{\cdot}$ $\boxed{5}$ $\boxed{x^2}$ $\boxed{=}$

To work out 2.7^3, key in $\boxed{2}$ $\boxed{\cdot}$ $\boxed{7}$ $\boxed{x^3}$ $\boxed{=}$

◉ Scientific calculators have a power (or index) key.

It can be shown by $\boxed{x^y}$ or $\boxed{y^x}$ or $\boxed{x^\blacksquare}$ or $\boxed{\wedge}$.

To work out 2.7^3, key in $\boxed{2}$ $\boxed{\cdot}$ $\boxed{7}$ $\boxed{x^y}$ $\boxed{3}$ $\boxed{=}$

◉ To work out square roots on a calculator use the $\boxed{\sqrt{}}$ key.

◉ To work out cube roots on a calculator use the $\boxed{\sqrt[3]{}}$ key.

Example 4   Use a calculator to work out $1.2^3 + 6.25$.

Method 1

[1][.][2][x^3][=] ← | Or you could key in 1.2 × 1.2 × 1.2 =

The result is 1.728.
1.728 + 6.25 = ← | Add the result to 6.25.
The answer is 7.978.

Method 2

[1][.][2][x^3][+][6][.][2][5][=] ← | Key in the whole calculation.

The answer is 7.978.

Exercise 1C

1   Work out

   a 2.5^2 b 3.2^2 c 47^2 d 1.8^2 e 17.9^2

2   Work out

   a 6^3 b 22^3 c 2.1^3 d 3.4^3 e 1.5^3

3   Work out

   a 2^5 b 11^4 c 3^5 d 12^4 e 5^6

4   Work out

   a $17^2 + 10$ b $2.4^2 + 15$ c $19^2 - 322$ d $2.7^2 + 5.42$

5   Work out

   a $2.1^3 + 1.96$ b $1.9^3 + 5.29$ c $2.5^3 - 7.29$ d $1.4^3 - 1.544$

Example 5   Use a calculator to work out $\sqrt{14.44}$.

[√][1][4][.][4][4][=] ← | On some calculators you first key in 14.44 and then press the square root key.

$\sqrt{14.44} = +3.8$ ← | Calculators always give the positive square root.

✤ **Exercise 1D**

1 Work out
   a $\sqrt{529}$ b $\sqrt{289}$ c $\sqrt{1156}$ d $\sqrt{625}$

2 Work out
   a $\sqrt{2.56}$ b $\sqrt{22.09}$ c $\sqrt{13.69}$ d $\sqrt{88.36}$

3 Work these out, giving your answers correct to one decimal place.
   a $\sqrt{150}$ b $\sqrt{80}$ c $\sqrt{124}$ d $\sqrt{240}$

4 Work out
   a $\sqrt[3]{216}$ b $\sqrt[3]{729}$ c $\sqrt[3]{343}$ d $\sqrt[3]{1728}$

> 💡 **Results**Plus
> **Examiner's Tip**
>
> Write down all the figures on your calculator display before you round your answer to one decimal place. (See Unit 2 Section 3.7 on Rounding.)

5 Work these out, giving your answers correct to one decimal place.
   a $\sqrt[3]{40}$ b $\sqrt[3]{200}$ c $\sqrt[3]{120}$ d $\sqrt[3]{84}$

6 Work out
   a $\sqrt{51.84} + 4.8$ b $\sqrt{841} - 21.3$ c $\sqrt[3]{9.261} - 1.9$ d $\sqrt[3]{1.728} + 1.8$

7 How far can you see?
To work out the distance, in kilometres, you can see:
  1 Find the height, in metres, of your eyes above sea level.
  2 Multiply this height by 13.
  3 Find the square root of the answer.

James is standing on a cliff, at J. His eyes are 20 metres above sea level.
Matthew is standing in a lighthouse, M. His eyes are 50 metres above sea level.
Which of the three boats, A, B and C, should James be able to see?
Which of the three boats should Matthew be able to see?

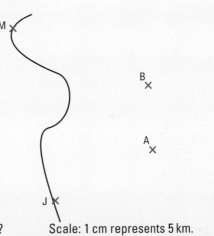

Scale: 1 cm represents 5 km.

1.4 Using a calculator to work out complex calculations

◎ Objective

○ You can use a calculator to work out complex calculations.

⬦ Why do this?

Engineers, architects, computer programmers and accountants all need to be able to work out complex calculations using a calculator.

⬥ Get Ready

1. Work out 1.5×4^2.
    2. Work out $3.5 + 2.5 \times 4$.
    3. Work out $\dfrac{20 - 10}{5}$.

Key Points

⊙ All scientific calculators carry out mathematical operations in the same order.
This order is sometimes abbreviated to BIDMAS (see Unit 2 Section 8.4).
You need to know about BIDMAS in order to use a scientific calculator properly.

⊙ On most scientific calculators you can key in calculations in the order in which they are written down.
To work out $(1.27 + 3.8)^2 \times 3.5$, for example, you would key in

$\boxed{(}\,\boxed{1}\,\boxed{\cdot}\,\boxed{2}\,\boxed{7}\,\boxed{+}\,\boxed{3}\,\boxed{\cdot}\,\boxed{8}\,\boxed{)}\,\boxed{x^2}\,\boxed{\times}\,\boxed{3}\,\boxed{\cdot}\,\boxed{5}\,\boxed{=}$

⊙ When you are doing a division calculation you must remember to divide by ALL of the denominator.
To work out $\dfrac{14.5}{1.32 + 1.28}$, for example, you must divide 14.5 by the result of $1.32 + 1.28$.

⊙ Most scientific calculators have the negative sign $\boxed{(-)}$. To enter the number -6, for example, key in $\boxed{(-)}\,\boxed{6}$.

Example 6

Work out the value of $\dfrac{16.3 + 7.82}{7.2 - 4.7}$.

Method 1

$\boxed{1}\,\boxed{6}\,\boxed{\cdot}\,\boxed{3}\,\boxed{+}\,\boxed{7}\,\boxed{\cdot}\,\boxed{8}\,\boxed{2}\,\boxed{=}$ ← Key in the numerator.

The result is 24.12.

$\boxed{7}\,\boxed{\cdot}\,\boxed{2}\,\boxed{-}\,\boxed{4}\,\boxed{\cdot}\,\boxed{7}\,\boxed{=}$ ← Key in the denominator.

The result is 2.5.

$\boxed{2}\,\boxed{4}\,\boxed{\cdot}\,\boxed{1}\,\boxed{2}\,\boxed{\div}\,\boxed{2}\,\boxed{\cdot}\,\boxed{5}\,\boxed{=}$ ← Divide the first result by the second result.

The value is 9.648.

> **ResultsPlus**
> **Examiner's Tip**
>
> If you work out the numerator and the denominator separately, make sure you write down the value of each.

Method 2

$\boxed{(}\,\boxed{1}\,\boxed{6}\,\boxed{\cdot}\,\boxed{3}\,\boxed{+}\,\boxed{7}\,\boxed{\cdot}\,\boxed{8}\,\boxed{2}\,\boxed{)}\,\boxed{\div}\,\boxed{(}\,\boxed{7}\,\boxed{\cdot}\,\boxed{2}\,\boxed{-}\,\boxed{4}\,\boxed{\cdot}\,\boxed{7}\,\boxed{)}\,\boxed{=}$

Put brackets around the numerator and around the denominator.

Exercise 1E

1 Work out

   a $(5.2 + 2.7)^2$ b $(12.4 - 9.71)^2$ c $(2.43 + 1.87)^3$ d $(5.1 - 3.7)^3$

2 Work out

   a $12^2 + 13^2$ b $34^2 + 6^3$ c $12^3 - 23^2$ d $38^2 - 18^2$

3 Work out

   a $\sqrt{17.8 + 13.56}$ b $\sqrt{415 - 159}$ c $\sqrt[3]{129 - 65}$ d $\sqrt[3]{1.85 + 1.525}$

E

4 Work out the value of each of these.
Write down all the figures on your calculator display.

a $\dfrac{4.78 - 1.42}{0.84}$ b $\dfrac{48.88}{3.62 + 5.78}$

c $\dfrac{12.24 \times 2.5}{6.8}$ d $\dfrac{35.36}{12.6 - 5.8}$

5 Work out the value of each of these.
Write down all the figures on your calculator display.

a $\dfrac{13.2 - 6.84}{2.8 + 3.41}$ b $\dfrac{5.6 \times 8.1}{12.5 - 3.9}$

c $\dfrac{4.37 \times 6.52}{2.8 + 7.19}$ d $\dfrac{17.6 + 9.82}{23.6 - 5.94}$

Chapter review

⦿ The **reciprocal** of a number is 1 divided by the number.

⦿ To find the reciprocal of a fraction, turn it upside down.

⦿ To work out reciprocals you can use the reciprocal key on a calculator.
It is usually shown by $\boxed{1/x}$ or $\boxed{x^{-1}}$.

⦿ Any number multiplied by its reciprocal gives the answer 1.

⦿ Zero has no reciprocal, because you cannot divide a number by zero.

⦿ You need to take care when writing down the answer from a calculator display.
Answers that are in pounds and pence should always be written with two figures after the decimal point.

⦿ You must make sure that your answer makes sense in the context of the question.
Sometimes the answer to a problem must be a whole number and if the calculator display shows a decimal you will need to think carefully about whether to round it up or round it down.

⦿ With a scientific calculator you can work out squares using the $\boxed{x^2}$ key.

⦿ Some scientific calculators have an $\boxed{x^3}$ key for working out cubes.

⦿ Scientific calculators have a power (or index) key.
It can be shown by $\boxed{x^y}$ or $\boxed{y^x}$ or $\boxed{x^\blacksquare}$ or $\boxed{\wedge}$.

⦿ To work out square roots on a calculator use the $\boxed{\sqrt{}}$ key.

⦿ To work out cube roots on a calculator use the $\boxed{\sqrt[3]{}}$ key.

⦿ All scientific calculators carry out mathematical operations in the same order. This order is sometimes abbreviated to BIDMAS. You need to know about BIDMAS in order to use a scientific calculator properly.

⦿ On most scientific calculators you can key in calculations in the order in which they are written down.

⦿ When you are doing a division calculation you must remember to divide by ALL of the denominator.

⦿ Most scientific calculators have the negative sign $\boxed{(-)}$.

Review exercise

1. Christine buys a calculator costing £3.99, a pencil case costing £1.65 and two rulers costing 28p each. She pays with a £10 note. How much change should she get from her £10 note?

2. Shares in a company cost £6.23 each. Tauqeer has £500. He buys as many shares as he can. Work out how many shares Tauqeer can buy.

3. A milk crate holds 24 bottles. Amraiz has 357 bottles of milk. Work out how many milk crates he can fill completely.

4. The table below shows the cost of each of three calculators.

Quicksum	£2.30
Basic	£2.15
Easycalc	£2.90

   a Emily buys one Quicksum calculator and two Easycalc calculators. She pays with a £10 note. How much change should she get?

   b Mrs Windsor wants to buy some Basic calculators. She has £60 to spend. Work out the greatest number of Basic calculators she can buy.

5. Work out
   a 2.9^2 b 12^3 c 3.7^2 d 2.2^3

6. Work out
   a $\sqrt{51.84}$ b $\sqrt{784}$ c $\sqrt[3]{512}$ d $\sqrt[3]{15.625}$

7. Work these out, giving your answers correct to one decimal place.
   a $2.8^2 + \sqrt{34}$ b $\sqrt{56} - 2.3^2$ c $4.7^2 - \sqrt{28}$ d $3.8^2 - \sqrt{50}$

8. Jonathan buys a can of cola and a roll.
   a Work out the total cost.

   Sachin buys a cup of tea, a cup of coffee and 2 sandwiches.
   b Work out the total cost.

   Kim buys a can of cola, a cup of coffee and a sandwich. She pays with a £5 note.
   c Work out how much change she should get.

Joe's Café

Prices

Cup of tea	70p
Cup of coffee	85p
Can of cola	75p
Roll	£1.60
Sandwich	£1.35

June 2007

9. Cans of drink are put into packs of 24. How many packs can be filled from 750 cans of drink?

10. There are 1230 students in a school. All the students go on a trip. Each bus can take 48 students. How many buses are needed?

11. Plain tiles cost 28p each.
    Patterned tiles cost £9.51 each.
    Julie buys 450 plain tiles and 15 patterned tiles.
    Work out the total cost of the tiles.

    Nov 2007

12. Use a calculator to work out
    $\sqrt{2.56} + 8.4$

    Nov 2008

13 Work out

    a $(3.7 + 2.64)^2$ **b** $\sqrt{17 + 25.25}$ **c** $(2.1 + 2.8)^2 \times 1.2$

14 Work out the value of each of these.

    Write down all the figures on your calculator display.

    a $\dfrac{5.68 - 1.52^2}{0.83}$ **b** $\dfrac{1}{3.58^2 - 2.87}$ **c** $\dfrac{8.7 + 5.92}{16.3 - 4.56}$

15 Work out the value of each of these.

    Write down all the figures on your calculator display.

    a $\dfrac{\sqrt{3.96 + 1.8}}{7.625 - 3.48}$ **b** $\sqrt{\dfrac{4.92 + 3.48}{9.2 - 3.75}}$

* 16 To work out a person's daily calorie requirement you can use one of these rules.

Gender	Daily calorie requirement
Female	$655 + (9.6 \times$ weight in kg$) + (1.8 \times$ height in cm$) - (4.7 \times$ age in years$)$
Male	$66 + (13.7 \times$ weight in kg$) + (5 \times$ height in cm$) - (6.8 \times$ age in years$)$

    The table below shows some information about four people.

Name	Gender	Age (years)	Weight (kg)	Height (cm)
Sophie	F	32	68	165
Chelsea	F	47	55	175
Kenny	M	27	98	191
Hassan	M	38	117	182

    Work out the recommended daily calorie intake for each person.

    Which person has the greatest daily calorie requirement?

    Which person has the smallest daily calorie requirement?

17 Find the reciprocal of   **a** $\frac{5}{8}$ **b** 2.5 **c** $\frac{1}{4}$

18 Use your calculator to work out $\dfrac{22.4 \times 14.5}{8.5 \times 3.2}$

    Write down all the figures on your calculator display.   *June 2007*

* 19

    A large tub of popcorn costs £3.80 and holds 200 g.

    A regular tub of popcorn costs £3.50 and holds 175 g.

    Rob says that the 200 g large tub is the better value for money.

    Linda says that the 175 g regular tub is the better value for money.

    Who is correct?

    Explain the reasons for your answer.

    You must show all your working.   *June 2006*

D

A03

D

20. Work out $\dfrac{4.6 + 3.85}{3.2^2 - 6.51}$

Write down all the numbers on your calculator display.

June 2009

A02 A03

21. Salma has £1.55.

She wants to buy a burger and fries.

a What are the different combinations that can she buy?

Mark buys 2 double burgers with cheese, 1 large fries and 1 large cola.

He pays with a £10 note

b He gets the best price. What change should he get?

Ben's Burger Bar

Burgers

Single Burger	£0.85
Single Burger with Cheese	£0.95
Double Burger	£1.55
Double Burger with Cheese	£1.70

Fries		Cola	
Regular	£0.65	Regular	£0.85
Large	£0.99	Large	£1.10

Meal Deals

Regular

Single Burger with Cheese regular Fries and regular Cola	£2.09

Large

Double Burger with Cheese large Fries and large Cola	£3.49

Scuba divers have to wear weights to overcome the natural buoyancy of their bodies, helping them to sink. The amount required depends on many factors, such as body fat, bone density and the thickness of wetsuit worn, but divers generally wear weights adding up to about 10% of their body weight. How much weight would you estimate that a diver with a body weight of 80 kg would need?

◎ Objectives

In this chapter you will:
- use a calculator to work out a percentage of a quantity
- use a calculator to increase or decrease a quantity by a given percentage
- express one number as a percentage of another.

◈ Before you start

You need to be able to:
- convert between and order percentages, fractions and decimals
- find a percentage of a quantity without using a calculator
- increase or decrease a quantity by a given percentage without using a calculator.

2.1 Finding percentages of quantities

Objectives

- You can work out a percentage of a quantity.
- You can use percentages in real-life problems.

Why do this?

This is useful if you need to work out your exam marks as a percentage of the total to see if you have reached the 75% pass mark.

Get Ready

1. Write 27% as a fraction.   **2.** Work out 50% of 70.   **3.** Work out 10% of 80.

Key Points

- You should know these percentages and their fraction and decimal equivalents.

Percentage	1%	10%	25%	50%	75%
Decimal	0.01	0.1	0.25	0.5	0.75
Fraction	$\frac{1}{100}$	$\frac{1}{10}$	$\frac{1}{4}$	$\frac{1}{2}$	$\frac{3}{4}$

- To work out a percentage of a quantity using a written method you should:
  - write the percentage as a fraction, and then
  - multiply the fraction by the quantity.

Example 1

The normal price of a television is £375.
Freya is given a discount of 24%.
Work out the discount that Freya is given.

To work out 24% of 375 it is quicker to use a calculator.

$24\% = \frac{24}{100}$ ← Change the percentage to a fraction.

$\frac{24}{100} \times 375 = 90$ ← Key in 2 4 ÷ 1 0 0 × 3 7 5 =

Freya is given a discount of £90.

Exercise 2A

Questions in this chapter are targeted at the grades indicated.

1 Work out
  a 12% of £40   b 86% of 45 kg   c 54% of £370   d 37% of 640 km
  e 48% of 330 ml   f 23% of $90   g 8% of £170   h 92% of 1500 m

2 There are 250 boats in a harbour. 46% of the boats are yachts.
How many yachts are there in the harbour?

3 Alan invested £1200 in a savings account. At the end of the year he received 4% interest.
Work out how much interest he received.

D

4 There are 225 students in Year 10.
24% of these students study history.
How many of the students study history?

5 Moira's salary is £48 000. Her employer agrees to increase her salary in line with inflation. The rate of inflation this year is 3%. Work out the amount her salary has increased by.

6 In a restaurant a service charge of 12.5% is added to the cost of the meal.
Work out the service charge when the cost of the meal is £60.

7 VAT is charged at the rate of $17\frac{1}{2}$%. Work out how much VAT will be charged on:
a   a ladder costing £84
b   a garage bill of £130.

8 The rate of simple interest is 3% per year. Work out the simple interest paid on £500 in one year.

9 The cash price of a washing machine is £670.
A Credit Plan requires a deposit of 5% of the cash price and 24 monthly payments of £28.
Which is the cheapest way to buy the washing machine. Explain your answer.

A02
A03

10 A 100 g tub of margarine has the following nutrional content.
fat   38 g
sodium   1.3 g
carbohydrate   2.8 g
protein   0.1 g
a   What percentage of the margarine is fat?
b   How many grams of fat would there be in a 250 g tub?

A02

C

11 Roger bought 50 pineapples at 80p each.
He sold all the pineapples.
On each of the first 36 pineapples he made a 35% profit.
On each of the remaining pineapples he made a 40% loss.
Work out the overall profit or loss that Roger made.

A03

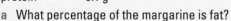

2.2 **Using percentages**

◉ Objectives

◉ You can increase and decrease a quantity by a given percentage.
◉ You can use a multiplier to work out a percentage increase or percentage decrease.

⚑ Why do this?

Banks and building societies use percentages for interest rates.

⬆ Get Ready

1. Work out 25% of 60.   **2.** Work out 30% of 90.   **3.** Work out 37% of 40.

Key Points

⊚ To increase a quantity by a percentage, work out the increase and add this to the original quantity.

⊚ To decrease a quantity by a percentage, work out the decrease and subtract this from the original quantity.

⊚ An alternative method is to work out the multiplier for an increase or decrease and then multiply the original amount by the multiplier to find the new amount. (See Example 2, method 2.)

A02

Example 2

In a sale all normal prices are reduced by 12%.
The normal price of a suit is £125.
Work out the sale price of the suit.

Watch Out!

Don't forget to add or subtract from the original amount.

Method 1

$\frac{12}{100} \times 125 = 15$ ← Work out the reduction.

$125 - 15 = 110$ ← Subtract to work out the sale price.

The sale price is £110.

Method 2

$100\% - 12\% = 88\%$ ← The sale price is 88% of the normal price.

$88\% = 0.88$ ← 0.88 is called the multiplier.

$0.88 \times 125 = 110$ ← Multiply the normal price by 0.88.

The sale price is £110.

Exercise 2B

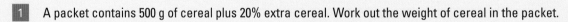

E

1   A packet contains 500 g of cereal plus 20% extra cereal. Work out the weight of cereal in the packet.

2   Karen's salary is £26 500. Her salary is increased by 3%. Work out her new salary.

3   The price of rail fares increased by 11%. Before the increase the price of a ticket was £87.
Work out the price of the ticket after the increase.

4   A travel company reduced the prices of its holidays by 12%.
What is the new price of a holiday which was originally priced at £695?

5   A car tyre costs £48 plus VAT at $17\frac{1}{2}$%. Work out the total cost of the car tyre.

6   VAT at $17\frac{1}{2}$% is added to a telephone bill of £76. Work out the total bill.

7   Katie invests £3600. The interest rate is 3.5% per year.
How much will Katie have in her account at the end of one year?

8   Vicky invests £1500 for 3 years at 4% simple interest.
Work out the value of her investment after one year.

9 Raja bought a car for £8000. In one year the value of the car depreciated by 10%.
Work out the value of the car one year after he bought it.

10 The normal price of a pack of croissants is £1.96.
The normal price is reduced by 25%.
Work out the price after the reduction.

11 A store reduced all normal prices by 15% in a two-day sale.
Work out the sale price of:
a a drill with a normal price of £70
b a lawnmower with a normal price of £180
c a tin of paint with a normal price of £14.

12 In a super-sale a shop reduces its sale prices by a further 10%.

> **SALE**
> $\frac{1}{2}$ off
> normal prices
>
> **PLUS**
> an extra
> 10% off
> sale prices

In the super-sale, Steve buys a camera with a normal price of £240.
How much does he pay?

13 Riverside Garage has a loyalty scheme for customers who buy their cars from the garage.
The scheme gives customers a discount on the cost of labour and the cost of parts.
The percentage discount depends on the age of the car.

Age of vehicle (years)	Labour discount	Parts discount
4	10%	5%
5	12.5%	5%
6	15%	5%
7	17.5%	10%
8	20%	10%
9	25%	10%
10 or older	30%	10%

Alan bought a new car from Riverside Garage in September 2005.
Today, Riverside Garage carried out some repairs on the car.

Copy and complete the bill for the repairs.

Item	Cost before discount	% discount	Cost after discount
Labour	£120	...............%	£...............
Parts	£84	...............%	£...............
Riverside Garage		Total before VAT	£...............
		VAT at $17\frac{1}{2}$%	£...............
		Total with VAT	£...............

2.3 Writing one quantity as a percentage of another

Objective

- You can write one quantity as a percentage of another.

Why do this?

Pay rises, profits and losses are often expressed as percentages.

Get Ready

1. Express 7 as a fraction of 10.
2. Express 48 as a fraction of 72.
3. $\frac{3}{10} = \frac{?}{100}$

Key Points

- To write one quantity as a percentage of another quantity:
  - write the first quantity as a fraction of the second quantity
  - convert the fraction to a percentage.

Example 3   Write 7 out of 20 as a percentage. Do not use a calculator.

$\frac{7}{20}$ ← Write 7 out of 20 as a fraction.

$\frac{7}{20} = \frac{35}{100}$ (×5) ← Make the denominator 100.

$\frac{35}{100} = 35\%$

Exercise 2C

G

1. a Write 7 out of 10 as a percentage.
   b Write £23 out of £50 as a percentage.
   c Write 13 kg out of 20 kg as a percentage.
   d Write 12p out of £1 as a percentage.
   e Write 120 ml out of 200 ml as a percentage.

2. There are 25 trees in a park. Of these trees, 18 are oak trees.
   What percentage of the trees are oak trees?

3. Tom planted 400 flower seeds. Of these seeds, 360 germinated.
   What percentage of the seeds germinated?

4. A glass contains 500 ml of drink. 400 ml of the drink is water. What percentage of the drink is water?

5. Chloe scored 24 out of 60 in a test. Write 24 out of 60 as a percentage.

6. 50 people in a club voted to elect a secretary.
   There were three candidates.
   Abi got 40% of the votes, Laura got 12 votes and Faisal got the remaining votes.
   What percentage of the votes did Faisal get?

A02

Example 4 A magazine has 72 pages. Forty-five of the pages have advertisements on them. What percentage of the pages have advertisements on them?

$\frac{45}{72}$ ← Write 45 out of 72 as a fraction.

$\frac{45}{72} = 0.625$ ← Change the fraction to a decimal using a calculator.

$0.625 \times 100 = 62.5$ ← Multiply the decimal by 100.

62.5% of the pages have advertisements.

Exercise 2D

1. a Write 525 g as a percentage of 750 g.
    b Write £8.40 as a percentage of £120.
    c Write 126 ml as a percentage of 350 ml.
    d Write 312 km as a percentage of 480 km.
    e Write 90p as a percentage of £2.50.

2. A football team played 45 matches. The team won 18 of these matches. What percentage of the matches did the team win?

3. There are 32 students in a class. On Friday, six of these students were absent. What percentage of the students were absent on Friday?

4. There are 1650 students in a school. 297 of the students are in Year 11. What percentage of the students are in Year 11?

5. 120 g of cheese contains 18.6 g of carbohydrates and 5.4 g of protein. What percentage of the cheese is:
    a carbohydrates   b protein?

6. A film audience consists of 108 males and 132 females. What percentage of the audience is female?

7. Sam is mixing sand and gravel. A mixture of 16 bucketfuls is 25% sand. He wants to make a mixture of 50% sand. How many bucketfuls of sand must Sam add to make the mixture 50% sand?

Chapter review

○ You should know these percentages and their fraction and decimal equivalents.

Percentage	1%	10%	25%	50%	75%
Decimal	0.01	0.1	0.25	0.5	0.75
Fraction	$\frac{1}{100}$	$\frac{1}{10}$	$\frac{1}{4}$	$\frac{1}{2}$	$\frac{3}{4}$

- To work out a percentage of a quantity using a written method you should:
  - write the percentage as a fraction, and then
  - multiply the fraction by the quantity.
- To increase a quantity by a percentage, work out the increase and add this to the original quantity.
- To decrease a quantity by a percentage, work out the decrease and subtract this from the original quantity.
- An alternative method is to work out the multiplier for an increase or decrease and then multiply the original amount by the multiplier to find the new amount.
- To write one quantity as a percentage of another quantity:
  - write the first quantity as a fraction of the second quantity
  - convert the fraction to a percentage.

Review exercise

G

1. In a survey, 42 out of 60 students said they would prefer to go to a theme park.
   Write 42 out of 60 as a percentage.

2. 180 of the 600 counters in a bag are red.
   Work out 180 as a percentage of 600.   *May 2009*

3. Write 9 out of 12 as a percentage.   *Nov 2008*

F

4. A hotel has 56 guests.
   35 of the guests are male.
   a Work out 35 out of 56 as a percentage.

   40% of the 35 male guests wear glasses.
   b Write the number of male guests who wear glasses as a fraction of the 56 guests.
   Give your answer in its simplest form.   *Nov 2007*

D

5. The weight of some biscuits is 125 g. 18% of the weight is fat. Work out the weight of the fat.

6. A furniture store reduced its prices in a sale. Work out the sale price of:
   a a bookcase with 50% off the normal price of £498
   b a bed with 40% off the normal price of £595
   c a fitted kitchen with 45% off the normal price of £12 000.

7. The population of a town is 54 000. In ten years' time the population is expected to have increased by 12%. What is the population expected to be in ten years' time?

*A03 *8. Jack wants to buy a new shed. There are three shops that sell the shed he wants.

Sheds For U	Garden World	Ed's Sheds
25% off normal price of £320	£210 plus VAT at $17\frac{1}{2}$%	$\frac{1}{3}$ off usual price of £345

Jack wants to pay as little as possible. From which of these three shops should Jack buy his shed?

D

9 A concert ticket costs £45 plus a booking charge of 15%.
Work out the total cost of a concert ticket.

Results Plus
Exam Question Report

84% of students answered this question poorly.
Many candidates incorrectly added £15 to £45,
giving an answer of £60.

June 2007

10 The normal price of a cat basket is £20.
In a sale, the manager reduces the price of the cat basket by 15%.
Work out the price of the cat basket in the sale.

Nov 2008

C

11 The normal price of a computer game is £21.30. The normal price is reduced by 20%.
What is its reduced price?

12 Students went to London or to York on a school trip.
The table shows the some information about the children.
  a What percentage of all the girls went to York?
  b What percentage of all those who went to London were boys?
  c What percentage of all the children went to London?

A02

	London	York
Boys	27	13
Girls	18	22

* 13 Rachael is a sales manager.
Last year, Rachael had a 10% pay rise. This year, she had a 5% pay rise.
Ziggy says, 'Rachael has had a 15% pay rise over the two years.'
Is Ziggy correct? Explain your answer.

A03

14

	Number of girls	Number of boys
Year 10	108	132
Year 11	90	110

A02

The table gives information about Year 10 and Year 11 at Mathstown School.
  a Work out the percentage of students in Year 10 who are girls.

Mathstown School had an end-of-term party.
40% of the students in Year 10 and 70% of the students in Year 11 went to the party.
  b Work out the percentage of all students in Years 10 and 11 who went to the party.

Nov 2004

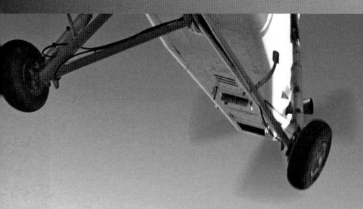

3 EQUATIONS

In algebra, letters are used to represent unknown numbers. A sky diver can work out how long it takes, t, to go from a speed of 4 metres per second to a speed of 20 metres per second. The sky diver would need to solve the equation $4 + 10t = 20$.

◉ Objectives

In this chapter you will:
- set up simple equations
- solve equations with one unknown value
- use equations to solve problems
- find approximate solutions to equations using trial and improvement.

◐ Before you start

You need to:
- know that letters can represent numbers
- be able to collect like terms
- know simple number bonds.

3.1 **Using simple equations**

Objectives

- You can write simple equations using letters.
- You can set up simple equations from word problems.
- You can solve simple equations using number bonds.

Why do this?

You might use a simple equation to work out how long it would take you to get drive to your friend's house as you would know the distance and the average speed you could travel.

Get Ready

1. Write down
   a 13×6
   b 7×19
   c 15×7

Key Point

- In an equation, a symbol or letter represents an unknown number. For example

  $5 \times \boxed{} + 2 = 17$ and

  $5x + 2 = 17$ are equations.

Example 1   Write these equations using letters.

     a $\boxed{} + 9 = 15$ **b** $4 \times \boxed{} - 3 = 21$

a $x + 9 = 15$ ← Replace $\boxed{}$ with a letter, usually x.

b $4x - 3 = 21$

Example 2   I think of a number.

I multiply the number by 3, and the answer is 21.

     a Write this problem as an equation.
     b What number did I think of?

a $3x = 21$ ← Let x stand for the number I thought of. Write $3 \times x$ as $3x$.

b $3 \times 7 = 21$ ← $21 \div 3 = 7$

The number I thought of was 7.

Exercise 3A

Questions in this chapter are targeted at the grades indicated.

In questions 1–10, write each equation using a letter.

1 $\boxed{} - 7 = 9$

2 $\boxed{} + 3 = 11$

3 $8 \times \boxed{} = 32$

4 $9 + \boxed{} = 20$

G

G

5 $7 \times \boxed{} - 3 = 32$

6 $\boxed{} \times 3 = 21$

7 $3 \times (\boxed{} + 1) = 24$

8 $\boxed{} \times 4 + 5 = 13$

9 $(5 + \boxed{}) \times 2 = 16$

10 $7 + 5 \times \boxed{} = 27$

In questions 11–15
a express the problem as an equation
b find the number.

11 Amy thinks of a number and adds 7 to it.
The answer is 11.

12 Ben thinks of a number and multiplies it by 5.
The answer is 45.

13 Irina thinks of a number. She adds 2 to it and multiplies the result by 4.
The answer is 24.

14 David thinks of a number. He multiplies it by 2 and subtracts 5 from the result.
The answer is 13.

15 Hannah thinks of a number. She multiplies it by 6 and adds 7 to the result.
The answer is 31.

3.2 Solving equations with one operation

Objective

You can use the balancing method of solving equations for one operation.

Why do this?

Equations can be used to work out unknown quantities.

Get Ready

Express each problem as an equation.
1. Chloe thinks of a number. She multiplies it by 3 and subtracts 4 from the result. The answer is 14.
2. Abdul thinks of a number. He multiplies it by 6 and adds 2. The result is 26.
3. Sarah thinks of a number. She multiplies it by 7 and subtracts 4. The result is 17.

Key Points

- You can solve an equation by rearranging it so that the letter is on its own on one side of the equation.
- To rearrange an equation you can:
  - add the same number to both sides
  - subtract the same number from both sides
  - multiply both sides by the same number
  - divide both sides by the same number.
- This is called the **balance method**.

Example 3 Solve the equation $d + 4 = 9$.

$$d + 4 = 9$$
$$d + 4 - 4 = 9 - 4 \quad \longleftarrow \boxed{\text{Subtract 4 from both sides.}}$$
$$d = 5$$

ResultsPlus
Examiner's Tip

'Solve' means find the value of the letter.

Example 4 Solve the equation $a - 7 = 4$.

$$a - 7 = 4$$
$$a - 7 + 7 = 4 + 7 \quad \longleftarrow \boxed{\text{Add 7 to both sides.}}$$
$$a = 11$$

Exercise 3B

Solve these equations.

1 $a + 6 = 7$	**2** $y + 3 = 5$	**3** $h + 2 = 9$
4 $p - 5 = 4$	**5** $q - 3 = 7$	**6** $d - 6 = 2$
7 $x + 3 = 3$	**8** $t - 4 = 0$	**9** $r + 7 = 10$
10 $k + 2 = 3$	**11** $n + 1 = 2$	**12** $x - 2 = 3$
13 $m + 7 = 12$	**14** $y - 7 = 9$	**15** $w + 5 = 5$
16 $q - 10 = 2$	**17** $5 + p = 7$	**18** $6 + t = 6$
19 $a + 19 = 31$	**20** $21 + x = 21$	**21** $p - 15 = 23$
22 $7 = a + 3$	**23** $6 = b + 5$	**24** $10 = v + 10$

F

Exercise 3C

Solve these equations.

1 $a + 5 = 10$	**2** $p - 4 = 7$	**3** $q - 3 = 5$	**4** $x + 7 = 15$
5 $y + 4 = 17$	**6** $s + 12 = 15$	**7** $x - 7 = 15$	**8** $y - 4 = 17$
9 $s - 12 = 15$	**10** $a + 5 = 6$	**11** $p - 5 = 6$	**12** $c + 17 = 21$
13 $5 + a = 6$	**14** $11 + p = 16$	**15** $12 + q = 12$	**16** $4 = a + 2$
17 $5 = b + 3$	**18** $12 = c - 3$	**19** $10 = p + 5$	**20** $11 = y - 10$
21 $15 = t + 10$	**22** $12 = p + 12$	**23** $12 = p - 12$	**24** $p + 12 = 12$

F

Example 5 Solve the equation $5x = 25$.

$$5x = 25$$

$$\frac{5 \times x}{5} = \frac{25}{5}$$ ← Divide both sides by 5.

$$x = \frac{25}{5} = 5$$ ← Cancel $\frac{5 \times x}{5} = x$

Exercise 3D

Find the value of the letter in these equations.

1	$3a = 6$	**2**	$4p = 8$	**3**	$5p = 15$
4	$6s = 18$	**5**	$2k = 10$	**6**	$7u = 28$
7	$2g = 14$	**8**	$5l = 35$	**9**	$6j = 12$
10	$8f = 32$	**11**	$3r = 27$	**12**	$5v = 45$

Example 6 Solve the equation $\frac{y}{3} = 2$.

$$\frac{y}{3} = 2$$

$$\frac{y \times 3}{3} = 2 \times 3$$ ← Multiply both sides by 3.

$$y = 2 \times 3$$
$$y = 6$$

Cancel $\frac{y \times 3}{3}$

Exercise 3E

Find the value of the letter in these equations.

1	$\frac{a}{2} = 5$	**2**	$\frac{b}{5} = 4$	**3**	$\frac{s}{4} = 3$
4	$\frac{c}{6} = 5$	**5**	$\frac{t}{4} = 6$	**6**	$\frac{s}{8} = 9$
7	$\frac{h}{6} = 12$	**8**	$\frac{f}{4} = 7$	**9**	$\frac{d}{3} = 15$
10	$\frac{a}{3} = 15$	**11**	$\frac{b}{5} = 8$	**12**	$\frac{r}{4} = 13$
13	$\frac{a}{12} = 5$	**14**	$\frac{b}{2} = 16$	**15**	$\frac{k}{3} = 16$

⚙ **Mixed exercise 3F**

Solve these equations.

1	$a + 4 = 5$	**2**	$b + 3 = 6$	**3**	$c + 4 = 9$
4	$p - 3 = 6$	**5**	$q - 2 = 2$	**6**	$d - 6 = 2$
7	$2p = 6$	**8**	$4r = 8$	**9**	$3s = 6$
10	$4 + r = 7$	**11**	$6 + e = 7$	**12**	$7 + p = 7$
13	$\dfrac{a}{2} = 6$	**14**	$\dfrac{b}{5} = 12$	**15**	$\dfrac{s}{5} = 6$

F

E

3.3 Solving equations with two operations

◎ **Objective**

◉ You can use the balancing method of solving equations for two operations.

⬆ **Get Ready**

Solve the equations.

1. $9 + q = 16$ **2.** $x - 5 = 11$ **3.** $5r = 30$ **4.** $\dfrac{p}{7} = 4$

🕐 **Key Points**

◉ In an equation with two operations, deal with the $+$ or $-$ first.
◉ Solutions to equations can be whole numbers, fractions or decimals.
◉ Solutions to **linear equations** can be negative.

📌 **Example 7** Solve

a $3a + 2 = 11$ **b** $4p - 3 = 13$ **c** $\dfrac{x}{5} + 2 = 6$

a $3a + 2 = 11$
    $3a + 2 - 2 = 11 - 2$ ⟵ Take 2 from both sides.
        $3a = 9$
    $3a \div 3 = 9 \div 3$ ⟵ Divide both sides by 3.
        $a = 3$

b $4p - 3 = 13$

$4p - 3 + 3 = 13 + 3$ ← Add 3 to both sides.

$4p = 16$

$4p \div 4 = 16 \div 4$ ← Divide both sides by 4.

$p = 4$

c $\dfrac{x}{5} + 2 = 6$

$\dfrac{x}{5} + 2 - 2 = 6 - 2$ ← Take 2 from both sides.

$\dfrac{x}{5} = 4$

$\dfrac{x}{5} \times 5 = 4 \times 5$ ← Multiply both sides by 5.

$x = 20$

Exercise 3G

Solve these equations.

1 $2a + 1 = 5$	**2** $2a - 1 = 5$	**3** $3a + 2 = 8$
4 $3a - 5 = 4$	**5** $3p + 7 = 7$	**6** $3p + 7 = 13$
7 $q + 5 = 17$	**8** $5r - 6 = 4$	**9** $6t - 12 = 18$
10 $7f - 12 = 9$	**11** $2r - 11 = 15$	**12** $10a - 5 = 5$
13 $10a + 5 = 5$	**14** $4d + 7 = 19$	**15** $5c - 2 = 18$
16 $\dfrac{a}{3} + 2 = 3$	**17** $\dfrac{z}{5} + 1 = 2$	**18** $\dfrac{r}{6} + 4 = 7$
19 $\dfrac{s}{4} + 6 = 9$	**20** $\dfrac{b}{3} + 7 = 13$	**21** $\dfrac{c}{4} - 2 = 4$
22 $\dfrac{f}{3} - 6 = 3$	**23** $\dfrac{h}{2} - 4 = -2$	**24** $\dfrac{x}{5} - 1 = 2$

Example 8   Solve $5m - 8 = 3$.

$5m - 8 = 3$

$5m - 8 + 8 = 3 + 8$ ← Add 8 to both sides.

$5m = 11$

$5m \div 5 = 11 \div 5$ ← Divide both side by 5.

$m = \dfrac{11}{5}$ or $2\dfrac{1}{5}$ or 2.2

ResultsPlus
Examiner's Tip

Unless the equation says give your answer in its simplest form, a mixed fraction such as $\dfrac{11}{5}$ is ok.

Exercise 3H

Solve the equations.

1	$2a + 3 = 6$	2	$2a - 4 = 3$	3	$3a + 7 = 15$
4	$3a - 6 = 7$	5	$5p + 7 = 15$	6	$5p - 7 = 15$
7	$5e + 3 = 3$	8	$4t + 3 = 9$	9	$8j - 7 = 5$
10	$7c - 4 = 7$	11	$8k + 3 = 5$	12	$3d - 7 = 3$
13	$9u + 7 = 9$	14	$4q - 4 = 5$	15	$7y + 6 = 15$

Example 9 Solve $3k + 11 = 2$.

$$3k + 11 = 2$$
$$3k + 11 - 11 = 2 - 11 \quad \longleftarrow \quad \text{Take 11 from both sides.}$$
$$3k = -9$$
$$3k \div 3 = -9 \div 3 \quad \longleftarrow \quad \text{Divide both sides by 3.}$$
$$k = -3 \quad \longleftarrow$$

Remember negative number $\div$ positive number = negative number (see Unit 2 Sections 1.8 and 1.9).

Exercise 3I

Solve these equations.

1	$2a + 3 = 1$	2	$2a + 5 = 1$	3	$2a + 9 = 1$
4	$3a + 8 = 5$	5	$3a + 7 = 1$	6	$5p + 12 = 2$
7	$2s + 7 = -3$	8	$5p - 2 = -12$	9	$4k - 5 = -9$
10	$8h + 10 = 2$	11	$4y + 12 = -8$	12	$3e + 47 = 20$
13	$6t - 12 = -12$	14	$3w + 4 = 1$	15	$2c + 15 = 11$
16	$13a + 9 = 9$				

Mixed exercise 3J

Solve these equations.

1	$2s + 4 = 10$	2	$5d + 3 = 18$	3	$8m - 7 = 33$
4	$4h - 2 = 14$	5	$4k + 7 = 43$	6	$3y + 7 = 13$

E

7	$5p + 2 = 9$	8	$4f + 4 = 17$	9	$3s - 6 = 5$
10	$-7g - 4 = 12$	11	$4f - 5 = 12$	12	$5k - 12 = 6$
13	$-3s - 15 = 2$	14	$6j - 3 = 19$	15	$9b + 7 = 2$
16	$-2r + 12 = 5$	17	$5t + 15 = -2$	18	$7y - 15 = -21$
19	$3e - 5 = -6$	20	$-4f - 7 = -2$	21	$5g + 17 = 15$
22	$4h + 4 = 0$	23	$-3c - 5 = 0$	24	$8s + 9 = 4$
25	$\frac{z}{2} + 2 = 4$	26	$\frac{x}{5} - 3 = 2$	27	$\frac{p}{2} - 5 = -3$
28	$\frac{c}{3} + 4 = -2$	29	$\frac{a}{8} - 1 = 5$	30	$-\frac{e}{3} + 2 = 10$

D

3.4 Solving equations with brackets

◉ Objective

● You can solve equations that have brackets.

⬙ Get Ready

Solve these equations.

1. $3x - 4 = 23$ **2.** $\frac{b}{6} + 2 = 4$ **3.** $-4x + 4 = 6$

◉ Key Point

◉ In an equation with brackets, expand the bracket first.

🔍 Example 10   Solve the equation $5(2x + 3) = 7$.

$$5(2x + 3) = 7$$
$$5 \times 2x + 5 \times 3 = 7 \quad \longleftarrow \quad \text{Multiply each term inside the bracket by 5 to expand the brackets.}$$
$$10x + 15 = 7$$
$$10x + 15 - 15 = 7 - 15 \quad \longleftarrow \quad \text{Take 15 from both sides.}$$
$$10x = -8$$
$$10x \div 10 = -8 \div 10 \quad \longleftarrow \quad \text{Divide both sides by 10.}$$
$$x = -\frac{8}{10} \text{ or } -\frac{4}{5} \text{ or } -0.8$$

Example 11 Solve the equation $\frac{y-7}{4} = 2$.

$\frac{y-7}{4} = 2$ ← In this expression $\frac{y-7}{4}$, the division sign acts as a bracket so $\frac{y-7}{4} = \frac{1}{4}(y-7)$.

$\frac{1}{4}(y-7) = 2$

$4 \times \frac{1}{4}(y-7) = 4 \times 2$ ← Multiply both sides by 4.

$y - 7 + 7 = 8 + 7$ ← Add 7 to both sides.

$y = 15$

Exercise 3K

Solve the equations.

1. $5(a-5) = 70$
2. $6(b+5) = 30$
3. $\frac{c}{6} = 4$
4. $3(d-5) = 15$
5. $5(e+2) = 40$
6. $\frac{f+4}{5} = 4$
7. $4g + 5 = 29$
8. $\frac{h}{3} - 5 = 2$
9. $4(m-4) = 12$
10. $9p - 1 = 2$
11. $6(q+5) = 30$
12. $5v + 3 = 7$
13. $\frac{x}{3} + 7 = 5$
14. $3(y-1) = 2$
15. $3c + 5 = 2$
16. $2(b-3) = 3$
17. $3(2d-5) = 27$
18. $\frac{n-3}{6} = 2$
19. $\frac{t+10}{6} = 1$
20. $\frac{3c+4}{3} = 2$

3.5 Solving equations with letters on both sides

Objective

You can solve equations that have letters on both sides.

Why do this?

Knowing how to solve equations helps you solve other problems such as finding one weight when given another.

Get Ready

Solve the equations.

1. $\frac{g+2}{4} = 6$
2. $\frac{a}{10-2} = 3$
3. $4(b-5) = 4$

Key Point

In an equation with a letter on both sides, use the balance method to rearrange the equation so that the letter is on one side only.

Example 12 Find the value of p in the equation $5p - 2 = 3p + 6$.

$5p - 2 = 3p + 6$

$5p - 3p - 2 = 3p - 3p + 6$ ← Take $3p$ from both sides.

$2p - 2 = 6$

$2p - 2 + 2 = 6 + 2$ ← Add 2 to both sides.

$2p = 8$

$p = 4$ ← Divide both sides by 2.

Exercise 3L

Solve the equations.

1. $2a + 9 = a + 5$
2. $3c - 1 = c + 9$
3. $5p - 7 = 2p + 11$

4. $8b + 9 = 3b + 14$
5. $9q - 8 = 2q + 13$
6. $x + 13 = 5x + 1$

7. $4d + 17 = 8d - 3$
8. $7y = 2y + 15$
9. $3n + 14 = 5n$

10. $5k + 1 = 2k + 1$
11. $4u + 3 = 2u + 8$
12. $7r - 3 = 2r + 9$

13. $6v - 7 = 3v + 7$
14. $9t + 5 = 4t + 9$
15. $7m - 2 = 3m + 8$

16. $3g + 4 = 9g - 1$
17. $5b + 6 = 7b + 5$
18. $2h + 7 = 8h - 1$

19. $3e = 7e - 18$
20. $9f = 3f + 4$

3.6 Solving equations with negative coefficients

◎ Objective

● You can solve equations with negative coefficients using the balance method.

⬥ Get Ready

Solve these equations.

1. $10a = 5a + 5$
2. $3b + 9 = 6b - 3$
3. $8c - 5 = 3c + 10$

⬥ Key Points

● A **coefficient** is the number in front of an unknown.
● You solve equations with negative coefficients using the balance method you have used in the previous sections.

Example 13   Solve the equations.

$$a \quad 7 - 3x = 19 \qquad\qquad b \quad 4 - 3x = 7 - 5x$$

a
$$7 - 3x = 19$$
$$7 = 19 + 3x \quad\longleftarrow \boxed{\text{Add } 3x \text{ to both sides.}}$$
$$7 - 19 = 19 - 19 + 3x \quad\longleftarrow$$
$$-12 = 3x \qquad\qquad \boxed{\text{Take 19 from both sides.}}$$
$$-12 \div 3 = 3x \div 3 \quad\longleftarrow$$
$$-4 = x \qquad\qquad \boxed{\text{Divide both sides by 3.}}$$
$$So \; x = -4 \quad\longleftarrow$$
$$\boxed{\text{Rewrite so that it is in the form } x =.}$$

b
$$4 - 3x = 7 - 5x \quad\longleftarrow \boxed{\text{Add } 5x \text{ to both sides.}}$$
$$4 + 2x = 7$$
$$2x = 3 \quad\longleftarrow \boxed{\text{Subtract 4 from both sides.}}$$

$$x = \frac{3}{2} \text{ or } 1\frac{1}{2} \quad\longleftarrow \boxed{\text{Divide both sides by 2.}}$$

Exercise 3M

Solve these equations.

1	$8 - x = 6$	**2**	$9 - 2x = 1$
3	$40 - 3x = 1$	**4**	$3x + 2 = 10 - x$
5	$4(x + 1) = 11 - 3x$	**6**	$9 - 2x = x$
7	$9 - 5x = 3x + 1$	**8**	$2 - x = x$
9	$1 - 6x = 9 - 7x$	**10**	$5 - 6x = 9 - 8x$
11	$3 - 4x = 8 - 9x$	**12**	$17 - 6x = 5 - 3x$
13	$3 - 4x = 15$	**14**	$7 - 6x = 7$
15	$8 - 2x = 3$	**16**	$5 + 2x = 8 - 3x$
17	$8 + 3x = 1 - 4x$	**18**	$5(4 - x) = 5 + 4x$
19	$13 - 2x = 3 - 7x$	**20**	$3 - 9x = 5 - 6x$

C

3.7 Using equations to solve problems

⊙ Objective

- You can set up equations from mathematical and practical situations and solve the problem.

⊙ Why do this?

You can use equations to solve problems, such as finding the distance travelled with a given starting velocity, time and acceleration.

⊙ Get Ready

1. Two of the angles in a triangle are 140° and 20°. What is the third angle?
2. There are three angles at a point. Two of the angles are 110° and 90°. What is the third angle?
3. The perimeter of a square is 40 cm. What are the side lengths?

Key Point

- You can solve problems in mathematics and other subjects by setting up equations and solving them.

Example 14 In the diagram, ABC is a straight line.
Work out the size of angle DBC.

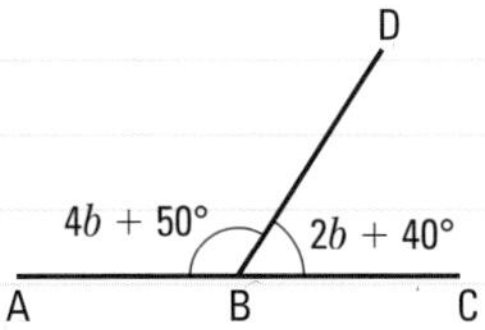

Angles: $4b + 50°$, $2b + 40°$ at B, with points A, B, C on the line and D above.

Write an equation in terms of b, using the sum of the angles on a straight line = 180°.

$$4b + 50 + 2b + 40 = 180$$
$$6b + 90 = 180$$

Collect the terms.

$$6b = 180 - 90$$
$$6b = 90$$
$$b = 15$$

Divide both sides by 6.

$$\text{angle DBC} = 2b + 40$$
$$= 2 \times 15 + 40$$
$$= 30 + 40$$
$$= 70°$$

Substitute $b = 15$.

⚙ Exercise 3N

E
A03

1. I think of a number. I multiply it by 7 and subtract 9.
The result is 47. Find the number.

A03

2. I think of a number. I multiply it by 3 and subtract the result from 50.
The answer is 14. Find the number.

D
A03

3. The sizes of the angles of a triangle are $a + 30°$, $a + 40°$ and $a - 10°$.
Find the size of the largest angle.

4 The diagram shows three angles at a point.
Find the size of each angle.

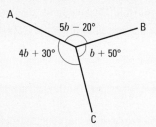

A03

C

5 The lengths, in centimetres, of the sides of a triangle are $3x - 4$, $x + 5$ and $15 - 2x$.
The perimeter of the triangle is 24 cm.
Find the length of each side.

6 I think of a number. I multiply it by 7 and subtract 6 from the result.
The answer is the same as when I multiply the number by 4 and add 27 to the result.
Find the number.

A03

7 The length of each side of a square is $2y - 5$ centimetres. The perimeter of the square is 36 cm.
Find the value of y.

A03

8 Gwen is 39 years older than her son. She is also 4 times as old as he is.
Find Gwen's age.

A03

9 The length of a rectangle is 3 cm greater than its width. The perimeter of the rectangle is 54 cm.
Find its length.

A03

10 The diagram shows a rectangle.
Find the values of x and y.

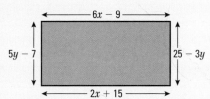

A03

3.8 Solving equations by trial and improvement

◎ Objective

◎ You can find approximate solutions to equations using trial and improvement.

⚙ Get Ready

1. The angles in a triangle are $x°$, $(2x + 20)°$ and $(3x + 40)°$. Find x.
2. I am 30 years older than my daughter. Our combined age is 54. How old is my daughter?
3. The length of each side of an equilateral triangle is $x + 3$ cm. The perimeter is 36 cm. Find x.

🔍 Key Points

◉ There are some equations that can only be solved using the method known as '**trial and improvement**'.
◉ It is helpful to set out your work in a table (see Example 15).

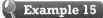 **Example 15** Use trial and improvement to solve the equation $x^3 + x = 16$.
Give your answer correct to 2 d.p.

> $x^3 + x = 16$ is a cubic equation. The highest power of x is cubed.

Method
Estimate a value for x.
Calculate $x^3 + x$ using your estimate.
Compare your answer with 16.
If your answer is too small, choose a bigger value for x.
If your answer is too big, choose a smaller value for x.
Keep repeating this process until you find a value for x correct to 2 d.p. which makes $x^3 + x$ as close as possible to 16.

x	$x^3 + x$	Bigger or smaller than 16?
2	10	Too small
3	30	Too big
2.5	18.125	Too big
2.4	16.224	Too big
2.3	14.467	Too small
2.35	15.327 875	Too small
2.36	15.504 256	Too small
2.37	15.682 053	Too small
2.38	15.861 272	Too small
2.39	16.041 919	Too big
2.385	15.951 416 63	Too small

> Try $x = 2.385$ to find out whether the solution is closer to 2.38 or 2.39.

The solution lies between 2.385 and 2.39.
So $x = 2.39$ to 2 d.p.

⚙ **Exercise 3O**

1. Use a trial and improvement method to solve $x^3 + x = 8$, giving your answer correct to 2 d.p.

2. Use trial and improvement to solve $\dfrac{x^2 + x}{5} = 17$, giving your answer correct to 2 d.p.

3. Use a trial and improvement method to solve $x^3 + 4x = 100$, giving your answer correct to 1 d.p.

4. Use trial and improvement to solve $\dfrac{x^3}{2 + x} = 50$, giving your answer correct to 1 d.p.

5. Use trial and improvement to solve $\dfrac{x^3 + 1}{x} = 10$, giving your answer correct to 2 d.p.

6. Use trial and improvement to solve $2x^3 + 2x = 50$, giving your answer correct to 2 d.p.

7. The equation $x^3 - 4x = 24$ has a solution between 3 and 4.
   Use a trial and improvement method to find this solution. Give your answer correct to 1 d.p.
   You must show all your working.

Chapter review

- In an equation, a symbol or letter represents an unknown number.
- You can solve an equation by rearranging it so that the letter is on its own on one side of the equation.
- To rearrange an equation you can:
  - add the same number to both sides
  - subtract the same number from both sides
  - multiply both sides by the same number
  - divide both sides by the same number.

  This is called the **balance method**.
- In an equation with two operations, deal with the $+$ or $-$ first.
- Solutions to equations can be whole numbers, fractions or decimals.
- Solutions to **linear equations** can be negative.
- In an equation with brackets, expand the bracket first.
- In an equation with a letter on both sides, use the balance method to rearrange the equation so that the letter is on one side only.
- A **coefficient** is the number in front of an unknown.
- You solve equations with negative coefficients using the balance method.
- You can solve problems in mathematics and other subjects by setting up equations and solving them.
- There are some equations that can only be solved using the method known as '**trial and improvement**'.

Review exercise

1 Solve these equations.

   a $a + 7 = 12$ **b** $c - 4 = 6$ **c** $3p = 21$

   d $\dfrac{d}{4} = 3$ **e** $5x + 4 = 19$ **f** $6b - 7 = 17$

   g $a + 7 = 3$ **h** $5b = -30$ **i** $c - 2 = -3$

   j $2e = 11$ **k** $3h + 7 = 1$ **l** $4m + 5 = 2$

   m $6p + 19 = 2$ **n** $6q + 7 = 3$

2 Solve these equations.

   a $2r + 7 = r + 10$ **b** $3x - 2 = x + 8$ **c** $5c + 4 = 2c + 19$ **d** $3b + 4 = b + 5$

   e $5d - 2 = 2d + 3$ **f** $7y - 9 = 2y - 5$ **g** $3t + 8 = 6t + 1$ **h** $2w = 8w - 15$

   i $7u - 6 = 4u - 15$ **j** $5w + 8 = 3w - 5$ **k** $3y - 5 = 7y + 5$

3 **a** Solve $4x - 1 = 7$ **b** Solve $5(2y + 3) = 20$

4 **a** Solve $4x + 3 = 19$ **b** Solve $4y + 1 = 2y + 8$ **c** Simplify $2(t + 5) + 13$

5 Solve $4(x + 3) = 6$

6 **a** Solve $2(x - 2) = 10$ **b** Solve $4(y + 1) = 10$

C

7 Solve these equations.

   a $3(a + 5) = a + 21$ **b** $5(b - 4) = 2b + 1$ **c** $7c - 2 = 3(c + 6)$

   d $6(d - 2) = 5(d - 1)$ **e** $8(e - 1) = 5(e + 2)$ **f** $9(f - 2) = 2(f + 3)$

   g $4(2m + 1) = 3(5m - 1)$ **h** $2(3t + 4) = 5(2t - 1)$ **i** $8 - a = 5$

   j $13 - 3b = 1$ **k** $5 - 4d = 3$ **l** $5 - 3g = 1$

   m $4 - 3p = 18$

8 The perimeter of a rectangle is 120 cm.

The length of a rectangle is 4 times its width.

Find the length of the rectangle.

9 In the diagram, all measurements are in centimetres.

ABC is an isosceles triangle.

$AB = 2x$

$AC = 2x$

$BC = 10$

   a Find an expression, in terms of x, for the perimeter of
the triangle. Simplify your own expression.

   b The perimeter of the triangle is 34 cm.
Find the value of x.

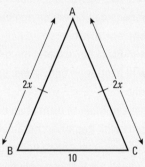

Diagram **NOT**
accurately drawn

10 Use the method of trial and improvement to find solutions to these equations.

   a $x^3 + 3x - 20 = 0$ (to 2 d.p.)   **b** $x^3 - 20x - 3 = 0$ (to 2 d.p.)

   c $x^3 - 4x^2 - 5 = 0$ (to 2 d.p.)   **d** $x^3 - 2x^2 = 25$ (to 2 d.p.)

   e $x^3 + 5x = 26$ (to 1 d.p.)   **f** $x^3 - 2 = 2x$ (to 2 d.p.)

11 The equation $x^3 + 10x = 21$ has a solution between 1 and 2. Use a trial and improvement method
to find this solution. Give your answer correct to 1 d.p. You must show ALL your working.

12 Tariq and Yousef have been asked to find the solution, correct to 1 decimal place, of the equation
$x^3 + 2x = 56$

   a Work out the value of $x^3 + 2x$ when $x = 3.65$.

Tariq says 3.6 is the solution.

Yousef says 3.7 is the solution.

   b Use your answer to part **a** to decide whether Tariq or Yousef is correct.
You must give a reason.

A03

13 In this quadrilateral, the sizes of the angles, in degrees, are

$x + 10$ $2x$ $2x$ 50

   a Use this information to write down an equation in
terms of x.

   b Work out the value of x.

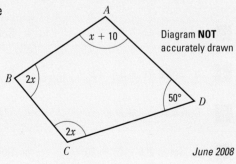

Diagram **NOT**
accurately drawn

June 2008

14 Uzma has £x. Hajra has £20 more than Uzma. Mabintou has twice as much as Hajra.
The total amount of money they have is £132.
Find how much money they each have.

A03

15 Jake has 3 sticks, A, B and C. Stick B is 5 cm longer than stick A. Stick C is 4 times the length of stick B.
Stick C is also 3 times the sum of the lengths of A and B.
Find the lengths of the 3 sticks.

A03

16
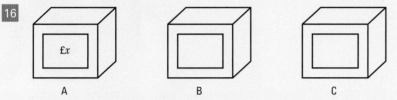

A   B   C

Here are 3 boxes. Box A has £x. Box B has £4 more than box A. Box C has one third of the money in box B. Altogether there is £24 in the 3 boxes.
Find the amount of money in the 3 boxes.

A03

17 Becky has 4 more CDs than Emil. Justin has twice as many CDs as Becky.
The total number of CDs they have altogether is 32.
a Form an equation.
b Work out how many CDs Justin has.

A02

18 **a** The equation $x^3 + 4x^2 = 100$ has a solution between 3 and 4.
Find this solution. Give your answer correct to one decimal place.
You must show ALL your working.
b The diagram shows a cuboid.
The base of the cuboid is a square.
The height of the cuboid is 4 cm more than the width.
The volume of the cuboid is 100 cm³.
Write down the height of the cuboid, correct to 1 decimal place.

Nov 2006 adapted

A03

19 A garden room is 3 metres longer than it is wide.
Given that its area is 14 m², use trial and improvement to find an estimate for its perimeter.

A03

4 INEQUALITIES

Often when shopping on the internet, you can search for items according to price. These goats are used on the Oxfam Unwrapped website where you can view gifts between £6 and £20, between £20 and £50 or gifts for £50+. This is an example of inequalities in action and it allows you to immediately see what is within your price range.

Objectives

In this chapter you will:
- understand and use inequality signs
- show inequalities on a number line
- solve inequalities.

Before you start

You need to be able to:
- solve equations with one unknown value.

4.1 Introducing inequalities

◎ Objectives

- ◉ You know and understand inequality signs.
- ◉ You can put in the correct inequality sign to make a statement true.

❓ Why do this?

Inequalities can be used to compare quantities.

The number of apples is greater than the number of pears.

◈ Get Ready

1. Put these numbers in order. Start with the smallest.

$-15 \quad -19 \quad 24 \quad 5 \quad 1.34$

Key Points

- ◉ $>$ means **greater than**.
- ◉ $\geq$ means **greater than or equal to**.
- ◉ $<$ means **less than**.
- ◉ $\leq$ means **less than or equal to**.

Example 1   Put the correct inequality sign between each pair of numbers to make a true statement.

     a 7, 8   **b** 9, 6

a $7 < 8$ ←   Use $<$ as 7 is less than 8.

b $9 > 6$ ←   Use $>$ as 9 is greater than 6.

ResultsPlus
Examiner's Tip

Sometimes in the examination the question will ask for integers. These are the same as positive and negative whole numbers.

Example 2   Write down the values of x that are whole numbers and satisfy these inequalities.

     a $3 < x < 8$ **b** $-3 \leq x < 2$

a $3 < x < 8$ ←   This means x is greater than 3 but less than 8. These whole numbers would satisfy this statement.
    $4, 5, 6, 7$

b $-3 \leq x < 2$ ←   This means x is greater than or equal to -3 and less than 2.
    $-3, -2, -1, 0, 1$ ←   Write the numbers in order of size.

Exercise 4A

Questions in this chapter are targeted at the grades indicated.

D

1 Put the correct sign ($<$ or $>$) between each pair of numbers to make a true statement.

a 4, 6   b 5, 2   c 12, 8   d 6, 6

e 15, 8   f 3, 24   g 10, 3   h 0, 0.1

i 6, 0.7   j 4.5, 4.5   k 0.2, 0.5   l 4.8, 4.79

2 Write down whether each statement is true or false. If it is false, write down the pair of numbers with the correct sign.

a $6 > 4$ b $2 > 6$ c $6 > 6$ d $6 > 8$

e $6 < 5$ f $8 = 14$ g $7 < 6.99$ h $6 > 6.01$

i $7 < 0$ j $4 < 4$ k $6 = 4$ l $6 > 0.84$

C

3 Write down the values of x that are whole numbers and satisfy these inequalities.

a $4 < x < 6$ b $3 < x < 8$

c $0 \leqslant x < 4$ d $3 < x < 6$

e $1 < x \leqslant 4$ f $2 < x < 6$

g $4 \leqslant x < 7$ h $-2 \leqslant x < 4$

i $-1 < x < 5$ j $-2 < x \leqslant 6$

k $-3 \leqslant x < 3$ l $-4 \leqslant x \leqslant 2$

m $0 < x < 5$ n $-1 < x \leqslant 4$

o $-5 \leqslant x < 0$ p $-3 \leqslant x \leqslant 3$

4.2 Representing inequalities on a number line

◉ Objective

● You can show inequalities on a number line.

⬦ Get Ready

Write the values of x that are whole numbers and satisfy these inequalities.

1. $-3 \leqslant x \leqslant 4$ **2.** $-5 \leqslant x < 2$ **3.** $-6 \leqslant x \leqslant 7$

🔍 Key Points

● You can show **inequalities** on a number line.
● An empty circle shows that the value is not included and a filled circle shows that the value is included (see Example 4).

Example 3 ▶ Draw a number line from 0 to 10. Show the inequality $x > 4$.

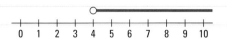

Draw an empty circle as the number is not included.

Example 4 ▶ Draw a number line from 0 to 10. Show the inequality $3 \leqslant x < 8$.

Draw a filled circle at 3 since the number 3 is included ($x \geqslant 3$).

Draw an empty circle at 8 since the number 8 is not included.

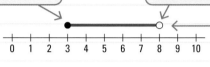

Draw a line between the circles at 3 and 8.

Example 5 ▶ Draw a number line from -5 to 5. Show the inequality $-3 < x \leqslant 4$.

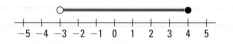

Empty circle at -3 as x is greater than -3.
Filled circle at 4 as x is less than or equal to 4.

Exercise 4B

1 Draw six number lines from 0 to 10. Show these inequalities.

a $x > 6$ b $x > 5$ c $x < 4$ d $x > 8$ e $x < 6$ f $x > 9$

2 Draw ten number lines from 0 to 10. Show these inequalities.

a $3 < x < 7$ b $5 < x < 8$ c $5 \leqslant x < 8$ d $7 < x \leqslant 9$

e $4 \leqslant x \leqslant 6$ f $2 < x \leqslant 8$ g $3 \leqslant x < 5$ h $4 < x < 7$

i $5 \leqslant x < 6$ j $2 < x \leqslant 5$

3 Draw ten number lines from -5 to 5. Show these inequalities.

a $-3 \leqslant x < 4$ b $-2 < x \leqslant 5$ c $-1 < x \leqslant 3$ d $-4 \leqslant x \leqslant 0$

e $0 < x < 4$ f $-3 < x \leqslant 2$ g $-4 \leqslant x < 1$ h $0 \leqslant x \leqslant 3$

i $-5 \leqslant x < 2$ j $-2 \leqslant x < 1$

4 Write down the inequalities represented on these number lines.

a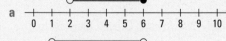

b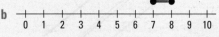

c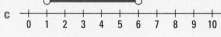

d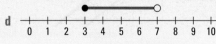

e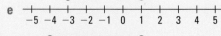

f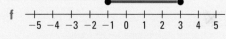

g (image)

h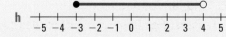

C

4.3 Solving inequalities

◎ Objective

● You can solve linear inequalities.

❓ Why do this?

Businesses use inequalities to help them maximise profits or minimise costs.

⬆ Get Ready

Show these on a number line.

1. $-6 < x < 2$ **2.** $-5 \leqslant x < 3$ **3.** $1 < x \leqslant 8$

🔍 Key Point

◎ You can solve inequalities in the same way as linear equations except you must not:

● multiply both sides by the same negative quantity
● divide both sides by the same negative quantity.

🔍 Example 6

a Solve the inequality $2x - 1 < 4$.

b Show the solution on a number line.

a $2x - 1 < 4$

$2x < 5$ ⟵ Add 1 to both sides.

$x < 2\frac{1}{2}$ ⟵ Divide both sides by 2.

b

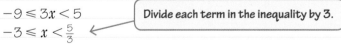

🔍 Example 7

a Solve the inequality $2x + 3 \leqslant 5x + 7$.

b Write down the smallest integer that satisfies this inequality.

a $2x + 3 \leqslant 5x + 7$

$3 \leqslant 3x + 7$ ⟵ Subtract $2x$ from both sides.

$-4 \leqslant 3x$ ⟵ Subtract 7 from both sides.

$x \geqslant -1\frac{1}{3}$ ⟵ Divide both sides by 3.

$-4 \leqslant 3x$ is the same as $3x \geqslant -4$

b The smallest integer that satisfies this inequality is -1.

🔍 Example 8

Find all the integers that satisfy the inequality $-9 \leqslant 3x < 5$. Draw a diagram to help.

$-9 \leqslant 3x < 5$

$-3 \leqslant x < \frac{5}{3}$ ⟵ Divide each term in the inequality by 3.

The integer solutions are $-3, -2, -1, 0, 1$

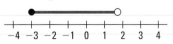

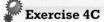

Exercise 4C

In questions 1–12, solve the inequality.

1	$x + 3 < 7$	2	$x - 1 \geqslant 5$	3	$2x \leqslant 12$
4	$\dfrac{x}{3} > 2$	5	$x - 4 < 5$	6	$5x > 20$
7	$x + 9 \geqslant 9$	8	$3x - 7 \leqslant 8$	9	$4x + 3 \geqslant 15$
10	$5x - 7 < 3$	11	$7x - 2 > 3x + 10$	12	$4x - 3 \leqslant 9x - 8$

In questions 13–18, solve the inequality and show the solution on a number line.

13	$4x > 11$	14	$6x \leqslant 3$	15	$3x + 7 \geqslant 1$
16	$8x - 3 > 7$	17	$2x + 5 < 2$	18	$7x - 5 \leqslant 3x - 2$

In questions 19–27, find all the integers that satisfy the inequality.

19	$4 \leqslant 2x \leqslant 8$	20	$-9 \leqslant 3x < 6$	21	$-15 < 5x \leqslant 5$
22	$0 \leqslant 6x < 24$	23	$-16 < 4x \leqslant 0$	24	$2 \leqslant 3x < 7$
25	$-7 < 5x \leqslant 15$	26	$-5 < 2x < 5$	27	$-10 < 3x < 0$

In questions 28–54, solve the inequality.

28	$8x < 20$	29	$4x \geqslant 3$	30	$5x > -15$
31	$3x \geqslant -8$	32	$\dfrac{x}{4} > -2$	33	$21 < 6x$
34	$4x - 9 \geqslant 2$	35	$6x + 7 \leqslant 3$	36	$8x - 1 > 6$
37	$9 < 7x + 2$	38	$5x + 3 \geqslant 2x + 9$	39	$7x + 2 \leqslant 3x - 2$
40	$8x - 1 > 5x - 6$	41	$9x - 7 < 5x + 3$	42	$2x + 9 \geqslant 7x - 6$
43	$2(x - 3) \geqslant 8$	44	$5(x + 2) > 10$	45	$3(x + 1) < x + 9$
46	$7 - x \leqslant 1$	47	$8 - 3x > 2$	48	$2 - 5x < 6$
49	$7 - 2x \geqslant 3x + 2$	50	$4(x - 3) \leqslant 3 - x$	51	$10 - 3x > 2x - 1$
52	$6 - 5x \leqslant 2 - 3x$	53	$3 - 5x \geqslant 4 - 7x$	54	$11 - 2x < 2 - 5x$

55 Solve the inequality $7x + 5 > 4x - 9$.
Write down the smallest integer that satisfies it.

56 Solve the inequality $3x + 4 \leqslant 1 - 2x$.
Write down the largest integer that satisfies it.

Chapter review

- $>$ means **greater than**.
- $\geqslant$ means **greater than or equal to**.
- $<$ means **less than**.
- $\leqslant$ means **less than or equal to**.
- You can show **inequalities** on a number line.
- An empty circle shows that the value is not included and a filled circle shows that the value is included.
- You can solve inequalities in the same way as linear equations except you must not:
  - multiply both sides by the same negative quantity
  - divide both sides by the same negative quantity.

Review exercise

1. Show each inequality on a number line.
   a $x > 1$
   b $x \leqslant 3$
   c $x \leqslant 0$
   d $-2 \leqslant x < 1$
   e $-1 < x \leqslant 3$
   f $1 \leqslant x < 4$

2. Write down the inequalities represented on these number lines.

   a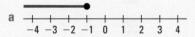
   b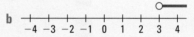

   c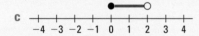
   d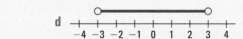

   e
   f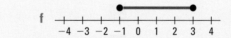

3. For each of these inequalities, list the integers that satisfy it.
   a $-3 \leqslant x < 1$
   b $0 < x \leqslant 3$
   c $-2 \leqslant x \leqslant 4$
   d $-4 < x < -1$

4. Solve each inequality.
   a $x - 6 > 4$
   b $6x \leqslant 30$
   c $2x - 5 < 4$
   d $5x + 11 \leqslant 1$
   e $8x + 9 \geqslant 4x + 3$
   f $7x - 1 < 4x - 1$
   g $3x - 1 < 5x$
   h $2(x - 3) < 7$
   i $4 - x \leqslant x + 8$

5. Solve each inequality and show the solution on a number line.
   a $2x < 5$
   b $4x \geqslant -2$
   c $3x - 4 > 1$
   d $6x + 7 \leqslant 1$
   e $9x - 5 < 4x + 5$
   f $6x + 7 < 8x + 7$

6. Solve the inequality $6x < 7 + 4x$.

7. a Solve $5 - 3x = 2(x + 1)$.
   b $-3 < y \leqslant 3$ y is an integer.
   Write down all possible values of y.

8 **a** Solve $7x > 21$.

   b Solve $5y + 1 \geqslant 3y + 13$.

9

Diagram **NOT** accurately drawn

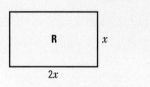

Here are 3 rods.

The length of rod A is x cm.

Rod B is 4 cm longer than rod A.

The length of rod C is twice the length of rod B.

The total length of all 3 rods is L cm.

a Show that $L = 4x + 12$.

The total length of all 3 rods must be less than 50 cm.

b Write down the inequality that must be satisfied.

c Work out the range of possible values of x.

Specimen Paper 2009

10 Tom has three parcels.

The weight of the first parcel is x kg.

The weight of the second parcel is 2 kg more than the first.

The weight of the third parcel is 3 kg more than the second.

The total weight of the parcels must be less than or equal to 20 kg.

Work out the largest possible weight of the heaviest parcel.

11

R x

2x

S

$x + 2$

The perimeter of the rectangle R is less than the perimeter of the square S.

Write down the range of values of x.

A02

A03

A02

C

5 QUADRATIC GRAPHS

The graph of a quadratic function is a curve called a parabola. A javelin would follow the path of a perfect parabola if air resistance, wind spin and rotation didn't affect it. Javelin throwing was part of the Ancient Greek Olympics. In one of the events competitors had to throw the javelin from the back of a galloping horse.

◉ Objectives

In this chapter you will:
- draw and interpret a range of linear and non-linear graphs
- use a table of values to draw quadratic graphs
- use graphs of quadratic functions to solve quadratic equations.

◈ Before you start

You need to know:
- how to plot a coordinate
- how to substitute a number for x in a linear equation
- how to plot a linear graph.

5.1 Interpreting real-life graphs

⊙ Objectives

- You can interpret and draw graphs of water filling different-shaped containers.
- You can interpret the shape of graphs, e.g. filling and emptying a bath.

⟳ Why do this?

You will often see graphs in newspapers and you need to be able to interpret the information on them.

⬧ Get Ready

1. Look at these graphs for the cost of using two mobile phones. One is pay as you go and one is for a contract: which is which? How might you choose which one is suitable for you?

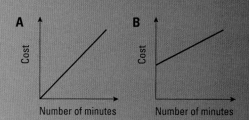

Key Points

- Containers with straight vertical sides fill at a **constant** rate.
- Containers with sides that bulge out fill quickly at first. The rate slows down until the widest point of the bulge, then the rate speeds up again.
- Containers with sides that curve in fill slowly at first. The rate speeds up until the narrowest point of the curve, then the rate slows down again.
- Containers that are thin fill faster than containers that are fatter.
- The thinner the container, the steeper the graph.
  You can see the difference in the graphs of these containers.
  They have the same height.

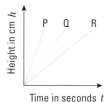

- Containers with slanting sides have curved line graphs. They start steep and get less steep as the diameter gets bigger.

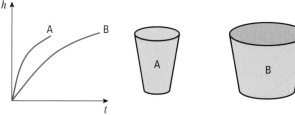

- Containers with sides that bulge out have a curved line graph and they start steep, get less steep and then get steep again.
- The graph for the top of the flask is a straight line.

Example 1   Match these containers to their graphs when they are filled with water at a constant rate.

A   B   C   D   E

A and 5 go together since A has straight sides and is thin.

B and 2 go together since B has straight sides and is wider than A.

C and 1 go together since C is wide with straight sides and then narrow with straight sides.

D and 3 go together since D is narrow with straight sides and then wide with straight sides.

E and 4 go together since E has three sections which can be identified on the graph.

Exercise 5A

Questions in this chapter are targeted at the grades indicated.

In questions **1** to **4**, liquid is poured at a constant rate into the containers. The height of the liquid in the container h in cm is plotted against the passage of time t in seconds.

1   Match these containers with their graphs.

A   B   C   D   E

2 Match these containers with their graphs.

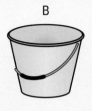  

A   B   C   D   E

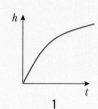 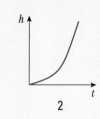  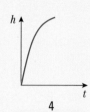 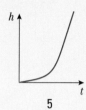

1   2   3   4   5

3 Match these containers with their graphs.

A   B   C   D   E

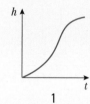 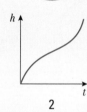 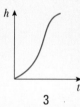 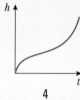 

1   2   3   4   5

4 Match these containers with their graphs.

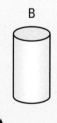   

A   B   C   D   E

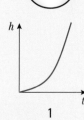  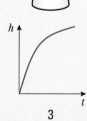

1   2   3   4   5

5 Liquid is poured into each of these containers at a constant rate.

For each set of containers draw, on the same graph, the height of the liquid h against the time t in seconds.

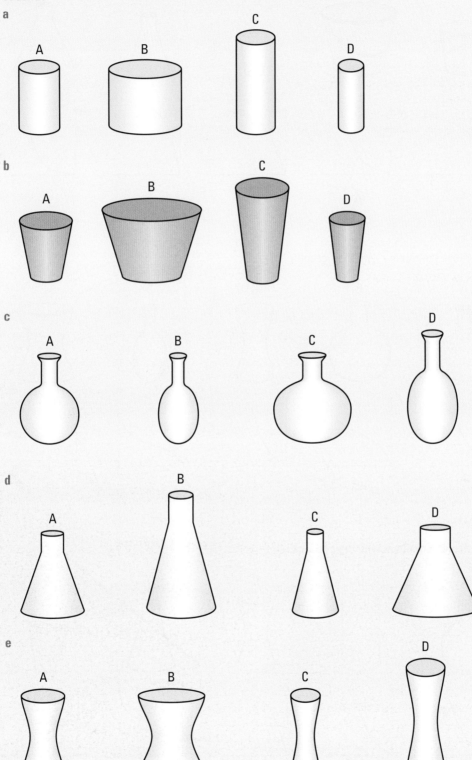

* **6** Here is a graph that shows the height of water in a bath. For each part of the graph, describe what may have happened.

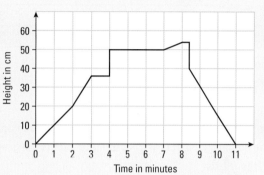

* **7** Here is a graph that shows the height, in cm, of the water in a bath.
Explain, giving the heights and the times, what happened at each stage of the process.

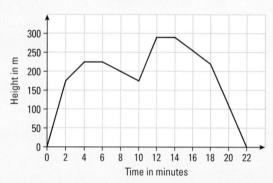

* **8** Here is a graph that shows the height, in metres, of a hot air balloon during a flight.

Describe the flight of the hot air balloon.

5.2 Drawing quadratic graphs

Objectives

- You can use a table of values to draw graphs of the form $y = ax^2 \pm b$.
- You can use a table of values to draw graphs of the form $y = ax^2 \pm bx \pm c$.
- You know the effect of putting a negative sign in front of the x^2.

Why do this?

You would be able to plot a graph of the trajectory of your ball if you were playing basketball.

Get Ready

Remember BIDMAS? (See Unit 2 Section 8.4.)
When you substitute numbers into these expressions you do the indices first and then the other processes.
e.g. Find the value of $3x^2$ when $x = 5$ $3 \times 5^2 = 3 \times 25 = 75$

1. When $x = 3$, find the value of
   a x^2 **b** $5x^2$ **c** $x^2 + 2x$
   d $4x^2 + 3x$ **e** $x^2 - 5x$ **f** $2x^2 - 10x$

Key Points

- To draw a quadratic graph (e.g. $y = x^2$):
  - make a table of values, selecting some values for x

x		−3	−2	−1	0	1	2	3
$y = x^2$								

  - substitute the values of x into $y = x^2$

x		−3	−2	−1	0	1	2	3
$y = x^2$		9	4	1	0	1	4	9

  - plot the points on a grid
  - draw in the line.

- For quadratic graphs such as $y = ax^2 + b$:
  - the number (b) that is on its own moves the graph up or down
  - the number (a) that is in front of the x^2 brings the graph closer to the y-axis
  - if there is a minus sign in front of the x^2 then the graph turns upside down.

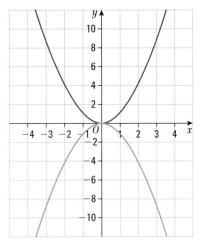

Example 2 On a coordinate grid with values of x from −3 to +3, draw the graphs of

     i $y = x^2$ **ii** $y = x^2 + 1$ **iii** $y = x^2 - 1$ **iv** $y = x^2 - 2$

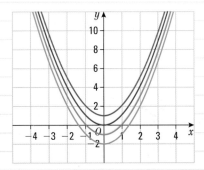

3. Plot the points on the grid.
4. Draw in the line.
5. Repeat for all the other lines.

1. Make a table of values, selecting some values for x.

x		−3	−2	−1	0	1	2	3
$y = x^2$								

2. Substitute the values of x into $y = x^2$.

x		−3	−2	−1	0	1	2	3
$y = x^2$		9	4	1	0	1	4	9

x		−3	−2	−1	0	1	2	3
$y = x^2 + 1$		10	5	2	1	2	5	10

x		−3	−2	−1	0	1	2	3
$y = x^2 - 1$		8	3	0	−1	0	3	8

x		−3	−2	−1	0	1	2	3
$y = x^2 - 2$		7	2	−1	−2	−1	2	7

Example 3

On a coordinate grid with values of x from -3 to $+3$, draw the graphs of

  i $y = x^2$ **ii** $y = 2x^2$ **iii** $y = 3x^2$

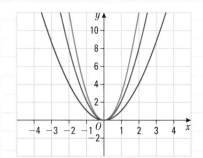

x	-3	-2	-1	0	1	2	3
$y = x^2$	9	4	1	0	1	4	9

x	-2	-1	0	1	2
$y = 2x^2$	8	2	0	2	8

x	-2	-1	0	1	2
$y = 3x^2$	12	3	0	3	12

Example 4

On a coordinate grid with values of x from -3 to $+3$, draw the graphs of

  i $y = x^2$ **ii** $y = -x^2$

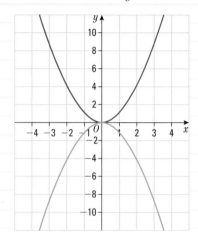

x	-3	-2	-1	0	1	2	3
$y = x^2$	9	4	1	0	1	4	9
$y = -x^2$	-9	-4	-1	0	-1	-4	-9

Exercise 5B

1   **a** Copy and complete the tables of values for these quadratic graphs.

   b Draw the graphs on a coordinate grid with x-axis drawn from -3 to $+3$ and y-axis drawn from -12 to $+12$.

i

x	-3	-2	-1	0	1	2	3
$y = x^2 + 2$		6		2		6	

ii

x	-3	-2	-1	0	1	2	3
$y = -x^2 - 2$		-6		-2		-6	

iii

x	-3	-2	-1	0	1	2	3
$y = -x^2 + 1$	-8			1			-8

iv

x	-3	-2	-1	0	1	2	3
$y = -x^2 + 4$		0		4			-5

v

x	-3	-2	-1	0	1	2	3
$y = x^2 + 3$		7				7	

C

2

a Copy and complete the tables of values for these quadratic graphs.

b Draw the graphs on a coordinate grid with x-axis drawn from -3 to $+3$ and y-axis drawn from -20 to $+20$.

i

x	-3	-2	-1	0	1	2	3
$y = 2x^2 + 1$		9		1		9	

ii

x	-3	-2	-1	0	1	2	3
$y = -2x^2 + 1$		-7		1		-7	

iii

x	-2	-1	0	1	2
$y = -3x^2 + 1$	-11		1		

iv

x	-3	-2	-1	0	1	2	3
$y = 2x^2 - 1$		7		-1			

v

x	-3	-2	-1	0	1	2	3
$y = -2x^2 - 1$		-9		-1			

3 Draw these quadratic graphs on a coordinate grid with x-axis drawn from -3 to $+3$ and y-axis drawn from -15 to $+15$.

a $y = x^2$ **b** $y = x^2 + 3$ **c** $y = x^2 - 3$ **d** $y = -x^2 + 3$ **e** $y = -x^2 - 3$

4 Draw these quadratic graphs on a coordinate grid with x-axis drawn from -3 to $+3$ and y-axis drawn from -20 to $+20$.

a $y = x^2$ **b** $y = -x^2$ **c** $y = 2x^2$ **d** $y = -2x^2$ **e** $y = -(x + 1)^2$

5 Draw these quadratic graphs on a coordinate grid with x-axis drawn from -3 to $+3$ and y-axis drawn from -30 to $+30$.

a $y = x^2$ **b** $y = 3x^2$ **c** $y = -3x^2 - 3$ **d** $y = -3x^2$ **e** $y = 3x^2 + 3$

Example 5   On a coordinate grid with values of x from -3 to $+3$, draw the graph of $y = x^2 + 2x - 5$.

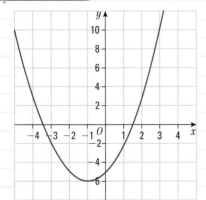

1. Make a table of values, selecting some values for x.

x	-3	-2	-1	0	1	2	3
x^2							
$2x$							
-5							
y							

2. Substitute the values of x into $y = x^2 + 2x - 5$.

x	-3	-2	-1	0	1	2	3
x^2	9	4	1	0	1	4	9
$2x$	-6	-4	-2	0	2	4	6
-5	-5	-5	-5	-5	-5	-5	-5
y	-2	-5	-6	-5	-2	3	10

Square x
Double x
Always -5

ResultsPlus

Watch Out!

Don't forget the rules of BIDMAS when filling in the table of values.

3. Plot the points on the grid.
4. Draw in the curved line.

Exercise 5C

1 **a** Copy and complete the tables of values for these quadratic graphs.

b Draw the graphs on a coordinate grid with x-axis drawn from -3 to $+3$ and y-axis drawn from -20 to $+20$.

i

x	-3	-2	-1	0	1	2	3
x^2	$+9$			0			
$2x$	-6			0			
$+1$	$+1$			$+1$			
$y = x^2 + 2x + 1$	4			1			

ii

x	-3	-2	-1	0	1	2	3
x^2		$+4$		0			
$3x$		-6		0			
$+2$		$+2$		$+2$			
$y = x^2 + 3x + 2$		0		2			

iii

x	-3	-2	-1	0	1	2	3
x^2	$+9$			0			
$2x$	-6			0			
-5	-5			-5			
$y = x^2 + 2x - 5$	-2			-5			

iv

x	-3	-2	-1	0	1	2	3
x^2	$+9$				$+1$		
$-2x$	$+6$				-2		
$+3$	$+3$				$+3$		
$y = x^2 - 2x + 3$	18				2		

v

x	-3	-2	-1	0	1	2	3
x^2	$+9$			0			
$-2x$	$+6$			0			
-3	-3			-3			
$y = x^2 - 2x - 3$	12			-3			

2 Draw these quadratic graphs on a coordinate grid with x-axis drawn from -3 to $+3$ and y-axis drawn from -15 to $+15$.

a $y = x^2$ **b** $y = x^2 + 3x$ **c** $y = x^2 - 3x$ **d** $y = -x^2 + 3x$ **e** $y = -x^2 - 3x$

3 Draw these quadratic graphs on a coordinate grid with x-axis drawn from -3 to $+3$ and y-axis drawn from -20 to $+20$.

a $y = x^2 + 2x + 3$ **b** $y = -x^2 + 2x + 3$ **c** $y = 2x^2 + x - 1$

d $y = -2x^2 + x + 1$ **e** $y = (x - 1)^2$ **f** $y = (x + 1)(x - 1)$

C

4 Draw these quadratic graphs on a coordinate grid with x-axis drawn from -3 to $+3$ and y-axis drawn from -30 to $+30$.

a $y = x^2 - 3x + 2$ b $y = 3x^2 - 4x$ c $y = -3x^2 + 4x$

d $y = -3x^2 + x$ e $y = 2x^2 - 3x$ f $(x + 2)(x - 1)$

5.3 Using graphs of quadratic functions to solve equations

◉ Objective

● You can use graphs of quadratic functions to solve quadratic equations.

⬆ Get Ready

Draw the graphs for these quadratic equations.

1. $y = -x^2 + 2x$ **2.** $y = 4x^2 - 2x$

🔍 Key Point

◉ You can solve a **quadratic equation** by drawing the graph and then finding where the graph crosses the x-axis, where $y = 0$.

🔍 Example 6

Solve the equations   a $x^2 - x - 3 = 0$ b $x^2 - x - 3 = 2$

Draw the graph of $y = x^2 - x - 3$.

Step 1 Make up a table of values.
Step 2 Plot the points.
Step 3 Draw the curve.
Step 4 Find where the curve cuts the line $y = 0$ (the x-axis).

x	-3	-2	-1	0	1	2	3
x^2	$+9$	$+4$	$+1$	0	$+1$	$+4$	$+9$
$-x$	$+3$	$+2$	$+1$	0	-1	-2	-3
-3	-3	-3	-3	-3	-3	-3	-3
$y = x^2 - x - 3$	9	3	-1	-3	-3	-1	$+3$

a $x = -1.3$ and $x = 2.3$

The curve meets the x-axis when $x = -1.3$ and 2.3. These are the answers, or the solutions, to the equation.

b $x = -1.8$ and $x = 2.75$

If the equation was $x^2 - x - 3 = 2$ then you would need to read off at $y = 2$. In this case the solutions would be $x = -1.8$ and 2.75.

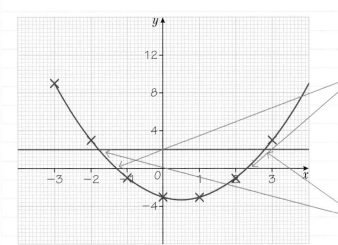

Exercise 5D

1 **a** Draw the graph of $y = 2x^2 - 3x - 2$ for values of x from -2 to $+4$.
 b Use your graph to solve the equations.
  i $2x^2 - 3x - 2 = 0$ **ii** $2x^2 - 3x - 2 = 10$

2 **a** Draw the graph of $y = x^2 - 3x - 2$ for values of x from -2 to $+5$.
 b Use your graph to solve the equations.
  i $x^2 - 3x - 2 = 0$ **ii** $x^2 - 3x - 2 = 5$

3 **a** Draw the graph of $y = 2x^2 - 3x$ for values of x from -2 to $+3$.
 b Use your graph to solve the equations.
  i $2x^2 - 3x = 0$ **ii** $2x^2 - 3x = 4$

4 **a** Draw the graph of $y = x^2 - 2x$ for values of x from -2 to $+4$.
 b Use your graph to solve the equations.
  i $x^2 - 2x = 0$ **ii** $x^2 - 2x = 3$

5 **a** Draw the graph of $y = x^2 - 4x + 3$ for values of x from -1 to $+5$.
 b Use your graph to solve the equations.
  i $x^2 - 4x + 3 = 0$ **ii** $x^2 - 4x + 3 = 2$

Chapter review

- The thinner the container, the steeper the graph.
- Containers with slanting sides have curved line graphs. They start steep and get less steep as the diameter gets bigger.
- Containers with sides that bulge out have a curved line graph and they start steep, get less steep and then get steep again.
- To draw a quadratic graph:
  - make a table of values, selecting some values for x
  - substitute the values of x into y
  - plot the points on a grid
  - draw in the line.
- For quadratic graphs such as $y = ax^2 + b$:
  - the number (b) that is on its own moves the graph up or down
  - the number (a) that is in front of the x^2 brings the graph closer to the y-axis
  - if there is a minus sign in front of the x^2 then the graph turns upside down.
- You can solve a **quadratic equation** by drawing the graph and then finding where the graph crosses the x-axis, where $y = 0$.

D A03

1 Here are six temperature/time graphs.
For each graph describe how the temperature changes with time.

A
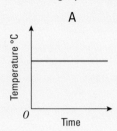

B
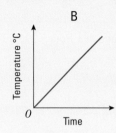

C
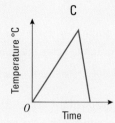

D
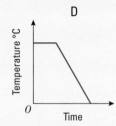

E
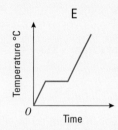

F
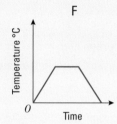

Nov 2008

C

2 **a** Copy and complete the table of values for
$y = x^2 - 4x - 2$.

x	-1	0	1	2	3	4	5
y		-2	-5			-2	3

b Copy the grid and draw the graph of
$y = x^2 - 4x - 2$.

c Use your graph to find estimates of the
solutions of $x^2 - 4x - 2 = 0$.

Nov 2008

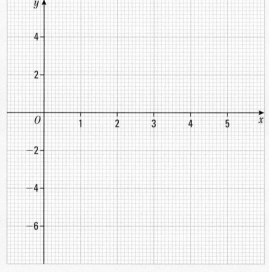

3 The graph of $y = x^2 - 2x$ has been drawn
on the grid.
Copy the graph and use it to find estimates
of the solutions of

a $x^2 - 2x = 0$

b $x^2 - 2x = 2$

c $x^2 - 2x = -1$

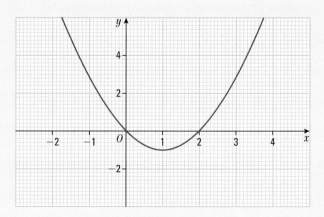

4 The diagram shows a square with sides of length x cm.

Part of the square is shaded as shown in the diagram.

Given that the shaded area is 3cm², find an estimate for the value of x.

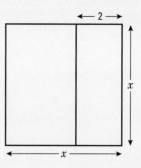

5 The diagram shows a rectangle.

All the measurements are in cm.

The width is x and the length is 3 cm more than the width.

The area of the rectangle is 20 cm².

a Draw a suitable graph.

b Find an estimate for the value of x.

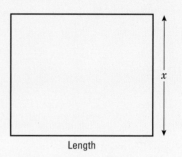

Length

6 FORMULAE

In the UK temperatures are normally given in Celsius. To convert Celsius to Fahrenheit, you multiply by $\frac{9}{5}$ and then add 32. So the formula is $°F = °C \times \frac{9}{5} + 32$. But what if you were in America and you heard the temperature in Fahrenheit and needed to know how much it was in Celsius? You would need to rearrange the formula to convert Fahrenheit to Celsius.

◎ Objectives

In this chapter you will:
- find the value of a term which is not the subject of the formula
- change the subject of a formula.

◊ Before you start

You need to know how to:
- use and write word formulae
- substitute numbers into expressions.

6.1 Finding the value of a term which is not the subject of a formula

◎ Objective

◉ You can work out a value in a formula when it is not the subject of the formula.

⬆ Get Ready

Solve these equations.

1. $2x + 4 = 10$ **2.** $24 = 2a - 8$ **3.** $6x = 30$

◯ Key Point

◉ To find out the value of a term which is not the subject of a formula, put the given values into the formula and then solve the resulting equation.

🔍 Example 1

$P = 2a + b$

Work out the value of a when $P = 25$ and $b = 7$.

$25 = 2a + 7$ ← Solve this equation.

$2a = 18$ ← Subtract 7 from both sides.

$a = 9$ ← Divide both sides by 2.

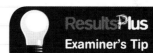

ResultsPlus

Examiner's Tip

Substitute the value of the term back into the formula to check your answer.

⚙ Exercise 6A

Questions in this chapter are targeted at the grades indicated.

1 $P = 6l$

Work out the value of l when

  a $P = 24$ **b** $P = 54$ **c** $P = 138$ **d** $P = 35.4$

F

2 $A = bh$

  a Work out the value of h when

    i $A = 45$ and $b = 5$ **ii** $A = 54$ and $b = 3$

  b Work out the value of b when

    i $A = 35$ and $h = 7$ **ii** $A = 120$ and $h = 8$

E

3 $E = F + V - 2$

  a Work out the value of F when

    i $E = 9$ and $V = 5$ **ii** $E = 21$ and $V = 9$

  b Work out the value of V when

    i $E = 15$ and $F = 10$ **ii** $E = 30$ and $F = 12$

D

D

4 $y = 2x + 3$

Work out the value of x when

a $y = 15$ **b** $y = 27$ **c** $y = -10$ **d** $y = -3$

5 $P = 2a + b$

a Work out the value of b when

     i $P = 15$ and $a = 6$ **ii** $P = 23$ and $a = 4.5$

b Work out the value of a when

     i $P = 11$ and $b = 5$ **ii** $P = 19$ and $b = 8$

6 $y = 4x - 5$

Work out the value of x when

a $y = 3$ **b** $y = -31$ **c** $y = 75$ **d** $y = -6$

7 $V = hwl$

Work out the value of h when

a $V = 24$, $l = 3$ and $w = 2$ **b** $V = 60$, $l = 6$ and $w = 2$ **c** $V = 80$, $l = 4$ and $w = 5$

8 $v = u + at$

a Work out the value of u when

     i $v = 19$, $a = 7$ and $t = 2$ **ii** $v = 25$, $a = 6$ and $t = 3$

b Work out the value of a when $v = 17$, $u = 5$ and $t = 2$.

c Work out the value of t when $v = 31$, $u = 3$ and $a = 7$.

9 $y = \dfrac{x}{5}$

Work out the value of x when

a $y = 4$ **b** $y = 17$ **c** $y = 7.4$ **d** $y = 0$

10 $t = \dfrac{d}{s}$

Work out the value of d when

a $t = 3$ and $s = 5$ **b** $t = 9$ and $s = -8$ **c** $t = 7.5$ and $s = 6$ **d** $t = 5.6$ and $s = -10.4$

6.2 Changing the subject of a formula

◉ Objective

● You can rearrange a formula to make a different variable the subject of the formula.

❓ Why do this?

If you wanted to find out the distance that you had left to travel but the subject of the formula was time, you could rearrange it to find out the distance.

⬆ Get Ready

Solve these equations.

1. $4 = 5 + 3x$ **2.** $18 = 2(x + 4)$ **3.** $24 = \frac{1}{3} \times 8x$

🔍 Key Point

● You can change the subject of a formula by carrying out the same operations on both sides of the equals sign.

Example 2   Make t the subject of the formula $v = u + at$.

$v = u + at$

$v - u = at$ ← Subtract u from both sides.

$t = \dfrac{v - u}{a}$ ← Divide both sides by a.

Example 3   Make l the subject of the formula $P = 2(l + b)$.

$P = 2(l + b)$

$P = 2l + 2b$ ← Multiply out the brackets.

$2l = P - 2b$ ← Subtract $2b$ from both sides.

$l = \dfrac{P}{2} - b$ ← Divide both sides by 2.

Alternatively, you can divide both sides by 2
$\dfrac{P}{2} = l + b$
and then subtract b from both sides
$l = \dfrac{P}{2} - b$

Example 4   Make h the subject of the formula $V = \frac{1}{3}Ah$.

$V = \frac{1}{3}Ah$

$3V = Ah$ ← Multiply both sides by 3.

$h = \dfrac{3V}{A}$ ← Divide both sides by A.

$h = \dfrac{V}{\frac{1}{3}A}$ is also correct but it is best not to have a fraction within another fraction.

Exercise 6B

Rearrange each formula to make the letter in square brackets the subject.

1   $P = 5d$ $[d]$ 2 $P = IV$ $[I]$ 3 $A = lw$ $[w]$

4   $C = \pi d$ $[d]$ 5 $V = lwh$ $[h]$ 6 $A = \pi rl$ $[r]$

7   $y = 4x - 3$ $[x]$ 8 $t = 3n + 5$ $[n]$ 9 $P = 2x + y$ $[y]$

10   $y = mx + c$ $[m]$ 11 $v = u - gt$ $[u]$ 12 $v = u - gt$ $[t]$

13   $A = \frac{1}{2}bh$ $[b]$ 14 $I = \dfrac{PRT}{100}$ $[T]$ 15 $T = \dfrac{D}{V}$ $[V]$

C

16 $\dfrac{PV}{T} = k$ $\quad$ [V]	**17** $\dfrac{PV}{T} = k$ $\quad$ [T]	**18** $I = m(v - u)$ $\quad$ [v]
19 $A = \frac{1}{2}(a + b)h$ $\quad$ [b]	**20** $y = \frac{1}{3}x - 2$ $\quad$ [x]	**21** $y = 2(x - 1)$ $\quad$ [x]
22 $x = 3(y + 2)$ $\quad$ [y]	**23** $H = 17 - \dfrac{A}{2}$ $\quad$ [A]	**24** $3x - 2y = 6$ $\quad$ [x]
25 $3x - 2y = 6$ $\quad$ [y]	**26** $P = 6(q - 7) - 5(q - 6)$ $\quad$ [q]	**27** $4y^2 - 2x = 6(x - 8y)$ $\quad$ [x]

Chapter review

- To find out the value of a term which is not the subject of a formula, put the given values into the formula and then solve the resulting equation.
- You can change the subject of a formula by carrying out the same operations on both sides of the equals sign.

Review exercise

E

1 You can use this rule to work out the cost, in pounds, of hiring a carpet cleaner.
Jill hires the carpet cleaner for 3 days.
a Work out the cost.
Carlos hires the carpet cleaner. The cost is £52.
b Work out for how many days Carlos hires the carpet cleaner.

> Multiply the number of days' hire by 6
> Add 4 to your answer

A03

June 2009

2 Navjeet uses this rule to work out his pay.

> Pay = Number of hours worked × rate of pay per hour

This week Navjeet worked for 10 hours.
His rate of pay per hour was £4.50.
a Use this rule to work out his pay.
Last week Navjeet's pay was £66.
He worked for 12 hours.
b Work out Navjeet's rate of pay per hour last week.

A03

June 2006

3 This word formula can be used to work out the total cost, in pounds, of running a car.

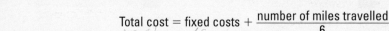

$$\text{Total cost} = \text{fixed costs} + \frac{\text{number of miles travelled}}{6}$$

a Flora's fixed costs were £500 and she travelled 9000 miles. Work out her total cost.
b Harry's total cost was £2700 and he travelled 12 000 miles. Work out his fixed costs.
c Ali's total cost was £1600 and his fixed costs were £400. Work out the number of miles he travelled.

D

4 The formula $v = u - gt$ can be used to work out velocity.
   a Work out the value of v when $u = 45$, $g = 10$ and $t = 3$.
   b Work out the value of u when $v = 8$, $g = 10$ and $t = 2$.

5 The cost, C in £, of buying t trees and b bushes together with delivery is given by the formula
$$C = 10t + 6b + 15.$$
Greg has £315 to spend and needs 35 bushes.
How many trees can he afford?

6 Tom the plumber charges £35 for each hour he works at a job, plus £50.
The amount Tom charges, in pounds, can be worked out using this rule.

> Multiply the number of hours
> he works by 35
> Add 50 to your answer

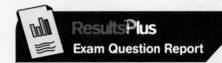
ResultsPlus
Exam Question Report

Tom charged a customer £260 for a job.
   a How many hours did Tom work?
Tom works h hours at a job.
He charges P pounds.
   b Write down a formula for P in terms of h.

86% of students did very well on part **a** of this question.

June 2007

7 The formula used to convert temperatures in Fahrenheit, F, into Celsius, C, is given by:
$$C = \frac{5(F - 32)}{9}$$
   a Find C when $F = 77$.
   b Use the formula to find the freezing point of water in Fahrenheit.
A newspaper headline read 'Phew, what a scorcher! Temperature soars into the 100s.'
   c What temperature unit are they saying? What is its equivalent in the other unit?

8 The formula $d = \dfrac{a + b}{3}$ can be used to work out the distance apart two bushes should be planted.
   a Work out the value of d when $a = 50$ and $b = 43$.
   b Work out the value of b when $d = 29$ and $a = 59$.

9 $F = 1.8C + 32$ is a formula which links temperatures in degrees Fahrenheit (F) with temperatures in degrees Celsius (C).
   a Use the formula to convert:
      i 20°C   **ii** 45°C   **iii** 70°C into °F.
   b Use the formula to convert:
      i 212°F   **ii** 122°F   **iii** 77°F into °C.

C

10 The width of a rectangle is x centimetres.
The length of the rectangle is $(x + 4)$ centimetres.
   a Find an expression, in terms of x, for the perimeter of the rectangle.
      Give your expression in its simplest form.
The perimeter of the rectangle is 54 centimetres.
   b Work out the length of the rectangle.

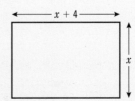

C

11   The diagram shows a trapezium.
All the lengths are in centimetres.
The perimeter of the trapezium is P cm.
Find a formula, in terms of a and b, for P.
Give your answer in its simplest form.

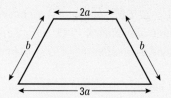

Diagram **NOT**
accurately drawn

12   $V = \frac{1}{3}\pi r^2 h$ is the formula for finding the volume of a cone.
Work out the volume of a cone with:
   a $r = 5$ cm and $h = 10$ cm   b $r = 7$ cm and $h = 15$ cm
   c $r = 4.6$ cm and $h = 9.2$ cm

13   a $S = 2p + 3q$
      Work out the value of S when $p = -4$ and $q = 5$.
   b $T = 2m + 20$
      Work out the value of m when $T = 30$.

14   Make b the subject of the formula $P = 2a + 2b$.

In questions 18–22 rearrange the formula to make the letter in square brackets the subject.

15   $P = 2x + y$ $[x]$

16   $s = \dfrac{a + b + c}{2}$ $[a]$

17   $T = \dfrac{D}{V}$ $[D]$

18   $A = \frac{1}{2}(a + b)h$ $[h]$

19   $y = \dfrac{5 - x}{2}$ $[x]$

ANGLES AND TWO-DIMENSIONAL SHAPES

Origami is the traditional Japanese art of paper folding. To challenge their accuracy, some origami makers try to make the shapes as small as possible. The smallest origami crane (the shape shown in the picture) was made from a square of paper measuring 0.1 mm by 0.1 mm using a microscope and special tools.

◎ **Objectives**

In this chapter you will:
- learn about polygons and their interior and exterior angles
- identify congruent shapes
- tessellate various shapes
- draw shapes accurately using a protractor or a pair of compasses
- learn about bearings and solve bearings problems
- use and interpret maps and scale drawings.

◑ **Before you start**

You need to be able to:
- use the angle properties of triangles and quadrilaterals
- recognise similar shapes
- measure and draw lines to the nearest mm and angles to the nearest degree.

7.1 Polygons

◉ Objectives

● You can recognise and name regular polygons.
● You can work out the sum of the interior angles of polygons.

❓ Why do this?

Polygons occur in both the natural and man-made world, for example, the pentagon shape can be seen in the vegetable okra and also the US department of defence building called The Pentagon.

⬆ Get Ready

1. Write down the name of the shape that has 3 equal sides and 3 equal angles.
2. Use one word to complete the following sentence.
   A square is a quadrilateral with 4 _____ sides and 4 _____ angles.

🔑 Key Points

● A **polygon** is a 2D shape with straight sides. The following shapes are all polygons:

Not all sides of a polygon need to be the same length.

Polygons can have sides which point inwards.

Polygons are closed shapes – there are no gaps in the perimeter.

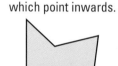

● A polygon is a **regular** polygon if its sides are all the same length and its angles are all the same size. You need to know the names of the following special polygons:

Equilateral triangle (3 sides)

Square (4 sides)

Pentagon (5 sides)

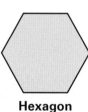

Hexagon
(6 sides)

Heptagon
(7 sides)

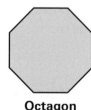

Octagon
(8 sides)

Decagon
(10 sides)

● The angle inside a polygon is called the interior angle.
The total of the **interior** angles of an n-sided polygon is $(n - 2) \times 180°$.

The interior angles of this pentagon can be found by dividing the shape into three triangles.
The sum of the interior angles of a triangle = 180°.
So the sum of the interior angles of the pentagon = $3 \times 180° = 540°$.
If the polygon is regular, each interior angle is the sum of all the interior angles divided by the number of sides.

● All regular polygons with the same number of sides, and all circles, are similar shapes.
(For more on similar shapes, see Unit 2 Section 15.3.)

polygon   regular   pentagon   hexagon   heptagon   octagon   decagon   interior

Example 1   **a** Find the total of the interior angles of a decagon.

             b The sum of the interior angles of a polygon is 2160°.
               Work out the number of sides of the polygon.

a   A decagon has 10 sides.
    The sum of its interior angles is $(10 - 2) \times 180° = 1440°$.

b   The sum of the interior angles of a polygon with n sides is $(n - 2) \times 180$.
    Therefore $(n - 2) \times 180 = 2160$
$$n - 2 = 2160 \div 180$$
$$n - 2 = 12$$
$$n = 12 + 2$$
$$n = 14$$
    The polygon has 14 sides.

Exercise 7A

Questions in this chapter are targeted at the grades indicated.

1   Name the following polygons.

    a   **b**   **c**

  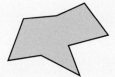

2   Calculate the sum of the interior angles of:

    a   a hexagon   **b**   an octagon   **c**   a 15-sided polygon   **d**   a 20-sided polygon.

3   The totals of the interior angles for some polygons are shown below.
    For each polygon calculate the number of sides.

    a   900°   **b**   1620°   **c**   3600°

F

D

7.2 **Exterior and interior angles**

◎ Objective

◦ You can use angle facts about interior and
exterior angles of a polygon to solve problems.

? Why do this?

To make a football you need to know how to
calculate the correct angles.

⊕ Get Ready

1. Find the value of the marked angle.

2. $x + 28 = 180$. Find x.

3. $3x = 240$. Find x.

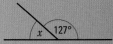

Key Points

- The angle outside a polygon is called the **exterior angle**.
  The exterior angles of a polygon add up to 360°.
- The interior angle and the exterior angle for any polygon
  add up to 180°.

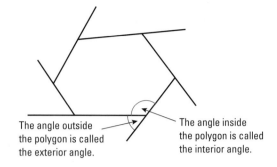

The angle outside the polygon is called the exterior angle.

The angle inside the polygon is called the interior angle.

Example 2

An *n*-sided regular polygon has an interior angle of 160°.

a Calculate the exterior angle of the polygon.

b Use your answer to part **a** to work out how many sides the polygon has.

a The interior angle and the exterior angle of the polygon add up to 180°.
Therefore 160° + exterior angle = 180°.
So the exterior angle = 20°.

b The exterior angles of a polygon add up to 360°.
So n × 20 = 360
              n = 360 ÷ 20
              n = 18.   The polygon has 18 sides.

ResultsPlus

Watch Out!

The formula exterior angles = 360° ÷ *n* does not work for irregular polygons.

Exercise 7B

E

1   Work out the size of the marked angles.

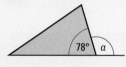  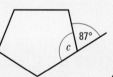 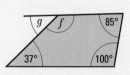

D
A03

2   Work out the exterior angle of:

   a   a pentagon   b   an equilateral triangle   c   a 20-sided polygon.

3   Use your answers to question 1 to work out the interior angle of each of the polygons.

C
A03

4   A regular polygon has an exterior angle of 12°. Work out how many sides it has.

A03

5   A regular polygon has an interior angle of 144°. Find the exterior angle and work out how many sides the polygon has.

7.3 Congruent shapes

◎ Objective

○ You can identify congruent shapes.

◈ Why do this?

Being able to identify if two shapes are an exact match can be a vital skill, particularly in the manufacturing industry where you need to remove defective products.

◈ Get Ready

1. Two of these shapes are exactly the same size. Which two?

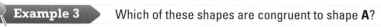

🔍 Key Point

◎ **Congruent** shapes are shapes that are exactly the same size and exactly the same shape.

🔍 Example 3

Which of these shapes are congruent to shape **A**?

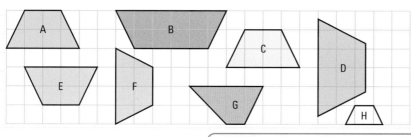

Shapes C, E and F. ⟵ These three shapes can all be cut out and will fit on A exactly. It does not matter if you turn them over or turn them round.

⚙ Exercise 7C

1 Write down the letters of three pairs of shapes that are congruent.

E

2 In each of the following, there is one pair of congruent shapes. Write down the letters of each pair.

E

3 On the grid, draw a shape that is congruent to the shaded shape but has been turned so it is not the same way up.

7.4 Tessellations

⊙ Objective

● You can tessellate various shapes.

❓ Why do this?

Tessellations can be found in nature. Bees tessellate hexagons when they build their honeycombs.

⬆ Get Ready

1. Is each floor covered with only one shape of tile?

a   b 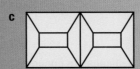   c

🔍 Key Points

● A **tessellation** is when a shape is drawn over and over again so that it covers an area without any gaps or overlaps. You often tessellate a shape to tile a floor.

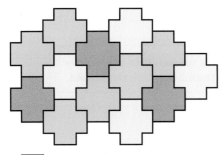

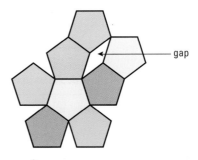
gap

This shape has been tessellated to cover a floor.

This pentagon cannot tessellate as gaps are formed.

● Tessellations can also be made using more than one shape. Here is a tessellation made from squares and regular octagons.

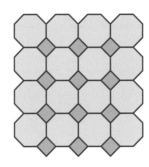

● Sometimes tessellations are used to create optical illusions. Here, a rhombus has been tessellated so that it looks as if there are lots of cubes.

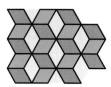

Example 4
Complete the following diagram to show how the shaded shape will tessellate.
You should draw at least six more shapes.

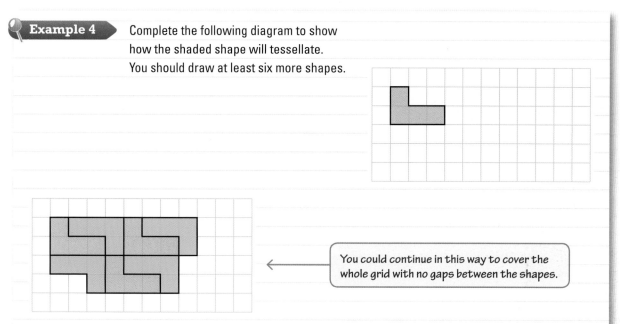

> You could continue in this way to cover the whole grid with no gaps between the shapes.

Exercise 7D

1 Show how each of the following shapes will tessellate.

a 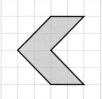 b 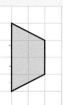 c 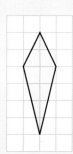 d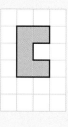

2 Copy and complete the following diagram to show how the shaded shape will tessellate.
You should draw at least five more shapes.

7.5 Accurate drawings

⊙ Objectives

● You can make accurate drawings of triangles and quadrilaterals.
● You can draw parallel lines.

⟨?⟩ Why do this?

Architects need to make accurate drawings of their structures.

⟨⬦⟩ Get Ready

1. Draw the following lines accurately using a pencil and ruler.
   a 6.8 cm   b 9.2 cm   c 76 mm   d 12.7 cm   e 83 mm

2. Draw the following angles accurately using a pencil, ruler and protractor.
   a 76°   b 42°   c 118°   d 55°   e 107°

◆ Key Points

● Most triangles can be drawn using three details about the triangle.
● To **construct** a triangle with the lengths of the sides given you should use a compass only.

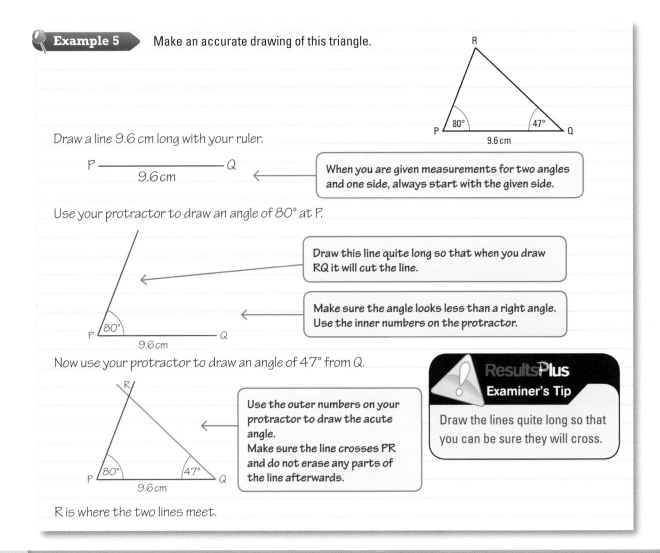

Example 5   Make an accurate drawing of this triangle.

Draw a line 9.6 cm long with your ruler.

> When you are given measurements for two angles and one side, always start with the given side.

Use your protractor to draw an angle of 80° at P.

> Draw this line quite long so that when you draw RQ it will cut the line.

> Make sure the angle looks less than a right angle. Use the inner numbers on the protractor.

Now use your protractor to draw an angle of 47° from Q.

> Use the outer numbers on your protractor to draw the acute angle.
> Make sure the line crosses PR and do not erase any parts of the line afterwards.

ResultsPlus
Examiner's Tip

Draw the lines quite long so that you can be sure they will cross.

R is where the two lines meet.

E

Exercise 7E

1   Make an accurate drawing of each of the following triangles.

a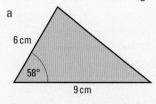

b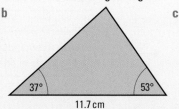

c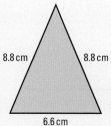

d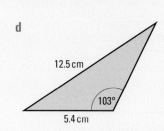

e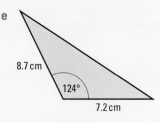

f

Example 6   Make an accurate drawing of this triangle.

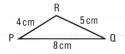

Draw a line 8 cm long with your ruler.

> It is useful to start with PQ, the horizontal line at the bottom of the triangle.

Set your compasses to 4 cm.
Put the point at P and draw an arc.

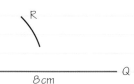

> Draw quite a big arc where you think the end of the line might be.

Now set your compasses to 5 cm.
Put the point at Q and draw another arc.

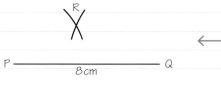

> Draw quite a big arc so that it cuts the arc drawn from P.

Draw a line from P to where the arcs meet
and a line from Q to where the arcs meet.

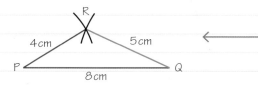

> Do NOT erase the arcs as they are a key part of your working for the accurate drawing.

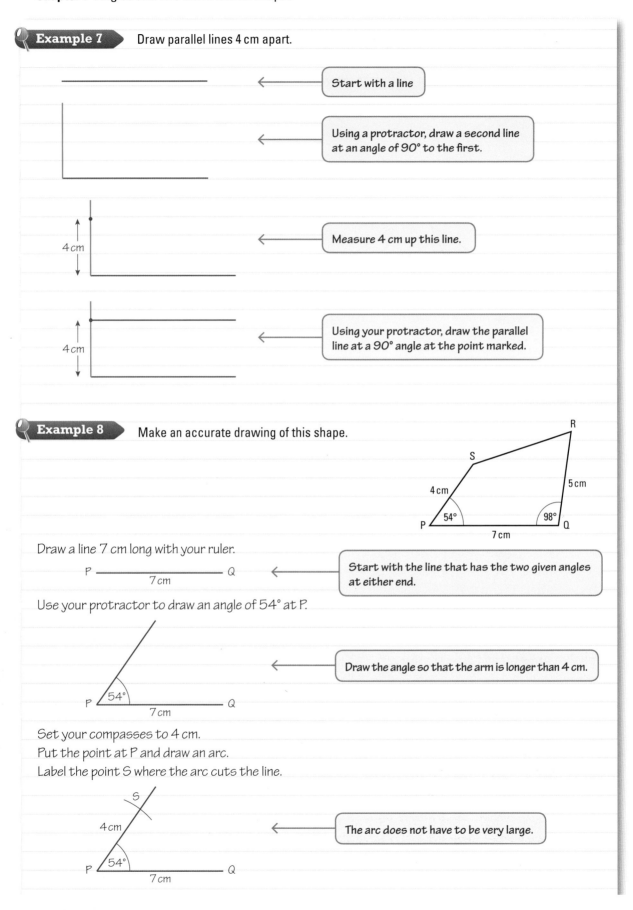

Example 7 Draw parallel lines 4 cm apart.

Start with a line

Using a protractor, draw a second line at an angle of 90° to the first.

4 cm | Measure 4 cm up this line.

4 cm | Using your protractor, draw the parallel line at a 90° angle at the point marked.

Example 8 Make an accurate drawing of this shape.

Draw a line 7 cm long with your ruler.

P ——————— Q
7 cm

Start with the line that has the two given angles at either end.

Use your protractor to draw an angle of 54° at P.

P 54°
7 cm Q

Draw the angle so that the arm is longer than 4 cm.

Set your compasses to 4 cm.
Put the point at P and draw an arc.
Label the point S where the arc cuts the line.

S
4 cm
P 54°
7 cm Q

The arc does not have to be very large.

Use your protractor to draw an angle of 98° at Q.

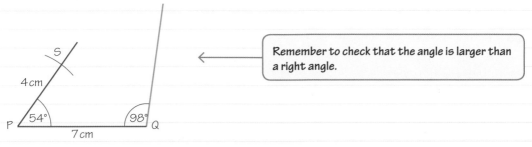

Remember to check that the angle is larger than a right angle.

Set your compasses to 5 cm. Put the point at Q and draw an arc.

Do NOT erase the arcs as they are a key part of your working for the accurate drawing.

Label the point R where this arc cuts the line just drawn. Join S to R.

Exercise 7F

1 Make an accurate drawing of each of the following sketches of triangles.

a 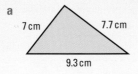 b   c 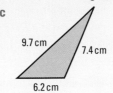 d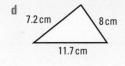

2 **a** Make an accurate drawing of this quadrilateral.

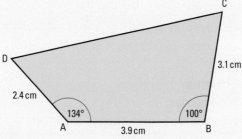

    b Measure the length of CD.

    c Measure the size of angle BCD.

3 In triangle EFG, EF = 9.3 cm, FG = 9.7 cm and angle FEG = 74°.

    a Draw a sketch of triangle EFG showing all three given measurements.

    b Make an accurate drawing of triangle EFG.

    c Measure the length of EG.

E

E

4   Using compasses, make an accurate drawing of triangle HJK where HJ = 10.6 cm, HK = 4.3 cm
     and JK = 5.1 cm. What problems do you find? Explain why.

5   Draw pairs of parallel lines that have a distance between them of:
     a 3 cm   **b** 5 cm   **c** 3.5 cm   **d** 4.5 cm

7.6 Bearings

⊙ Objectives

- You know what a bearing is.
- You can solve problems involving bearings by
  calculation and drawing.

⟳ Why do this?

You would use bearings when orienteering.

⟳ Get Ready

1. Copy and complete this
   diagram showing the
   8 points of the compass.

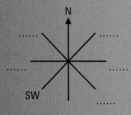

2. Use a protractor to measure angle a.

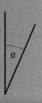

3. Draw angle ABC = 138°.
4. Write down the size of the marked angles.

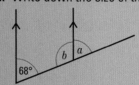

🔍 Key Points

- Bearings are used to describe directions with angles.
  - If you begin facing north then turn clockwise until you face the church,
    you have turned through 50°.
  - The angle you turn is called the **bearing**.
  - It is always written as a three-figure number.
  - When there are less than three digits in the angle, you need to add zeros
    to make a three-figure number. For example, 9° = 009°.
  - You write the bearing of the church as 050°.

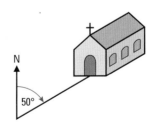

- Bearings are always measured from north in a clockwise direction.
  In this diagram the bearing of London from Birmingham is 135°.
  The bearing of Birmingham from London is 315°.

Exercise 7G

1. Complete the following sentences using one of the eight points of the compass.
   a The ship is _____ of the lighthouse.
   b The lighthouse is _____ of the airport.
   c The lighthouse is _____ of the harbour.

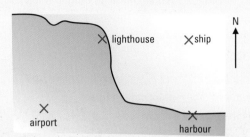

2. In each of the following, write down the bearing of B from A.

a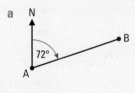

b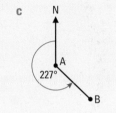

c

d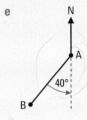

e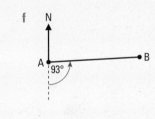

f

3. Write down the bearing of:
   a B from A
   b C from B
   c B from C.

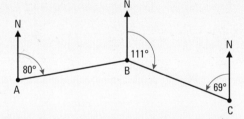

Example 9 Measure and write down the bearing of B from A.

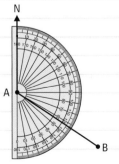

Use a protractor to measure the angle between the north line and AB.

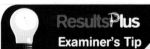

ResultsPlus
Examiner's Tip

Remember to measure bearings only in a clockwise direction.

The angle is 123°. So the bearing of B from A is 123°.

Example 10

The bearing of A from B is 75°.
Work out the bearing of B from A.

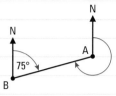

The bearing of B from A is the reflex angle at A.
Angle $x = 75°$ alternate angles
So the bearing of B from A $= 180° + 75°$
$$= 255°$$

Exercise 7H

D

1 In each of the following diagrams measure the bearing of T from S.

a

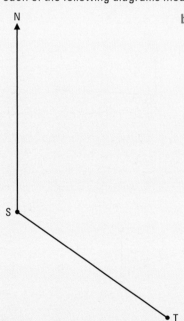

b   c

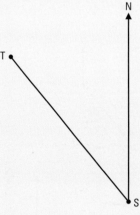

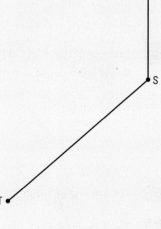

2 Use a protractor to draw bearings of:
   a 085°   b 147°   c 238°.

3 Use a protractor to find the bearings of:
   a Q from P
   b P from R
   c R from Q.

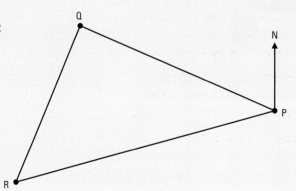

4 Paul is using the map below to find the bearing from Tavistock to:

  a Tiverton

  b Plymouth

  c Bodmin.

Write down these bearings.

5 Three ships, A, B and C, are at sea.

The bearing of B from A is 065°.

The bearing of B from C is 125°.

The bearing of C from A is 040°.

Draw a sketch to show the positions of the three ships.

6 The bearing of P from Q is 055°.

Work out the bearing of Q from P.

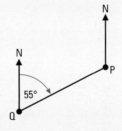

7 The bearing of T from S is 168°. Work out the bearing of S from T.

8 The bearing of Blackburn from Rochdale is 303°. What is the bearing of Rochdale from Blackburn?

9 The bearing of Hull from York is 115°. What is the bearing of York from Hull?

10 The diagram shows the positions of three lighthouses A, B and C.

The bearing of B from A is 048°.

The bearing of C from A is 126°.

Lighthouse B and C are the same distance from A.

Work out the bearing of lighthouse C from B.

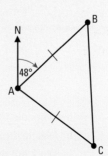

A02
A03

A03

A02

A03

7.7 Maps and scale drawings

◎ Objectives

- ● You can use and interpret maps and scale drawings.
- ● You can construct accurate scale drawings.
- ● You can draw lines and shapes to scale and estimate lengths on scale drawings.
- ● You can work out lengths using a scale factor.

❓ Why do this?

When planning to build an extension to a house, accurate scale drawings have to be made.

◈ Get Ready

1. Convert   **a** 56 000 mm into cm   **b** 5.6 m into cm.
2. Divide 36 g in the ratio
   a 1 : 2   **b** 3 : 1   **c** 3 : 6   **d** 8 : 4

🔍 Key Points

- ◉ Maps and plans are accurate drawings from which measurements are made.
- ◉ A **scale** is a ratio which shows the relationship between a length on a drawing and the actual length in real life. (There is more about ratios in Unit 2 Chapter 6.)
- ◉ Ordnance Survey Pathfinders maps, used by hill walkers, are on a scale of 1 to 25 000, written 1 : 25 000. 1 cm on the map represents 25 000 cm in real life, which is 250 m or a quarter of a kilometre.
- ◉ Drawing diagrams to scale and using bearings means you can measure and calculate missing angles and distances.

🔍 Example 11

The scale on a road map is 1 : 200 000.
Sunderland and Newcastle are 9 cm apart on the map.

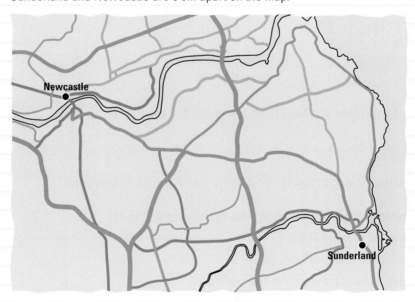

a Work out the real distance, in km, between Sunderland and Newcastle.
b Middlesbrough is 55 km in a straight line from Newcastle.
   Work out the distance of Middlesbrough from Newcastle on the map.

a The distance on the map is 9 cm.

> Remember:
> 100 cm = 1 m
> 1000 m = 1 km

real distance = 9 cm × 200 000 = 1 800 000 cm

real distance = 18 000 m ← Divide by 100 to convert cm to m.

The real distance between Sunderland and Newcastle is 18 km. ← Divide by 1000 to convert m to km.

b The real distance is 55 km.

real distance = 55 × 1000 = 55 000 m ← Multiply by 1000 to convert km to m.

real distance = 55 000 × 100 = 5 500 00 cm ← Multiply by 100 to convert m to cm.

Distance on the map = $\frac{5500000}{200000}$ = 27.5 cm ← Divide by 200 000 to find the distance on the map.

Example 12

Irie walks for 2 miles on a bearing of 060° from home.
She then walks a further 4 miles on a bearing of 300°.
How far is Irie from home?
What bearing must Irie walk on to get back home?
Use a scale of 2 cm to represent one mile.

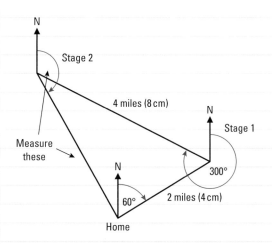

Step 1   Draw the bearing of 060° from home.
Step 2   As the scale is 2cm for 1 mile, you need to draw a line that is 4 cm long.
Step 3   Put in a new north line at the end of Stage 1.
Step 4   Draw the bearing of 300° from Stage 1.
Step 5   Make the line 8 cm long (4 miles is 4 × 2 cm).
Step 6   Put in a new north line at the end of Stage 2.
Step 7   Measure the distance from Stage 2 to home.
Step 8   Measure the bearing from Stage 2 to home.

Answer   Irie is about 3.5 miles from home and must walk on a bearing of 150°.

Exercise 7I

1   The scale on a map is 1 cm to 2 km.
The distance between Ashton and Dacreville is 5.5 cm on the map.
How many kilometres apart are Ashton and Dacreville in real life?

D

D

2 A map is drawn on a scale of 3 cm to 1 km.
  a Work out the real length of a lake, which is 4.2 cm long on the map.
  b The distance between the church in Canwick and the town hall in Barnton is 5.8 km.
     Work out the distance between them on the map.

3 Jane walks for 10 miles on a bearing of 060°.
  Use a scale of 1 cm to represent 1 mile to show the journey.

4 Sam runs for 4 km on a bearing of 120°. Use a scale of 1 cm to represent 2 km to show the journey.

5 Witley is 2 km due south of Milford. The bearing of Hydestile from Milford is 125° and the distance from Milford to Hydestile is 2.8 km.
  a Make a scale drawing to show the three villages. Use a scale of 1 : 25 000.
  b Use your drawing to find
     i the distance of Hydestile from Witley
     ii the bearing of Hydestile from Witley.

6 Ian sails his boat from the Isle of Wight for 20 km on a bearing of 135°.
  He then sails on a bearing of 240° for 10 km.
  How far is Ian from his starting point?
  What bearing does he need to sail on to get back to the start?
  Use a scale of 1 cm to represent 2 km.

7 Peg Leg the pirate buried his treasure 100 yards from the big tree on a bearing of 045°. One-Eyed Rick dug up the treasure and moved it 50 yards on a bearing of 310° from where it had been buried.
  How far is the treasure from the big tree now?
  What bearing is the new hiding place of the treasure?
  Use a scale of 1 cm to represent 10 yards.

8 Ray flew his plane on a bearing of 300° for 200 km. He then changed direction and flew on a bearing of 150° for 100 km.
  What bearing must Ray fly on to get back to the start?
  How far is he away from the start?

9 This is a sketch of Arfan's bedroom. It is *not* drawn to scale.
  Draw an accurate scale drawing on cm squared paper of Arfan's bedroom.
  Use a scale of 1 : 50.

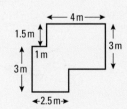

Chapter review

- A **polygon** is a 2D shape with straight sides.
- A polygon is a **regular** polygon if its sides are all the same length and its angles are all the same size.
- The angle inside a polygon is called the interior angle.
  The total of the interior angles of an n-sided polygon is $(n - 2) \times 180°$.
- All regular polygons with the same number of sides are similar shapes.
- The angle outside a polygon is called the **exterior angle**. The exterior angles of a polygon add up to 360°.

- The interior angle and the exterior angle for any polygon add up to 180°.
- **Congruent** shapes are shapes that are exactly the same size and exactly the same shape.
- A **tessellation** is when a shape is drawn over and over again so that it covers an area without any gaps or overlaps.
- Most triangles can be drawn using three details about the triangle.
- To **construct** a triangle with the lengths of the sides given you should use a compass only.
- **Bearings** are measured clockwise from north and are always written as a three-figure number.
- Maps and plans are accurate drawings from which measurements are made.
- A **scale** is a ratio which shows the relationship between a length on a drawing and the actual length in real life.

Review exercise

1 Here are 6 shapes drawn on a grid.

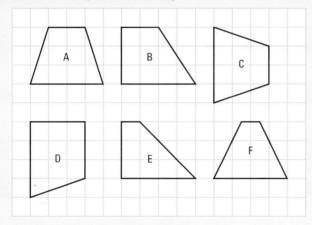

Two of these shapes are congruent.

a Write down the letters of these two shapes.

b On a copy of the grid below, draw a shape that is congruent to shape **P**.

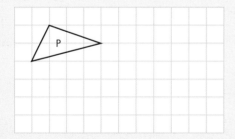

June 2009

2 Work out the value of x.

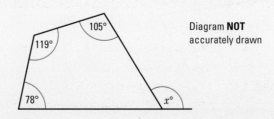

Diagram **NOT** accurately drawn

Nov 2007

87

E

3 On the grid, show how this shape will tessellate.
You should draw at least 8 shapes.

June 2007

4 The diagram shows the position of a farm F and a bridge B on a map.
   a Measure and write down the bearing of B from F.

   A church C is on a bearing of 155° from the bridge B.
   On a copy of the map, the church is 5 cm from B.
   b Mark the church with a cross (✕) and label it C.

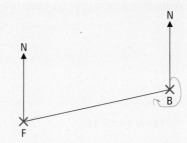

Nov 2006

5 A car is 4 m long and 1.8 m wide.
A model of the car, similar in all respects, is 5 cm long. How wide is it?

6 A model of a car is 12 cm long and 5.2 cm high.
If the real car is 3.36 m long, how high is it?

7 AB = 8 cm.   AC = 6 cm.   Angle A = 52°.
Make an accurate drawing of triangle ABC.

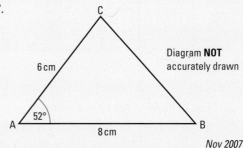

Diagram **NOT**
accurately drawn

Nov 2007

8 Here is a sketch of a triangle.
The lengths of the sides of the triangle are
9 cm, 7 cm and 5 cm.
Use ruler and compasses to make an
accurate scale drawing of the triangle.

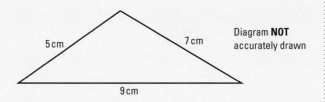

Diagram **NOT**
accurately drawn

9

Diagram **NOT**
accurately drawn

Make an accurate drawing of the quadrilateral ABCD.

June 2007

10 This shape is a regular polygon.

  a Write down the special name for this type of regular polygon.

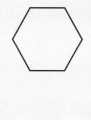

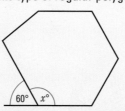

  b **i** Work out the size of the angle marked $x°$.

   ii Give a reason for your answer.

June 2007

11 **a** Find the bearing of B from A.

  b On a copy of the diagram, draw a line on a bearing of 135° from A.

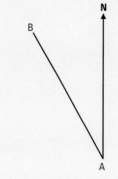

Nov 2006

12 The diagram shows a regular hexagon.

  a Work out the size of angle x.

  b Work out the size of angle y.

Diagram **NOT** accurately drawn

Nov 2006

13 The diagram shows the position of two airports, A and B.

A plane flies from airport A to airport B.

  a Measure the size of the angle marked x.

  b Work out the real distance between airport A and airport B. Use the scale 1 cm represents 50 km.

Airport C is 350 km on a bearing of 060° from airport B.

  c On the diagram, mark airport C with a cross (×). Label it C.

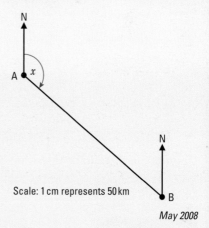

Scale: 1 cm represents 50 km

May 2008

14 The diagram shows part of a regular 10-sided polygon. Work out the size of the angle marked x.

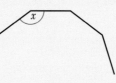

Diagram **NOT** accurately drawn

Nov 2008

D

C

In zorbing or sphereing a participant inside an inner capsule in a large, transparent ball rolls along the ground or downhill. The record for the fastest speed in a sphere is a rather scary 52 km per hour.

◉ **Objective**

In this chapter you will:
○ learn how to work out the area and circumference of circles and part circles.

◈ **Before you start**

You should be able to identify and name parts of a circle, including:
○ circumference   ○ radius
○ diameter   ○ arc
○ chord   ○ tangent
○ segment   ○ sector.

8.1 Circumference of a circle

⊙ Objective

⊙ You can remember and use the formula to find the circumference of a circle.

⦾ Why do this?

Bicycle designers might need to know how far a wheel goes on each revolution.

⬥ Get Ready

1. Name each part of the circle, centre O, drawn in red.

a   **b**   **c**

2. Copy and complete the following statements by putting a number on the dotted line.

   a The diameter $-$ the radius $\times$ ......

   b The radius $=$ the diameter $\times$ ......

🌐 Key Points

◉ Draw some circles and measure the circumference and diameter of each one.
You should find that the circumference of any circle is just over 3 times the diameter.
This value cannot be worked out exactly but it is about 3.142.
We use the Greek letter π (pi) for this value. You can find it on your calculator.

◉ For all circles: $\dfrac{\text{circumference}}{\text{diameter}} = \dfrac{C}{d} = \pi$

◉ This gives us a formula to calculate the circumference of a circle:
$C = \pi \times d$ or $C = \pi d$.

◉ As the diameter is twice the radius, we can also use this formula:
$C = 2 \times \pi \times r$ or $C = 2\pi r$.

ResultsPlus

Examiner's Tip

You will need to learn these formulae for your exam.

🔍 Example 1

A circle has a radius of 5.7 cm.
Work out the circumference of the circle.
Give your answer to 1 decimal place.

5.7 cm

$C = 2\pi r$

$= 2 \times \pi \times 5.7$ ← You need to write down all the numbers you are putting into your calculator.

$= 35.81415$ ← Always show your unrounded answer before you round it.

$= 35.8\,\text{cm (to 1 d.p.)}$ ← This number rounds to 35.8.

Example 2

Find the circumference of a circle with diameter 13 cm.
Give your answer to 1 decimal place.

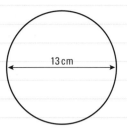

13 cm

$C = \pi d$ ←

> Use this formula as we are given the diameter.

$= \pi \times 13$ ←

> Use the π key or use $\pi = 3.142$.

$= 40.8407$ ←

> Write down at least six digits from your calculator.

$= 40.8$ cm (to 1 d.p.) ←

> Give the units with your answer.

ResultsPlus
Examiner's Tip

Do not just write down the formula. Make sure you write down the numbers you are putting into the formula.

Exercise 8A

Questions in this chapter are targeted at the grades indicated.

C

1 Work out the circumferences of circles with the following radii.
   a 6.3 m   b 9.5 cm   c 4.2 cm   d 12.5 mm   e 29.4 cm

2 Work out the circumferences of circles with the following diameters.
   a 6.9 cm   b 10.1 mm   c 5.3 cm   d 9.7 cm   e 5 m

3 A circular pond has a radius of 1.8 metres. Work out the circumference of the pond.

4 A circular plate has a radius of 16 cm. Work out the circumference of the plate.

5 A penny-farthing bicycle has a large wheel and a small wheel.
   The large wheel has a diameter of 1.43 metres and the small wheel has a radius of 0.15 metres.

   a Work out the circumference of the large wheel.
   b Work out the circumference of the small wheel.
   c Work out how many times the small wheel has to turn when the large wheel turns once.
   Give your answers to 2 decimal places.

Example 3   The circumference of a circle is 78.4 cm. Work out its radius.
Give your answer to 2 decimal places.

$C = 2\pi r$

> If you divide both sides by 2π, you can use this formula.

$r = \dfrac{C}{2\pi}$

$r = \dfrac{78.4}{2\pi} = 12.477747$

> On the calculator you need to press: $78.4 \div 2 \times \pi$.

$= 12.48\,\text{cm}$ (to 2 d.p.)

> Note that the number is rounded to 2 d.p.

> In the same way, if you are asked to find the diameter, given the circumference, you can use the formula
> $$d = \dfrac{C}{\pi}$$

Exercise 8B

Give your answers to 1 decimal place in each of the following questions.

1   Work out the diameters of circles with the following circumferences.
    a 45.6 m   b 20 cm   c 58.1 cm   d 37.2 mm   e 100 cm

2   Work out the radii of circles with the following circumferences.
    a 30.4 cm   b 71.8 mm   c 64 cm   d 93.2 cm   e 49.5 m

3   A trundle wheel is used to measure a garden path.
    The circumference of the trundle wheel is 188 cm.

    Work out the diameter of the trundle wheel.

C

8.2 Area of a circle

⊙ Objective

● You can remember and use the formula to find the area of a circle.

❓ Why do this?

Being able to work out the area of a circle could be helpful if you want to use a square or rectangular cake tin instead of a circular one.

⬆ Get Ready

Use your calculator to work out the following calculations.
Give your answers correct to 2 decimal places.

1. $\pi 5^2$　　　　**2.** $3^2 \pi$　　　　**3.** $(7\pi)^2$　　　　**4.** $(9\pi)^2$

🔵 Key Points

● Take a circle and cut it into lots of equal sectors.

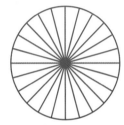

Circumference $= C$
radius $= r$

● Rearrange these sectors as shown in the diagram.

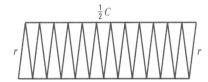

● When there are lots of sectors this gets closer to a rectangle.

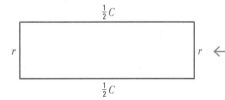

Half of the circumference is at the top of the rectangle with the other half at the bottom.

● The area of the circle $=$ the area of the rectangle

$$= \tfrac{1}{2}C \times r \quad \longleftarrow \boxed{\text{Area of a rectangle} = \text{base} \times \text{height}}$$

$$= \tfrac{1}{2} \times 2\pi r \times r$$

$$= \pi r^2$$

$$A = \pi r^2 \quad \longleftarrow \boxed{\text{Area} = \pi \times \text{radius} \times \text{radius}}$$

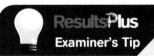

ResultsPlus
Examiner's Tip

You will need to learn this formula for your exam.

Example 4 A circle has a radius of 8.2 cm.
Work out the area of the circle.
Give your answer to 3 significant figures.

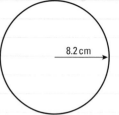

> Show what you have substituted into the formula.

$A = \pi r^2$
  $= \pi \times 8.2^2$
  $= \pi \times 67.24$
  $= 211.24069$
  $= 211 \text{ cm}^2$ (to 3 s.f.)

> Always square the radius before multiplying by π.

> Write down all the digits from your calculator.

> Rounding to 3 s.f. means you only want 3 digits in the answer.

Example 5 Find the area of the circle with diameter 20 cm.
Give your answer to 1 decimal place.

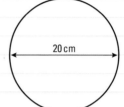

> You need to halve the diameter to find the radius for the formula.

$A = \pi r^2$
  $= \pi \times 10^2$
  $= \pi \times 100$
  $= 314.159 \text{ cm}^2$
  $= 314.2 \text{ cm}^2$ (to 1 d.p.)

> $10^2 = 10 \times 10 = 100$

> Give the units of area with your answer.
> As the 2nd decimal place is a 5 you have to round up.

Exercise 8C

Give your answers to 3 significant figures in each of the following questions.

1 Work out the areas of circles with the following radii.
   a 5.1 m b 3 cm c 8.7 cm d 15.2 mm e 9.4 cm

2 Work out the areas of circles with the following diameters.
   a 30 cm b 24.4 mm c 7.4 cm d 12.3 cm e 8 m

3 A goat is tied to a post in the middle of a field covered in grass.
   He is tied so that he can eat the grass within 3.8 m of the post.
   Work out the area of grass from which he cannot eat.

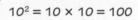

4 Rosie makes some jam. She covers the tops of the jars with
   circular pieces of material of diameter 8.6 cm.
   Work out the area of material covering one jar.

5 The diagram shows a square of side 9 cm inside a circle of radius 11 cm.
   a Work out the area of the circle.
   b Work out the area of the square.
   c Work out the area of the shaded part.

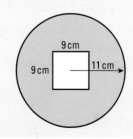

C

6   The diagram shows a rectangular card measuring 32 cm by 16 cm.
Eight circles of radius 2 cm are cut out so that the card can hold
eight pots of yoghurt.
Work out the area of the card that is left.

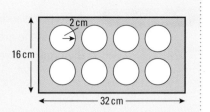

8.3   Area and perimeter of half and quarter circles

◎ Objective

● You can find the perimeter and area of a half
circle and a quarter circle.

⑦ Why do this?

Many shapes come in half circles and quarter
circles such as flower beds and you may need to
calculate the area to know how much soil to get.

⬆ Get Ready

Use your calculator to work out the following, giving your answer to 2 decimal places.

1. $\dfrac{7^2\pi}{2}$ 2. $\dfrac{(2\pi)(31)}{4}$ 3. $\dfrac{(5\pi)^2}{2}$ 4. $\dfrac{21\pi}{4}$

◉ Key Points

● The perimeter of a **semicircle** is the diameter + half the circumference.
● The perimeter of a quarter circle is the diameter + one quarter the circumference.
● The area of a semicircle is half the area of the circle.

⚲ Example 6

A semicircle has a diameter of 24 cm.
Work out its perimeter.
Give your answer to 3 significant figures.

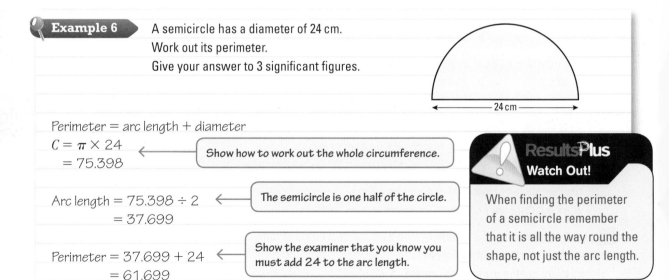

Perimeter = arc length + diameter

$C = \pi \times 24$
    $= 75.398$ ← *Show how to work out the whole circumference.*

Arc length = 75.398 ÷ 2 ← *The semicircle is one half of the circle.*
           $= 37.699$

Perimeter = 37.699 + 24 ← *Show the examiner that you know you must add 24 to the arc length.*
          $= 61.699$
            $= 61.7$ cm (to 3 s.f.) ← *Put the units with your answer.*

ResultsPlus
Watch Out!

When finding the perimeter
of a semicircle remember
that it is all the way round the
shape, not just the arc length.

Exercise 8D

Give your answers to 3 significant figures in each of the following questions.

1 Calculate the perimeter and the area of each sector.

a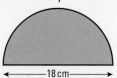
← 18 cm →

b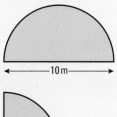
← 10 m →

c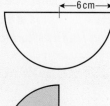
← 6 cm →

d
← 4 cm →

e
← 6.2 cm →

f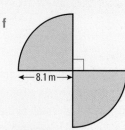
← 8.1 m →

2 A door is in the shape of a rectangle with a semicircle on top.
The width of the door is 1.2 m.
The height of the rectangular part of the door is 2.2 m.
a Calculate the area of the door.
The door is to be covered with brown leather. The leather costs £22.49 per square metre and comes in 2 m widths.
b What is the cost of covering the door?

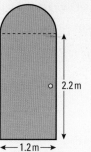
2.2 m
← 1.2 m →

3 The diagram shows a triangle inside a quarter of a circle.
a Work out the area of the shaded segment.
b Work out the perimeter of the whole shape.

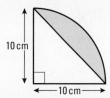
10 cm
← 10 cm →

Chapter review

- To find the circumference (C) of a circle when given the radius (r) or diameter (d), use the formulae
  $C = \pi d$
  $C = 2\pi r$
- To find the diameter (or radius) of a circle when given the circumference, use the formula
  $d = \dfrac{C}{\pi}$
- To find the area (A) of a circle when given the radius (or diameter), use the formula $A = \pi r^2$.
- The perimeter of a **semicircle** is the diameter + half the circumference.
- The perimeter of a quarter circle is the diameter + one quarter the circumference.
- The area of a semicircle is half the area of the circle.

Review exercise

C

1 A circle has a radius of 6 cm.
A square has a side of length 12 cm.
Work out the difference between the area of the
circle and the area of the square.
Give your answer correct to one decimal place.

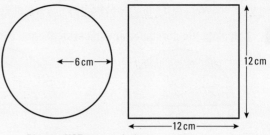

Diagram **NOT** accurately drawn

Nov 2008

2 The diagram shows two small circles inside a large circle.
The large circle has a radius of 8 cm.
Each of the two small circles has a diameter of 4 cm.
a Write down the radius of each of the small circles.
b Work out the area of the region shown shaded in the diagram.
Give your answer correct to one decimal place.

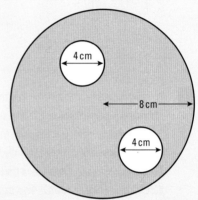

Diagram **NOT** accurately drawn

Nov 2008

3 The radius of this circle is 8 cm.
Work out the circumference of the circle.
Give your answer correct to 2 decimal places.

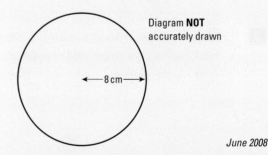

Diagram **NOT**
accurately drawn

June 2008

4 The diagram shows a semicircle.
The radius of the semicircle is 10 cm.
Calculate the area of the semicircle.
Give your answer correct to 3 significant figures.
State the units of your answer.

Diagram **NOT**
accurately drawn

Nov 2007

5 The diagram shows a circle.
The radius of the circle is 10 cm.
Calculate the area of the circle.
Give your answer correct to 3 significant figures.
State the units with your answer.

Diagram **NOT**
accurately drawn

Nov 2007

C

6 The diameter of a wheel on Harry's bicycle is 0.65 m.
Calculate the circumference of the wheel.
Give your answer correct to 2 decimal places.

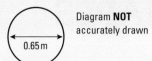

Diagram **NOT**
accurately drawn

0.65 m

June 2007

7 Here is a tile in the shape of a semicircle.

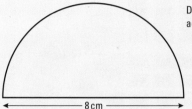

Diagram **NOT**
accurately drawn

8 cm

The diameter of the semicircle is 8 cm.
Work out the perimeter of the tile.
Give your answer correct to 2 decimal places.

ResultsPlus
Exam Question Report

89% of students answered this question poorly.
Many students incorrectly used the formula for
area of a circle (πr^2).

June 2009

8 The top of a table is a circle.
The radius of the top of the table is 50 cm.
a Work out the area of the top of the table.

The base of the table is a circle.
The diameter of the base of the table is 40 cm.

b Work out the circumference of the base of the table.

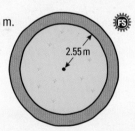

June 2007

9 A ring-shaped flowerbed is to be created around a circular lawn of radius 2.55 m.
Roses costing £4.20 are to be planted approximately every 50 cm around the
flowerbed.
How much money will be needed for roses?

A02
A03

2.55 m

10 The diagram shows a garden that includes a lawn, a vegetable patch, a circular pond and
a flowerbed. All measurements are shown in metres.
The lawn is going to be re-laid with turf costing £4.60 per square metre.
How much will this cost?

A02
A03

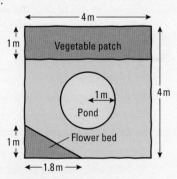

4 m

1 m

Vegetable patch

1 m
Pond

4 m

1 m

Flower bed

1.8 m

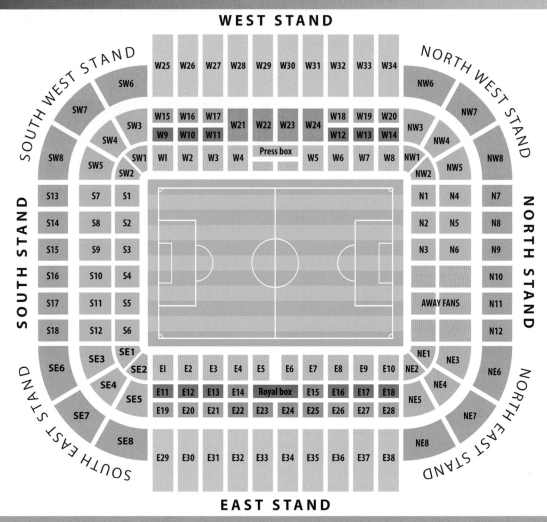

When you book tickets for a football match or a concert, you often chose the area you want to sit in from a picture like this. This picture is a plan – it's the view from above. An elevation is a view from the side. You would need an elevation to see which of the stands in this stadium was the highest.

Objectives

In this chapter you will:
- learn how to draw nets and recognise solids from their nets
- learn how to draw and interpret plans and elevations
- find the volumes and surface areas of cylinders
- understand the effect of enlargement for perimeter, area and volume of shapes and solids
- convert between area and volume measures.

Before you start

You need to be:
- familiar with two-dimensional shapes.

9.1 Nets

⊙ Objective

⊙ You can draw nets and recognise solids from their nets.

⦾ Why do this?

A designer making a 3D container needs to draw an accurate 2D plan to show how to make the container from a flat piece of card or other material.

⬙ Get Ready

How many faces do each of these 3D objects have?

1. A cube   **2.** A square-based pyramid   **3.** A hexagonal prism

⬙ Key Points

⊙ A **net** is a pattern of flat (2D) shapes that can be folded to make a hollow **solid** shape.

This cuboid can be made from a piece of card shaped like this.

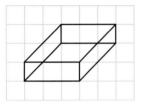 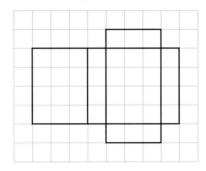

There are other possible nets to make the same cuboid.

⚙ Exercise 9A

> Questions in this chapter are targeted at the grades indicated.

1   The diagrams below show some solids.

      1   2   3   4

Three nets are shown below (not drawn to scale).

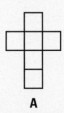   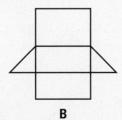

      A   B   C

   a   Write which net can be folded to make each solid.

   b   Draw a net for the missing solid.

E

2 Sketch the following solids and their nets.

    a hexagonal prism   **b** tetrahedron

A02
A03

3 Charlie has some sheets of metal of length 2 m and width 1.5 m.

He wants to make containers to collect different types of rubbish.

What shape should he use for the container for

    a the collection of waste paper from an office

    b the collection of waste engine oil from a garage?

In each case, make a sketch of the net for the container.

Explain why you have chosen a container of this shape.

9.2 Plans and elevations

◉ Objective

● You can draw and interpret plans and elevations.

ⓦ Why do this?

Architects, engineers and draughtsmen must be able to represent 3D objects with accurate 2D drawings.

⬆ Get Ready

1. A, B and C have been drawn from a different viewpoint. For each, write down the letter of the congruent 3D shape.

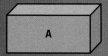
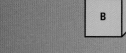

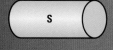

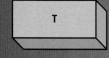

🌐 Key Points

● **Plans** and **elevations** show the 2D view of a 3D object drawn from different angles.

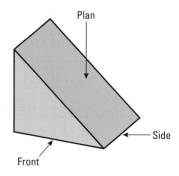

● The view from above
is called the plan.

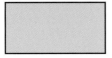

● The view from the front
is called the **front elevation**.

● The view from the side
is called the **side elevation**.

Example 1 Use squared paper to help you to draw the plan, front elevation and side elevation of this triangular prism.

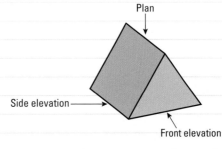

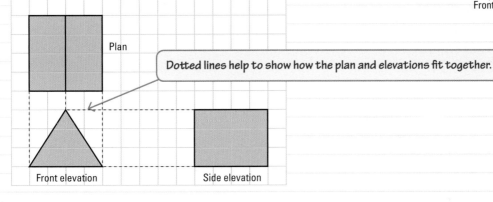

Dotted lines help to show how the plan and elevations fit together.

Exercise 9B

1 Use squared paper to make an accurate drawing of the plan, front elevation and side elevation for this cuboid.

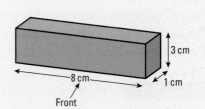

3 cm
8 cm
1 cm
Front

2 Sketch the plan, front elevation and side elevation for these shapes.

a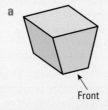

Front

b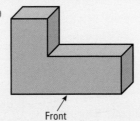

Front

c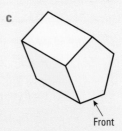

Front

D

A03

D
A03

3 The diagram shows the plan and front elevation of an object.

  a Sketch the side elevation.

  b Draw a 3D sketch of the shape.

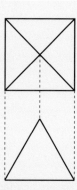

9.3 Volume and surface area of a cylinder

⊚ Objectives

● You can find the volume and surface area
of a cylinder.
● You can use volume to solve problems.

⦾ Why do this?

The surface area is the amount of space on an object
available for design, information or advertising.

⬆ Get Ready

1. Find the area of these two-dimensional shapes.

  a   3.8 cm

  b   4.3 cm

🔍 Key Points

◉ A cylinder is a prism with a circular cross section.
◉ The volume of a cylinder is the area of the circular cross-section × height.
Volume $= \pi r^2 h$
◉ You can use the volumes of cuboids, prisms and cylinders to solve real-life problems.
◉ The surface area of a cylinder is the area of the net which can be used to build the shape.
Surface area $= 2\pi rh + 2\pi r^2$

📌 Example 2   Work out the volume of this cylinder.

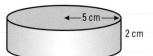
5 cm
2 cm

Volume of a cylinder = Area of the circular end × height

$= \pi \times r^2 \times h$

$= \pi \times 5 \times 5 \times 2 \quad = 50\pi$

$= 157.0796327$

$= 157$ cm^3 (to 3 significant figures)

> Put in the values you know for the
> radius and the height.

> Use the π button on your calculator.

Exercise 9C

In this exercise give your answers to 3 significant figures. Do not forget to give the units.

1 Find the volume of these cylinders.

a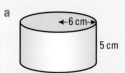

b

c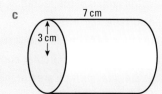

2 A cylinder has a height of 2 cm. If the volume of the cylinder is 50 cm³, calculate the radius of the cross-section.

3 A water tank on a farm is in the shape of a cylinder. It has a radius of 2 m and a height of 2.5 m and A02 A03 it is full of water.

The farmer uses water from the tank to fill troughs for horses. The trough is shown below.

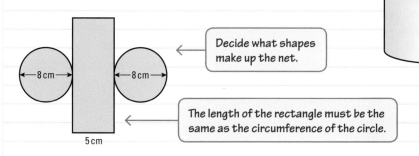

The cross-section of the trough is a pentagon of area 0.8 m².
Each trough is 1.2 m long.
Work out:

a how many troughs the farmer can fill from the water tank

b how much water is left over.

Example 3 Work out the surface area of this cylinder.

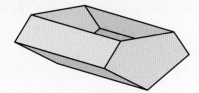

Decide what shapes make up the net.

The length of the rectangle must be the same as the circumference of the circle.

Circumference = $\pi d = 8\pi = 25.13$ cm
Area circle = $\pi r^2 = \pi \times 4 \times 4 = 50.27$ cm²
Area rectangle = $5 \times 25.13 = 125.65$ cm²
Total surface area of a cylinder = $2 \times$ circle + rectangle
$= 2 \times 50.27 + 125.65$
$= 226.19$ cm²

ResultsPlus
Examiner's Tip

Showing your method ensures you get all the marks!

E

Exercise 9D

1 The diagram shows a sketch of the net of a cylinder.

   a Work out the length of the rectangle which makes up the covered surface.

   b Work out the area of the curved surface.

   c Work out the area of the circular ends.

   d Work out the total surface area of the cylinder.

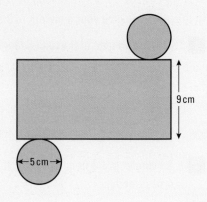

2 Find the surface area of these cylinders.

   a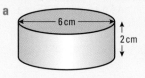   **b**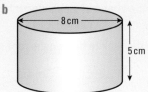

3 The diagram shows a can of food.

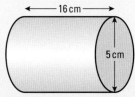

A label giving information about the product completely covers the curved surface area.
Work out the area of the label.

9.4 Perimeter, area and volume

◎ Objectives

● You understand the effect of enlargement for perimeter, area and volume of shapes and solids.

● You understand that enlargement does not have the same effect on area and volume.

● You can use simple examples of the relationship between enlargement and area and volume of simple shapes and solids.

⊘ Why do this?

When using scale models it is important to be able to find the surface area and volume of the full-sized object.

⊕ Get Ready

Find the area of these shapes.

1.   **2.**   **3.**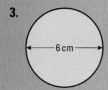

> **Key Points**

● The diagram shows squares of side 1 cm, 2 cm, 3 cm and 4 cm.
  The squares are all similar.

Square A has side 1 cm   perimeter 4 cm   It takes 1 cm² to fill the square.

Square B has side 2 cm   perimeter 8 cm   It takes 4 cm² to fill the square.

Square C has side 3 cm   perimeter 12 cm   It takes 9 cm² to fill the square.

Square D has side 4 cm   perimeter 16 cm   It takes 16 cm² to fill the square.

● When a shape is enlarged each length is multiplied by the scale factor.
  Enlarged perimeter = original perimeter × scale factor

● The area is length × length. Both lengths must be multiplied by the scale factor.
  Enlarged area   = (length × scale factor) × (length × scale factor)
                 = length × length × scale factor × scale factor
                 = original area × scale factor²

● The diagram shows a cube of side 1 cm,
  a cube of side 2 cm and a cube of side 3 cm.

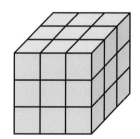

● The volume of the cube of side 1 cm is 1 × 1 × 1 = 1 cm³.
● The volume of the cube of side 2 cm is 2 × 2 × 2 = 8 cm³.
● The volume of the cube of side 3 cm is 3 × 3 × 3 = 27 cm³.
● Enlarged volume = (length × scale factor) × (length × scale factor) × (length × scale factor)
                 = length × length × length × scale factor × scale factor × scale factor
                 = original volume × scale factor³

> **Example 4**   The diagram shows rectangles A and B made up of cm squares.
>   Rectangle A has a perimeter of 10 cm and an area of 6 cm².
>   Rectangle A is enlarged by a scale factor of 3 to become rectangle B.

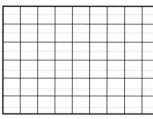

Find   **a**   the perimeter of rectangle B.
        b   the area of rectangle B.

a Perimeter of A = 10 cm
   Perimeter of B = 3 × 10 = 30 cm ←

> Multiply the perimeter
> by the scale factor.

> Multiply the area by the
> square of the scale factor.

ResultsPlus
Examiner's Tip

Show the examiner evidence
that you know the scale factor is
squared when you are looking for
the area. This will be worth a mark!

b Area of A = 6 cm²
   Area of B = 6 × 3² = 6 × 9 = 54 cm²

Exercise 9E

1 The diagram shows a rectangle A.
   a Find the perimeter of rectangle A.
   b Find the area of rectangle A.
   c On squared paper draw an enlargement P of rectangle A with scale factor 2.
   d Find the perimeter of rectangle P.
   e Find the area of rectangle P.
   f On squared paper draw an enlargement R of rectangle A with scale factor 3.
   g Find the perimeter of rectangle R.
   h Find the area of rectangle R.
   i Work out the value of   i $\dfrac{\text{Perimeter P}}{\text{Perimeter A}}$ ii $\dfrac{\text{Perimeter R}}{\text{Perimeter A}}$
      Write down anything you notice about these results.
   j Work out the value of   i $\dfrac{\text{Area P}}{\text{Area A}}$ ii $\dfrac{\text{Area R}}{\text{Area A}}$
      Write down anything you notice about the results.
   k S is an enlargement of rectangle A with scale factor 8.
      i What is the perimeter of rectangle S?
      ii What is the area of rectangle S?

2 A rectangle with length 4 cm and width 5 cm is enlarged with scale factor 4.
   a Find the new length and width.
   b Find the perimeter of the enlarged rectangle.
   c Find the area of the enlarged rectangle.

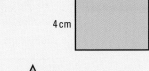

3 The triangle shown with area 20 cm² is enlarged with scale factor 3.
   Find the area of the new triangle.

4 The diagram shows a scale drawing of a flowerbed.
   The real flowerbed is 50 times bigger than the drawing.
   a The perimeter of the drawing is 1.2 m.
      Find the perimeter of the real flowerbed.
   b The area of the drawing is 1 m².
      Find the area of the real flowerbed.

5 A triangle with base 4 cm and area 6 cm² is enlarged.
The enlarged triangle has base 12 cm.
Work out the area of the enlarged triangle.

6 A photograph with length 4 cm and width 6 cm is enlarged.
The enlarged rectangle has length 16 cm.
Work out the perimeter and area of the enlargement.

A02

Example 5 The diagram shows a cuboid P with length 10 cm and volume 40 cm³.
The cuboid is enlarged with scale factor 4.
Find:
  a the length of the enlarged cuboid
  b the volume of the enlarged cuboid.

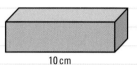

10 cm

a Length = 4 × 10 cm = 40 cm.
b Volume = 4 × 4 × 4 × 40 = 2560 cm³.

Exercise 9F

1 **a** Find the scale factor of the enlargement.
   b Find the volume of cuboid B.

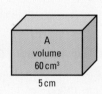

A
volume
60 cm³

5 cm

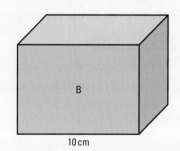

B

10 cm

2 The small cylinder has volume 20 cm³.
The large cylinder is an enlargement of the small cylinder.
Find the volume of the large cylinder.

5 cm

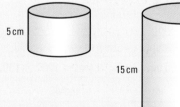

15 cm

A03

3 Two similar jugs have heights 4 cm and 7 cm respectively.
The smaller jug holds 50 cm³.
How much does the larger jug hold?

4 Two cylindrical tins have heights 5 cm and 9 cm.
The large tin is an enlargement of the small tin.
The volume of the small tin is 375 cm³.
Find the volume of the large tin.

C A02 A03

5 A cereal company is designing a large box to hold individual packets of cereal.
The individual packets are cuboids with height 10 cm, width 8 cm and depth 4 cm.
The large box must be an enlargement of an individual packet.
Work out the height, width and depth of a large box which will hold 25 packets.

9.5 Converting units of measure

◎ Objectives

● You can convert between area measures.
● You can convert between volume measures.
● You can convert between units of volume and units of capacity.

? Why do this?

When objects are enlarged it is often necessary to use different units. Measurements on a map may be in millimetres or centimetres, whilst in real life they are in miles or kilometres.

⊕ Get Ready

1. Convert the following measurements to the units given.

   a 250 cm to m   **b** 350 mm to cm   **c** 6.3 m to cm
   d 350 m to km   **e** 1.5 km to m   **f** 3.6 cm to mm

Converting area measures

🔍 Key Points

● The two squares A and B are congruent. They are exactly the same size and shape.
The area of square A is $1\,m \times 1\,m = 1\,m^2$.
The area of square B is $100\,cm \times 100\,cm = 10\,000\,cm^2$.
$$1\,m^2 = 10\,000\,cm^2$$

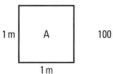

● There are similar results for other units.

Length	Area
1 cm = 10 mm	$1\,cm^2 = 10 \times 10 = 100\,mm^2$
1 m = 100 cm	$1\,m^2 = 100 \times 100 = 10\,000\,cm^2$
1 km = 1000 m	$1\,km^2 = 1000 \times 1000 = 1\,000\,000\,m^2$

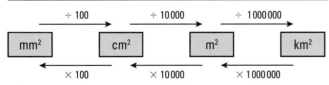

● When converting from a large unit to a smaller one, multiply.
● When converting from a small unit to a larger one, divide.

🔍 Example 6   Change 3.6 m² to cm².

$3.6\,m^2 = 3.6 \times 10\,000 = 36\,000\,cm^2$. ← | Metres are bigger than cm so the answer must be bigger. This is a clue to multiply.

Example 7   Convert 4 375 000 m² to km².

> Metres are smaller than km so the answer must be smaller. This is a clue to divide.

$$4\,375\,000 \text{ m}^2 = 4\,375\,000 \div 1\,000\,000 = 4.375 \text{ km}^2.$$

Exercise 9G

1   Convert to cm².
    a   3 m²   b   4.5 m²   c   300 mm²   d   34 mm²

2   Convert to m².
    a   6 km²   b   0.4 km²   c   20 000 cm²   d   3450 cm²

3   The area of a pane of glass is 14 500 cm².
    Write down the area of the pane of glass in m².

4   A plan shows the area of a square flowerbed as 225 cm².
    The real flowerbed is also a square but its sides are 10 times bigger.
    Find the area of the real flowerbed, giving your answer in m².

5   A door has height 2 m and width 70 cm.
    a   Write down the area of the door in m².
    b   Write down the area of the door in cm².

6   Dave is tiling the wall in a bathroom. The wall is 3 m long and is to be tiled to a height of 1.5 m.
    The tiles are square with length 15 cm.
    How many tiles are needed?

7   The diagram shows a wall with a window in it.
    Work out the shaded area.

             4.5 m   180 cm   75 cm   2.9 m

8   The perimeter of a rectangle is 1.5 m.
    The length of the longest side is 45 cm.
    Find the area of the rectangle.

Converting volume measures

Key Points

- The two cubes A and B are congruent.
  They are exactly the same size and shape.
  The volume of cube A is 1 m × 1 m × 1 m = 1 m³.
  The volume of cube B is 100 cm × 100 cm × 100 cm = 1 000 000 cm³.

$$1 \text{ m}^3 = 1\,000\,000 \text{ cm}^3$$

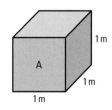

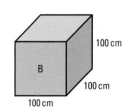

◉ There are similar results for other units.

Length	Volume
1 cm = 10 mm	$1\,cm^3 = 10 \times 10 \times 10 = 1000\,mm^3$
1 m = 100 cm	$1\,m^3 = 100 \times 100 \times 100 = 1\,000\,000\,cm^3$
1 km = 1000 m	$1\,km^3 = 1000 \times 1000 \times 1000 = 1\,000\,000\,000\,m^3$

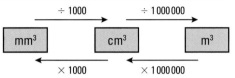

◉ Litres are often used to measure the capacity or amount a container can hold.

1 litre $= 1000\,cm^3$

$1\,cm^3 = 1\,ml$

> **Example 8** a Convert $7\,m^3$ to cm^3 b Convert $500\,000\,cm^3$ to m^3
>
> a $7 \times 1\,000\,000 = 7\,000\,000\,cm^3$
> b $500\,000 \div 1\,000\,000 = 0.5\,m^3$

> **Example 9** a Convert 2.5 litres to cm^3 b Convert $5000\,cm^3$ to litres
>
> a $2.5 \times 1000 = 2500\,cm^3$
> b $5000 \div 1000 = 5$ litres

Exercise 9H

C

1 Convert to cm^3.
   a $4\,m^3$
   b $4.5\,ml$
   c $400\,mm^3$
   d 3 litres

2 Convert to litres.
   a $400\,ml$
   b $5600\,cm^3$
   c $1\,m^3$
   d $3500\,mm^3$

3 How many mm^3 are there in 1 litre?

4 The diagram shows a cuboid.
   Work out the volume of the cuboid in
   a cm^3
   b mm^3.

   4 cm
   3 cm
   12 cm

5 The petrol tank of a car holds 42 litres of fuel.
   How many cm^3 is this?

A02 6 A bottle of medicine holds 0.5 litres.
   How many $5\,cm^3$ doses are contained in the bottle?

A02 7 A swimming pool has length 50 m, width 9 m and depth 1.5 m.
   How much water does it hold?
   Give your answer in litres.

8   Individual bars of soap are cuboids of size 8 cm × 6 cm × 4 cm.
The bars are placed in the large cardboard container shown in the diagram.
How many bars can be packed into the container?

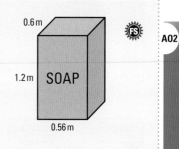

0.6 m

1.2 m   SOAP

0.56 m

A02   C

9   A path is to be resurfaced with 1 cubic metre of concrete.
The path is 20 m long and 2.4 m wide.
What is the depth of the concrete in cm?

A02

10   A cylinder holds 26 litres of molten metal.
The metal is to be made into cubes of side 3 cm.
How many cubes can be made?

A02
A03

Chapter review

- A **net** is a pattern of flat (2D) shapes that can be folded to make a hollow **solid** shape.
- **Plans** and **elevations** show the 2D view of a 3D object drawn from different angles.
- The view from above is called the plan.
- The view from the front is called the **front elevation**.
- The view from the side is called the **side elevation**.
- A cylinder is a prism with a circular cross section.
- The volume of a cylinder is the area of the circular cross-section × its length.
- The surface area of a cylinder is the area of the net which can be used to build the shape.
- When a shape is enlarged each length is multiplied by the scale factor.
  Enlarged perimeter = original perimeter × scale factor.
- Enlarged area = original area × scale factor^2.
- Enlarged volume = original volume × scale factor^3.

Length	Area
1 cm = 10 mm	1 cm^2 = 10 × 10 = 100 mm^2
1 m = 100 cm	1 m^2 = 100 × 100 = 10 000 cm^2
1 km = 1000 m	1 km^2 = 1000 × 1000 = 1 000 000 m^2

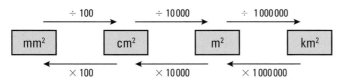

÷ 100   ÷ 10 000   ÷ 1 000 000

mm^2 cm^2 m^2 km^2

× 100   × 10 000   × 1 000 000

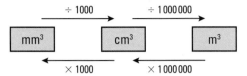

Length	Volume
1 cm = 10 mm	$1 \text{ cm}^3 = 10 \times 10 \times 10 = 1000 \text{ mm}^3$
1 m = 100 cm	$1 \text{ m}^3 = 100 \times 100 \times 100 = 1\,000\,000 \text{ cm}^3$
1 km = 1000 m	$1 \text{ km}^3 = 1000 \times 1000 \times 1000 = 1\,000\,000\,000 \text{ m}^3$

```
        ÷ 1000          ÷ 1 000 000
     ┌──────────┐    ┌──────────────┐
  ┌─────┐    ┌─────┐        ┌─────┐
  │ mm³ │    │ cm³ │        │ m³  │
  └─────┘    └─────┘        └─────┘
     └──────────┘    └──────────────┘
        × 1000          × 1 000 000
```

Litres are often used to measure the capacity or amount a container can hold.

1 litre = 1000 cm³

$1 \text{ cm}^3 = 1 \text{ m}l$

Review exercise

E

1 The diagram shows a pyramid with a square base.

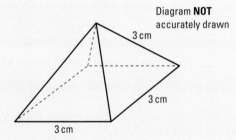

Diagram **NOT**
accurately drawn

3 cm

3 cm

3 cm

The length of each side of the base is 3 cm.

The length of each sloping edge is 3 cm.

On a copy of the grid of centimetre squares, draw an accurate net of the pyramid.

Nov 2008

2 The diagram shows some nets and some solid shapes.
An arrow has been drawn from one net to its solid shape.
Draw an arrow from each of the other nets to its solid shape.

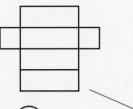

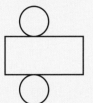
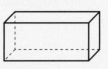

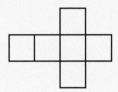
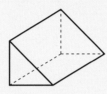

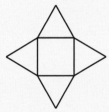

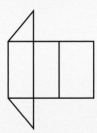
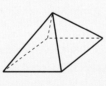

Nov 2008

3 The diagram shows a prism drawn on a centimetre isometric grid.

a On a centimetre grid, draw the front elevation of the prism from the direction marked by the arrow.

b On a centimetre grid, draw a plan of the prism.

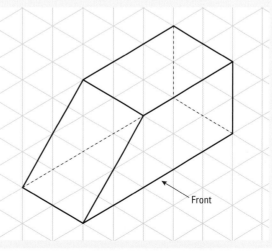

Front

Nov 2007

E

4 The diagram shows a solid object made of 6 identical cubes.

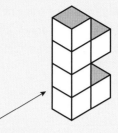

a On a centimetre grid, draw the side elevation of the solid object from the direction of the arrow.

b On a centimetre grid, draw the plan of the solid object.

June 2007

5 The diagram shows a cuboid.
The cuboid has
a volume of 300 cm³,
a length of 10 cm,
a width of 6 cm.
Work out the height of the cuboid.

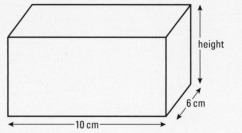

height

Diagram **NOT** accurately drawn

6 cm

10 cm

Nov 2006

6

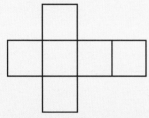

Here is a net of a 3D shape.
The diagrams show four 3D shapes.

A   B   C   D

Write down the letter of the 3D shape that can be made from the net.

June 2007

D

7 The diagram represents a solid made from 5 identical cubes.
On the grid below, draw the view of the solid from direction A.

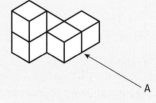

A

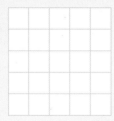

Nov 2008

8 Here are the front elevation, side elevation and the plan of a 3D shape.
Draw a sketch of the 3D shape.

Front elevation   Side elevation

Plan

June 2008

9

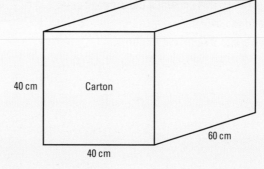

A02
A03 **D**

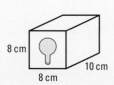

A light bulb box measures 8 cm by 8 cm by 10 cm.
Light bulb boxes are packed into cartons.
A carton measures 40 cm by 40 cm by 60 cm.
Work out the number of light bulb boxes which
can completely fill **one** carton.

ResultsPlus
Exam Question Report

85% of students answered this question poorly.
Some students calculated that there were 5 in a
row, 5 high and 6 back, but added these numbers
together rather than multiplying them.

June 2007

10 Louise makes chocolates.
Each box she puts them in has
Volume $= 1000 \text{ cm}^3$
Length $= 20$ cm
Width $= 10$cm.

a Work out the height of a box.

Louise makes 350 chocolates.
Each box will hold 18 chocolates.

b Work out

   i how many boxes Louise can fill completely,

   ii how many chocolates will be left over.

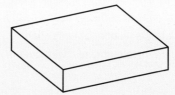

11 A piece of plastic has been designed as part of a game.
The plan and front elevation of a prism have been
drawn on centimetre squared paper.

a On squared paper draw a side elevation of the shape.

b Draw a 3D sketch of the shape.

c Find the volume of the prism.

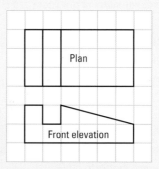

C

12 A solid cylinder has a radius of 4 cm and a height of 10 cm.
Work out the volume of the cylinder.
Give your answer correct to 3 significant figures.

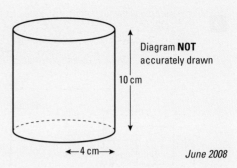

Diagram **NOT**
accurately drawn

10 cm

←4 cm→

June 2008

13 An oil drum is in the shape of a cylinder.
The lid has been removed.
Calculate the surface area of the oil drum without the lid.

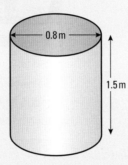

0.8 m

1.5 m

14 Rainfall on a flat rectangular roof 10 m by 5.5 m flows into a cylindrical tub of diameter 3 m.
Find, in cm, the increase in depth of the water in the tub caused by a rainfall of 1.2 cm.
Give your answer correct to 2 significant figures.

15 Cylindrical cans of radius 4 cm and height 10 cm are filled from a drum containing 0.5 m³ of oil.
a Calculate the number of cans filled.
b Calculate the quantity of oil left over in cm³.

* 16 Danni is going to redecorate her bedroom.
She wants to wallpaper all four walls and fit new carpet and underlay.
The dimensions of her room are shown in the diagram.

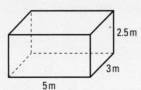

2.5 m

3 m

5 m

The carpet that she likes costs £18.50 per m² and the underlay £3.50 per m² fully fitted.
The wallpaper costs £25 per roll and the shop has a handy table that she can use to estimate how many
rolls she needs to buy.

Room perimeter (m)	Height (m)			
	2.1 to < 2.25	2.25 to < 2.4	2.4 to < 2.55	2.55 to < 2.7
10	4	5	5	5
11	5	5	5	5
12	5	6	6	6
13	6	6	7	7
14	6	7	7	7
15	7	7	8	8
16	7	8	9	9
17	8	8	9	9
18	8	9	10	10
19	9	9	10	10
20	10	10	12	12

Calculate how much Danni will have to budget for the decoration.

17 You are planning a party for 30 children.
You buy some concentrated orange squash and some plastic cups.

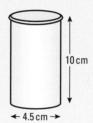

Each plastic cup will have 150 ml of drink in it. (150 ml = 150 cm^3)

a Check that the plastic cup shown can hold 150 ml of drink. Use the formula:
$$\text{volume} = \frac{\pi \times h \times d^2}{4}$$

Each of the 30 children at the party will have a maximum of three drinks of orange squash.
Each plastic cup is to be filled with 150 ml of drink.
The squash needs to be diluted as shown on the bottle label.
A bottle of concentrated orange squash contains 0.8 litres of squash and costs £1.25.

b How many bottles of concentrated orange squash do you need for the party?
How much will they cost in total?

18 The triangular prism has length 10 cm and volume 90 cm^3.
The small prism is a scale model for a larger prism which is a part for
a piece of machinery.
The length of the larger prism is 30 cm.
All of its lengths are enlarged by the same scale factor.
Find the volume of the larger prism.

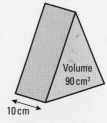

Volume
90 cm^3

10 cm

A03

119

C

19 The volume of the cube is 125 cm³.
    Change 125 cm³ into mm³.

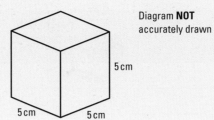

Diagram **NOT**
accurately drawn

5 cm

5 cm   5 cm

Nov 2009 adapted

20 The volume of this cube is 8 m³.
    Change 8 m³ to cm³.

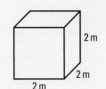

Diagram **NOT**
accurately drawn

2 m

2 m

2 m

June 2007

21 a Change 2.5 m² to cm².
    b Change 734.9 mm² to cm².

22 The area of a large farm is 6 540 000 m².
    Change 6 540 000 m² to km².

10 CONSTRUCTIONS AND LOCI

 BBC ACTIVE

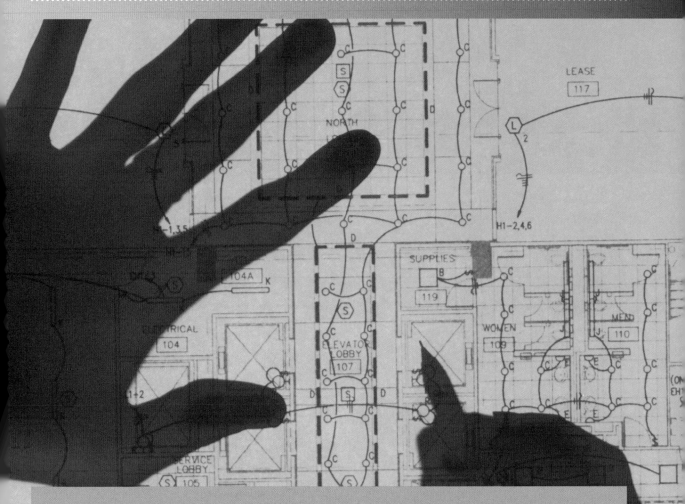

Architects do scale drawings of projects they are working on for both planning and presentation purposes. Originally these were done on paper using ink and copies had to be made by hand. Later they were done on tracing paper so that copying was easier. Today, computer-generated drawings have largely taken over. The first program that could create these was released in the 1960s and now for many of the top architecture firms these have been replaced by architectural animation.

⊙ Objectives

In this chapter you will:
- learn how to draw the five basic constructions using a ruler and compass only
- learn how to accurately construct the locus of a set of points and draw regions associated with loci.

◇ Before you start

You need to:
- know that 'bisect' means 'cut in half'
- be able to measure and draw lines accurately
- be able to draw circles and arcs to a given radius
- have a pencil, eraser, ruler, protractor and compasses.

10.1 Constructions

⟐ Get Ready

1. Draw a line of length 5 cm.
2. Draw a circle of radius 5 cm.

Key Points

● Constructing an angle of 60°.

A   B

Start with a line.

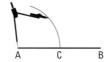

A   C   B

Open your compasses.
Put the point at A and draw an arc that cuts the line.
Label the point C.

A   C   B

Keeping your compasses the same width, put the point at C. Draw an arc to cut the first one.

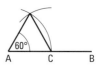

A   C   B

Join up to get a 60° angle. This is an equilateral triangle.

● Bisecting an angle.

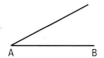

A   B

Start with an angle.

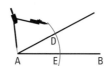

A   E   B

Put the point of the compasses at A and draw an arc that cuts both lines. Label the points D and E.

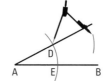

A   E   B

Put the point at D and draw an arc between the two sides of the angle. Without adjusting your compasses, place the point at E and draw an arc to cut the first one. Label the point where they cross F.

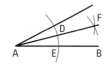

A   E   B

Draw a straight line from F to A to bisect the angle.

● To construct angles of sizes other than 60°, use the idea of starting with 60°, or a multiple of 60°, and bisecting the angle. For example, to construct an angle of 30°, first construct an angle of 60° and then bisect it.

● Bisecting a line.

A   B

Start with a line.

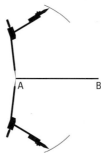

A   B

Open your compasses to more than half the line length. Put the point at A and draw an arc above and below the line.

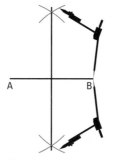

A   B

Keeping your compasses the same, put the point at B and draw arcs above and below the line to cross the other arcs.

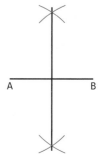

A   B

Join the crosses to make a line. This line will bisect AB.

◉ Constructing a perpendicular line from a point on a given line.

 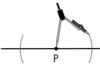 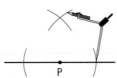 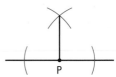

Start with a line and a point P on that line.

Put your compass on point P and draw arcs on the line either side of point P.

From each of the arcs drawn, use compasses to draw two intersecting arcs above the line.

Join the intersecting arcs to point P. This line is perpendicular to the given line at P.

◉ Constructing a perpendicular line from a point to a given line.

 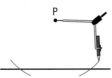

Start with a line and a point P above that line.

Put your compass on point P and draw arcs on the line either side of point P.

From each of the arcs drawn, use compasses to draw two intersecting arcs below the line.

Use the intersecting arcs to draw a line from point P to the line below. This line is perpendicular to the given line.

Example 1 Construct a regular hexagon inside a circle.

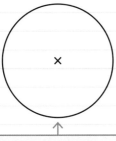 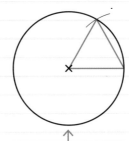 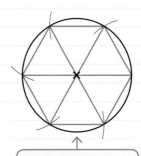

Start with a circle. A regular hexagon has angles at the centre which are each $\frac{360}{6} = 60°$.

Draw an angle at the centre which is 60°. Draw in a triangle.

Draw in all the other 60° angles, drawing in the triangles.

Exercise 10A

Questions in this chapter are targeted at the grades indicated.

For each of the following questions use one or more of the five constructions.

1 Construct each of the following angles.
a 60°   b 90°   c 30°   d 45°   e 15°

2 Draw lines of the lengths shown. Then bisect each of the lines.
a 8 cm   b 6 cm   c 7 cm   d 9 cm

3 Construct equilateral triangles with sides of the following lengths.
a 5 cm   b 8 cm   c 7 cm   d 6 cm

C

C

4   Construct squares with sides of the following lengths.

      a   6 cm   b   4 cm   c   8 cm   d   5 cm

5   Draw a triangle. Bisect each of its sides.

      Extend each of the bisectors so they meet at a point X. Put the point of your compass at point X. Draw a circle through each of the vertices of the triangle.

6   Draw a 5 cm line. Mark a point P on your line. Construct a perpendicular line at point P.

7   Draw a 5 cm line. Mark a point P at least 4 cm above your line. Construct a perpendicular line from point P down to the line.

8   Construct an equilateral triangle of side 6 cm. Construct a perpendicular line from a vertex to the opposite side of the triangle.

9   Draw a regular hexagon in a circle of radius 4 cm.

10   Draw a regular octagon in a circle of radius 4 cm.

11   Draw a regular pentagon in a circle of radius 4 cm.

10.2 Loci

◉ Objectives

- You can interpret a locus as a set of points.
- You can draw a locus that obeys a rule.
- You can use constructions to draw loci.

◈ Why do this?

Seismologists can use loci to work out the area that an earthquake is likely to affect and damage.

⬆ Get Ready

1. Draw accurately an equilateral triangle of side 5 cm.

🔑 Key Points

◉ The locus is a set of points that obey a given rule. Loci is the plural of locus.

◉ The **locus** of points which are the same distance (**equidistant**) from a single point is a circle.

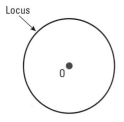

◉ The locus of points that are the same distance from two points is a line that is the **perpendicular bisector** of the line joining the two points.

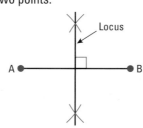

◉ The locus of points the same distance from two lines is the **bisector** of the angle between the lines.

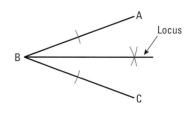

Example 2

Here is a line AB.

Draw the locus of points that are equidistant from the line AB.

A ———————————— B

> Points can be placed that are the same distance above and below the line.
> So parts of the locus are parallel lines above and below AB.

> However, more points can be placed at an equal distance (radius) around the end points A and B.
> The loci of the points are semicircles at each end.

> This is now a complete locus.

ResultsPlus
Examiner's Tip

Always remember to show your construction arcs when using constructions to draw loci.

Exercise 10B

1 Draw a line of length 5 cm. Draw the locus of points that are 2 cm from this line. **A03**

2 Plot a point P on your page. Draw the locus of points that are 4 cm from point P. **A03**

3 Draw two points, A and B, 8 cm apart.
Draw the locus of points that are the same distance from point A and from point B. **A03**

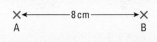

4 Plot a point T on your page. Draw the locus of points that are 6 cm from point T. **A03**

5 Copy this diagram.
Draw the locus of points that are the same distance from AB and BC. **A03**

6 The diagram shows two lighthouses which are 5 km apart.
A ship wants to sail a route that keeps it the same distance from lighthouse P and lighthouse Q.
Using a scale of 1 cm = 1 km, draw an accurate diagram to show the route the ship must take. **A02**

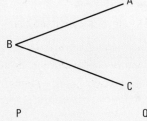

7 Draw a square with sides of length 5 cm.
Draw the locus of points that are 3 cm from the sides of the square. **A03**

C

A03

8   This rectangle has a width of 3 cm and a length of 5 cm.

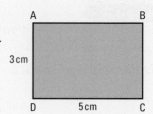

 a Within the rectangle, draw the locus of points that are 1 cm from DC.

 b Draw the locus of points that are the same distance from AD
    and from DC.

A03

9   Copy this equilateral triangle.

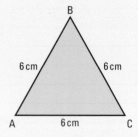

 a Within the triangle, draw the locus of points that are 2 cm from point A.

 b Draw the locus of points that are the same distance from
    AB and from BC.

A03

10   Points S and T are 6 cm apart.
     Draw the locus of points that are the same distance
     from point S as from point T.

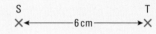

A03

11   This triangle represents a field.
     The scale of the plan is 1 cm = 2 m.
     The farmer places an electric wire 1 m from each side of
     the field to stop the cows getting near to the perimeter
     of the field.
     Copy the plan and draw on it where the electric
     wire should be placed.

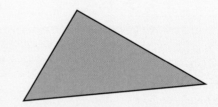

A03

12   Copy the triangle from question 11.
     Draw the locus of points that are equidistant from two adjacent sides.
     Then draw the locus of points that are equidistant from another two adjacent sides, and then the third
     set of adjacent sides.
     Mark clearly the point where all three loci meet.

10.3 Regions

⊙ Objectives

- You can interpret a locus as a region.
- You can draw a region that obeys a rule.
- You can use constructions to draw regions.

⊘ Why do this?

A school may only take students from a certain
catchment area. Understanding regions would
enable you to work out if you lived in the
necessary area.

⊕ Get Ready

1. Plot a point P on your page. Draw the locus of points that are 5 cm from point P.
   What shape have you drawn? What do all the points within the shape have in common?

Key Points

- Sometimes the locus is a **region** of space.
- The locus of points that are no more than a given distance from a single point is the area within a circle.

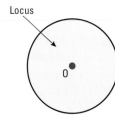
Locus

- The diagram shows the locus of points that are closer to BC than AB.

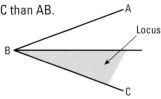
Locus

Example 3

This diagram is a plan of a yard.
A light at corner L can illuminate the
yard up to a distance of 3 m from the
light. Indicate this region on the plan.

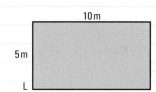
10 m
5 m
L

A02

The region is part of a circle
of radius 3 m from corner L.
The region inside this quarter
circle should be shaded.

ResultsPlus
Watch Out!

Don't forget to shade the region.

The shaded region represents that part of the yard that
can be illuminated from corner L.

Exercise 10C

1 Copy the point A.
Shade the region that is less than 3 cm from point A.

✕ A

A03

2 Copy the rectangle ABCD.
  a Shade the region of points that are less than 2 cm from B.
  b Shade the region of points that are less than 1 cm from BC.

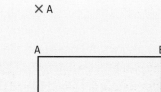
A   B
2 cm
D   3 cm   C

A03

3 Copy the rectangle PQRS.
  a Shade the region of points that are closer to PR than to PS.
  b Shade the region of points that are less than 1 cm from SR.
  c Shade the region of points that are both closer to PR than
    to PS, **and** are less than 1 cm from SR.

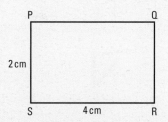
P   Q
2 cm
S   4 cm   R

A03

4 The diagram represents a garden.

Plants must be planted in the garden so they are more than 1 metre from the edges of the garden.

a Copy the diagram and shade the region in which the plants must **not** be planted.

b A sprinkler is placed at C. It can spread water up to 2 m from the sprinkler. On your diagram, shade the region that can be watered by the sprinkler.

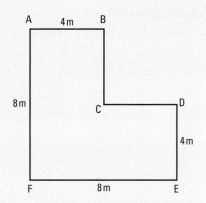

5 This rectangle is a plan of a swimming pool. The half of the pool nearest to side AB is reserved for school lessons.

Copy the rectangle and shade the region of the pool reserved for school lessons.

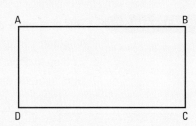

6 The diagram represents three radio masts.

Signals from each radio mast can be received up to 20 km away.

Copy the diagram and shade the region in which signals from all three masts can be received.

Scale: 1 cm = 10 km.

7 In the diagram, AB represents the coast, with a lighthouse at point L.

Ships cannot come nearer than 2 km from the coast.

a Use a scale of 1 cm = 1 km to represent this on a plan.

b On a foggy night the light can only be seen up to 3 km from the lighthouse. Show this on your plan.

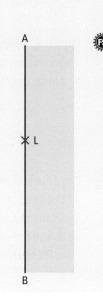

8   Copy this triangle.
    a   Show the region of points that are less than 2 cm from A.
    b   Show the region of points that are less than 2 cm from BC.
    c   Shade the region of points that are nearer to AB than AC.
    d   Is there a region in which there are some
        points that satisfy all three of these
        conditions?
        Indicate this clearly on
        your diagram.

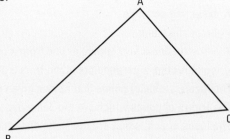

9   Copy this rectangle.

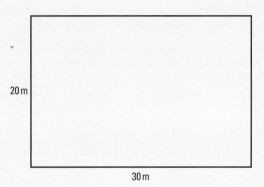

The rectangle represents a plan of a compound which has dimensions of 20 m by 30 m, and a scale of
1 cm = 5 m. Lights are placed on the walls all around the compound. The lights can illuminate a region
no more than 5 m from the compound wall, both inside and outside the compound. Shade the region
illuminated on your plan.

10

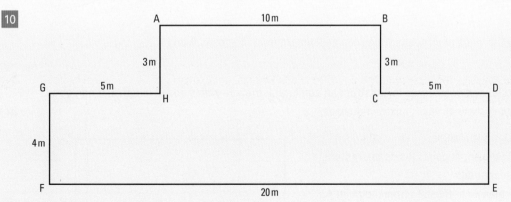

The above is a plan of a hall. Draw an accurate plan, using a scale of 1 cm = 2 m.
Then draw the following regions on the plan.
a   The locus of points that are nearer to BC than AB.
b   The locus of points that are within 3 m of point H or of point C.
c   The locus of points that are more than 2 m from FE.
Indicate clearly any points that are within all of the regions indicated.

Chapter review

- You have learnt the following constructions:
  - constructing an angle of 60°
  - bisecting an angle
  - bisecting a line
  - constructing a perpendicular line from a point on a given line
  - constructing a perpendicular line from a point to a given line.
- The locus is a set of points that obey a given rule. Loci is the plural of locus.
- The **locus** of points which are the same distance (**equidistant**) from a single point is a circle.
- The locus of points that are the same distance from two points is a line that is the **perpendicular bisector** of the line joining the two points.
- The locus of points the same distance from two lines is the **bisector** of the angle between the lines.
- Sometimes the locus is a **region** of space.
- The locus of points that are no more than a given distance from a single point is the area within a circle.
- The diagram shows the locus of points that are closer to BC than AB.

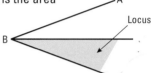

Review exercise

1 Use ruler and compasses to construct the bisector of angle ABC.
You must show all your construction lines.

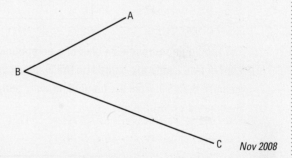

Nov 2008

2 Draw the locus of all points which are equidistant from the points A and B.

A✕   ✕B

Nov 2008

3 Use ruler and compasses to construct an equilateral triangle with sides of length 6 centimetres.
You must show all your construction lines.

June 2008

4 ABCD is a rectangle.
Shade the set of points inside the rectangle which are **both**
more than 4 centimetres from the point A
and more than 1 centimetre from the line DC.

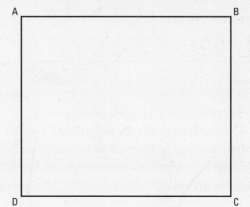

5   ABC is a triangle. Make an accurate copy of ABC. Shade the region inside the triangle which is **both** less than 4 centimetres from the point B **and** closer to the line AC than the line BC.

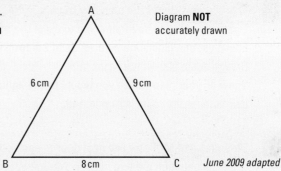

Diagram **NOT** accurately drawn

June 2009 adapted

6   There are two sprinklers in the garden, C and D.

They are 5 m apart. Draw a plan of this situation.
The sprinklers can water the garden for up to a distance of 3 m in all directions.
Show on your plan the part of the garden that is getting double the water.

7   This diagram shows a quadrangle.
Copy the plan shown, using a scale of 1 cm = 5 m.
  a   A path goes from D so that it is the same distance from AD as from CD.
   Draw this path on your plan.
  b   A flower bed is dug into the quadrangle at C so that the plants are no further than 5 m from C.
   Draw the flower bed on your plan.
  c   A fence is put up that is exactly 5 m from side BC. Draw this fence on your plan.

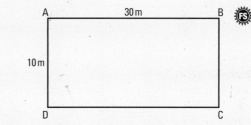

8   A goat is tied to one wall of a shed.
The shed has dimensions 8 m by 4 m.
Draw a diagram to show the area of grass that can be eaten by the goat when the rope has a length of **a** 2 m and **b** 4 m.

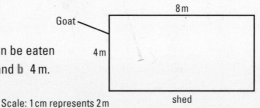

Scale: 1 cm represents 2 m

9   A gardener plants two shrubs 60 cm apart. This is the minimum distance that can be allowed between the shrubs that he is planting. Draw a diagram to show the gardener the area in which a third shrub cannot be planted.

10   The diagram shows a plan of a compound.
The compound has a length of 32 m and a width of 20 m, and is surrounded by a fence.
Draw a scale plan of the compound.
  a   A security guard walks around the outside of the compound at a distance of 3 m from the fence.
   Draw the path taken by the security guard on your plan.
  b   Another guard walks around the inside of the compound at a distance of 2 m from the fence. On your plan show the path taken by this guard.

A03

A03

A03

A03

A03

C
AO3

11 This diagram shows the plan of a room.
Lights are going to be fitted to the walls of the room.
Each light can illuminate an area up to 2 m from where the light is fixed.
Draw a scale plan of the room.
Show on your plan where you would fix the lights so that the entire
perimeter of the room is illuminated.

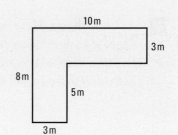

AO3

12 Mr Jones and Mr Parry live next door to each other. Their houses are 24 m apart. A cable needs
to be run between the two houses. Mr Jones and Mr Parry want the cable to be laid as far from their
houses as possible. Draw a plan to show how the cable could be laid so they are both happy.

AO3

13 As a bicycle moves along a flat road, draw the locus of
  a the yellow dot, a point on the centre of the wheel
  b the green dot, a point on the circumference of the wheel.

11 TRANSFORMATIONS

Many fairground rides use rotation, and the G-forces created, to thrill their riders. Can you tell the order of rotational symmetry for this ride? Where do you think the centre of rotation is?

◎ Objectives

In this chapter you will:
- learn how to distinguish between the four main transformations
- learn how to carry out and describe single and multiple transformations.

◁ Before you start

You need to:
- be able to spot patterns in shapes in real-life situations, for example in wallpaper
- have a pencil, eraser, ruler, squared paper and tracing paper for some transformations.

11.1 Introduction

⊙ **Objectives**

○ You can recall the names of the four main transformations.
○ You can identify simple transformations.

❓ **Why do this?**

Transformations are useful for producing designs for tiles, mosaics, wallpaper and rugs.

⬆ **Get Ready**

1. Pick out any letters that you think might be symmetrical in some way.

A B C D E F G H I J K L M N O P Q R S T U V W X Y Z

🔍 **Key Point**

◉ There are four main **transformations**.

Reflection	Rotation	Translation	Enlargement

⚙ **Exercise 11A**

Questions in this chapter are targeted at the grades indicated.

In each of the following cases, identify which of the four transformations is being shown.

E

E

11.2 **Translations**

◉ Objectives

- ○ You can recognise a translation.
- ○ You can carry out a translation.
- ○ You can describe a translation.

◈ Why do this?

In sport, any movement can be described as a translation, from a set piece in football to a gymnastics routine.

⬆ Get Ready

1. You are standing at point A on the grid.
   You are facing to the right.
   You want to move along the lines of the grid to get to point B.
   Describe a number of moves you could make to get to point B.

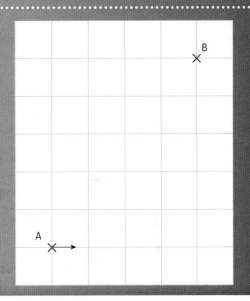

Key Points

◉ A **translation** is a sliding movement made from one or more moves.

In a simple translation you need to describe the distance and direction of each move.

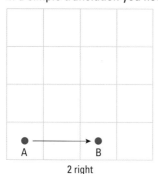

2 right

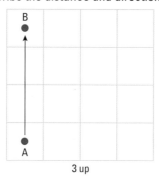

3 up

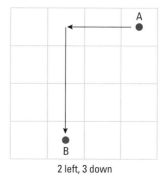

2 left, 3 down

◉ You can describe a translation by using a **column vector**, e.g. $\begin{pmatrix} 3 \\ 2 \end{pmatrix}$.

The top number describes the movement to the right, the bottom number the movement up.

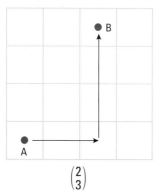

$\begin{pmatrix} 2 \\ 3 \end{pmatrix}$

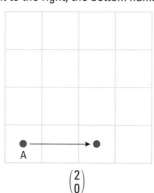

$\begin{pmatrix} 2 \\ 0 \end{pmatrix}$

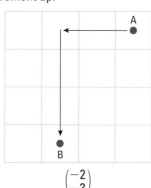

$\begin{pmatrix} -2 \\ -3 \end{pmatrix}$

Notice the negative signs mean the opposite direction: left instead of right, down instead of up.

◉ In a translation:

  ◉ the lengths of the sides of the shape do not change

  ◉ the angles of the shape do not change

  ◉ the shape does not turn.

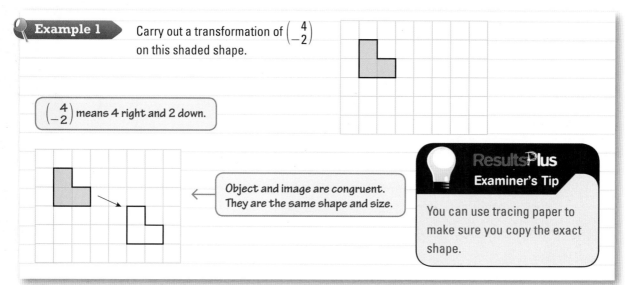

Example 1 Carry out a transformation of $\begin{pmatrix} 4 \\ -2 \end{pmatrix}$ on this shaded shape.

$\begin{pmatrix} 4 \\ -2 \end{pmatrix}$ means 4 right and 2 down.

Object and image are congruent. They are the same shape and size.

ResultsPlus
Examiner's Tip

You can use tracing paper to make sure you copy the exact shape.

Example 2 Describe, as a column vector, the transformation that moves triangle A to triangle B.

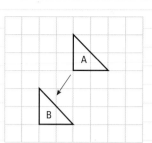

The transformation is a translation.

The movement is 2 left and 3 down.

ResultsPlus
Watch Out!

Don't forget the negative signs when writing column vectors.

The description using a column vector is

'A translation of $\begin{pmatrix} -2 \\ -3 \end{pmatrix}$.'

Exercise 11B

1   Copy each shape and carry out the translation described.

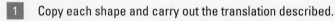

a $\begin{pmatrix} 2 \\ 3 \end{pmatrix}$

b $\begin{pmatrix} 3 \\ 0 \end{pmatrix}$

c $\begin{pmatrix} 1 \\ 2 \end{pmatrix}$

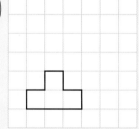

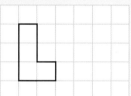

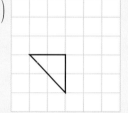

d $\begin{pmatrix} 3 \\ -1 \end{pmatrix}$

e $\begin{pmatrix} 0 \\ -2 \end{pmatrix}$

f $\begin{pmatrix} -2 \\ -4 \end{pmatrix}$

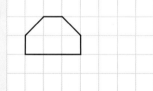

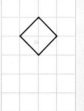

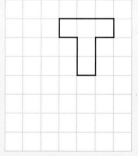

g $\begin{pmatrix} -2 \\ 4 \end{pmatrix}$

h $\begin{pmatrix} -1 \\ -3 \end{pmatrix}$

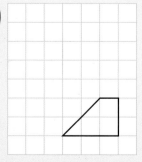

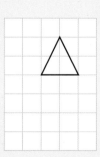

C

C

2   Carry out these translations on the shaded shape.

a $\begin{pmatrix}2\\3\end{pmatrix}$ Label the shape A.

b $\begin{pmatrix}3\\2\end{pmatrix}$ Label the shape B.

c $\begin{pmatrix}-1\\2\end{pmatrix}$ Label the shape C.

d $\begin{pmatrix}4\\-2\end{pmatrix}$ Label the shape D.

e $\begin{pmatrix}-3\\0\end{pmatrix}$ Label the shape E.

f $\begin{pmatrix}3\\-2\end{pmatrix}$ Label the shape F.

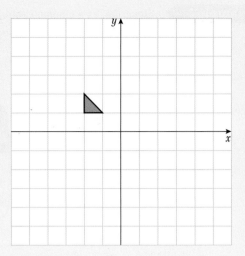

3   Describe, as a column vector, each transformation given below.

a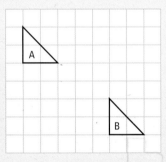
b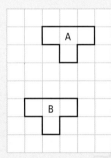
c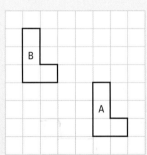

d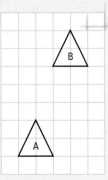
e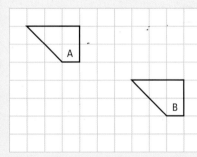

f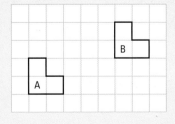
g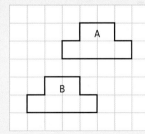
h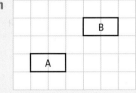

C

4 Describe, using a column vector, the transformation that moves the following shapes.

a A to B

b C to B

c B to D

d D to B

e B to A

f A to C

11.3 **Rotations**

◎ Objectives

◉ You can recognise a rotation.

◉ You can carry out a rotation.

◉ You can describe a rotation.

❓ Why do this?

Engineers need to check the path of a fairground ride as it rotates to make sure it does not crash into anything.

⬆ Get Ready

1. Write down the order of rotation of each of these shapes.

a   b 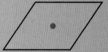   c   d

🌐 Key Points

◉ A **rotation** can be described as a fraction of a turn, or as an angle of turn.

◉ The direction of rotation can be **clockwise** ↻ or **anticlockwise** ↺.

◉ The point about which the shape is turned is called the **centre of rotation**.

◉ It is useful to use tracing paper to assist in rotating a shape.

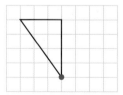

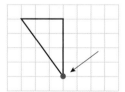

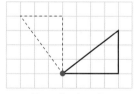

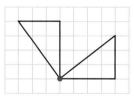

| Trace the shape onto tracing paper. | Hold the tracing paper down at the point of rotation, and rotate the tracing paper as requested. | Trace the shape in the new position. | Rotation complete. |

◉ The centre of rotation can sometimes be given as coordinates on a coordinate grid.

◉ In a rotation:

  ◉ the lengths of the sides of the shapes do not change

  ◉ the angles of the shape do not change

  ◉ the shape turns.

Example 3 Draw the image of the triangle after it has been rotated 90° clockwise about point O. Label the image B.

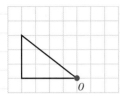 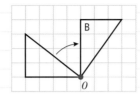

> Object and image are congruent. They are the same shape and size.

Exercise 11C

1 Copy each diagram. Draw the image of each shape after the rotation requested, using the point shown as centre of rotation.

a

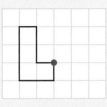

$\frac{1}{4}$ turn
clockwise

b

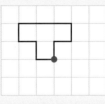

$\frac{1}{2}$ turn

c

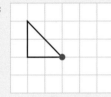

90° turn
anticlockwise

d

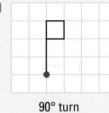

90° turn
clockwise

2 Copy each diagram. Draw the image of each shape after the rotation requested, using the point shown as centre of rotation.

a

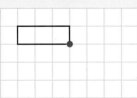

90° turn
anticlockwise

b

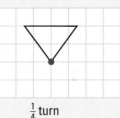

$\frac{1}{4}$ turn
clockwise

c

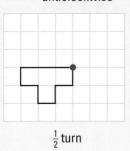

$\frac{1}{2}$ turn

d

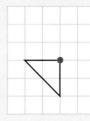

180° turn

D

3 Copy each diagram. Draw separate images for each shape after a rotation of 90° anticlockwise about each of the centres marked.

a
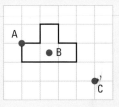

b
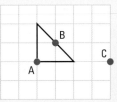

c
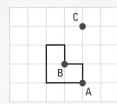

d
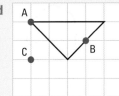

4 Copy each diagram. Draw separate images for each shape after the rotation requested, using the given point as centre of rotation.

a   A rotation of A clockwise 90° about (1, 0)

b   A rotation of B 90° clockwise about (−1, 2)

c   A rotation of C 180° about (2, −2)

d   A rotation of A anticlockwise 90° about (1, −1)

e   A rotation of B 180° about (0, 3)

f   A rotation of C clockwise 90° about (2, 2)

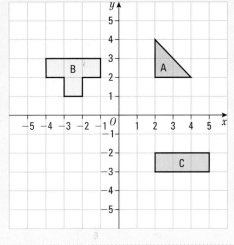

C

Example 4   Describe fully the transformation that maps shape A onto shape B.

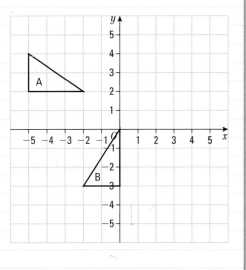

This is a rotation.

From A to B the direction is anticlockwise, and it is a 90° turn.

Using tracing paper or drawing lines (as shown) you can identify the centre of rotation as (0, 2), so the complete description is 'A rotation, 90° anticlockwise, centre (0, 2).'

> It is important to state that your transformation is a rotation.

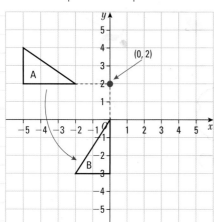

> Marks are given for stating three facts:
> (1) transformation is a rotation
> (2) direction and angle
> (3) centre of rotation.

Exercise 11D

D

1 Describe fully the rotation that maps shape A onto shape B.

a

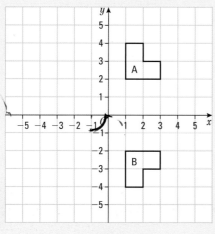

b

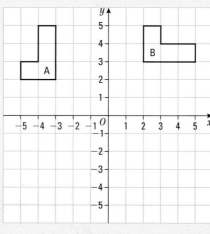

c

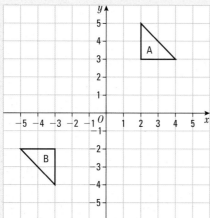

d

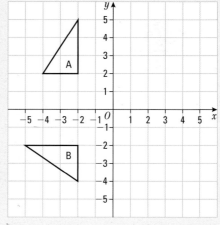

2 Describe fully the transformation that maps shape A onto shape B.

a

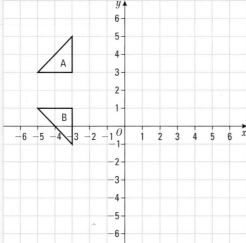

b

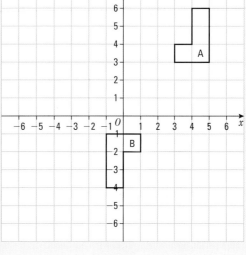

c

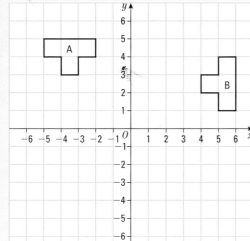

d

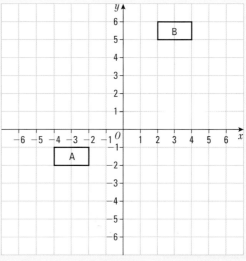

11.4 Reflections

Objectives

- You can recognise a reflection.
- You can carry out a reflection.
- You can describe a reflection.

Why do this?

Reflections are evident in everyday life, particularly in nature, for example on butterfly wings.

Get Ready

1. Below is a set of four shapes. Write down the number of lines of symmetry of each shape.

a
b
c
d

🔍 **Key Points**

- ◉ Images of a shape that are formed by reflecting a given shape about a **line of reflection** (or mirror line) are called **reflections** of the shape.
- ◉ In a reflection:
    - ◉ the lengths of the sides of the shape do not change
    - ◉ the angles of the shape do not change.
- ◉ It is useful to use tracing paper to assist in reflecting a shape.

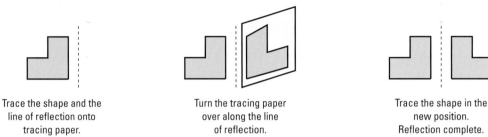

| Trace the shape and the line of reflection onto tracing paper. | Turn the tracing paper over along the line of reflection. | Trace the shape in the new position. Reflection complete. |

- ◉ The reflection can sometimes be given on a coordinate grid.
- ◉ The line of reflection can be given as the equation of a line.

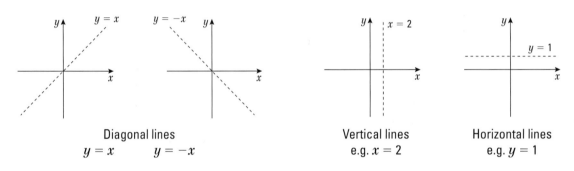

Diagonal lines
$y = x$ $y = -x$

Vertical lines
e.g. $x = 2$

Horizontal lines
e.g. $y = 1$

🔍 **Example 5**   Draw the image of this shape after it has been reflected in the mirror line.

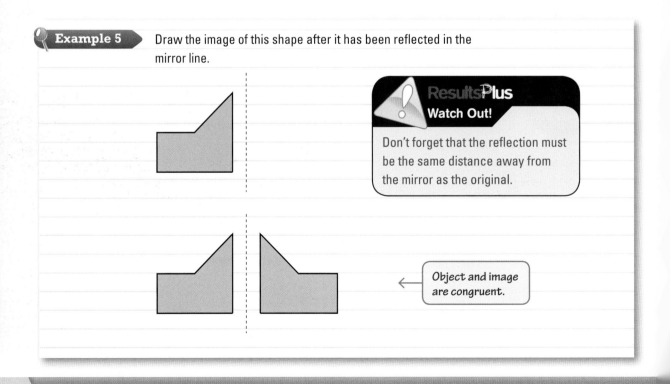

Results Plus

Watch Out!

Don't forget that the reflection must be the same distance away from the mirror as the original.

Object and image are congruent.

Exercise 11E

1. In each of these diagrams the dotted line is a line of reflection.
   Copy each diagram and draw the reflection of the shape in the line.

a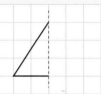

b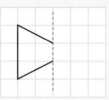

c

d

e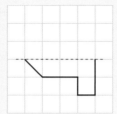

f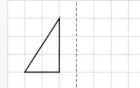

g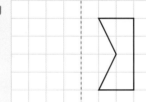

h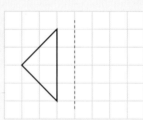

2. In each of these diagrams the dotted line is a line of reflection.
   Copy each diagram and draw the reflection of the shape in the line.

a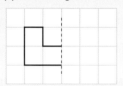

b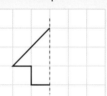

c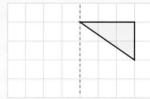

d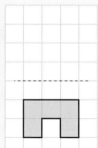

e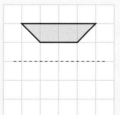

f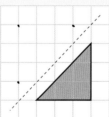

g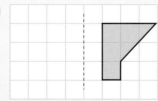

h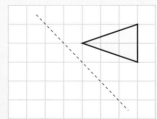

Example 6   Describe fully the transformation that maps shape A onto shape B.

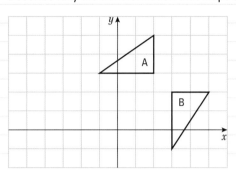

Marks are given for stating two facts:
(1) transformation is a reflection
(2) the line in which the shape has been reflected.

This is a reflection.

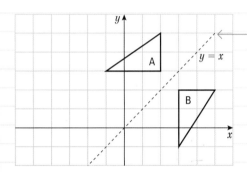

First draw the line of symmetry.
This is the line $y = x$.

The complete description of the transformation is:
'A reflection in the line $y = x$.'

Exercise 11F

D

1   Describe fully the reflection that maps shape A onto shape B.

a

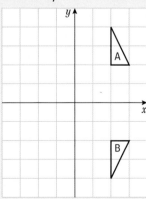

b

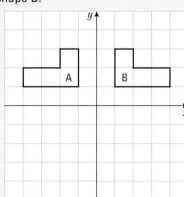

D

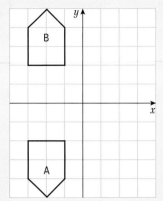

c

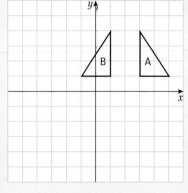

d

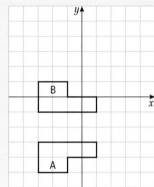

e

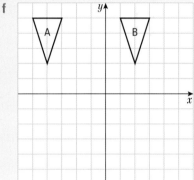

f

2 Describe fully the reflection that maps

    a F onto G

    b D onto F

    c A onto H

    d A onto G

    e F onto E

    f B onto C

    g C onto H.

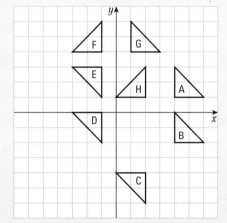

3 Describe fully the reflection that maps shape A onto shape B.

    a

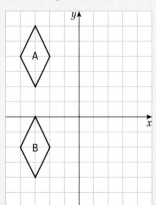

    b

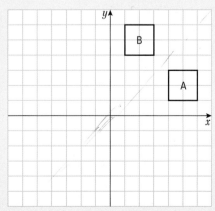

C

c

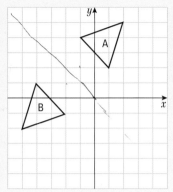

d

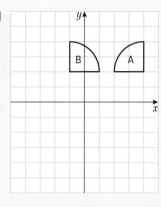

e

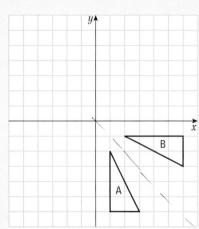

f

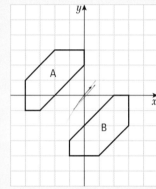

11.5 Enlargement

◉ Objectives

- You can recognise an enlargement.
- You can carry out an enlargement.
- You can describe an enlargement.

❓ Why do this?

Once an original for something exists, it can be enlarged. This can be seen in the case of Russian dolls, where each enlargement contains a smaller version of itself.

⬆ Get Ready

1. Draw this picture of a robot onto a copy of the larger grid, making the picture twice as big.

Key Points

- An **enlargement** changes the size of an object. It changes the length of its sides, but does not change its shape.
- The **scale factor** of the enlargement is the value that lengths in the original object are multiplied by to get the lengths in the image.
  For example, a scale factor of $1\frac{1}{2}$ means all the lengths are $1\frac{1}{2}$ times what they were in the original shape.
- Shapes can be enlarged from a point called the **centre of enlargement**.
- To find or use the centre of enlargement, draw in additional lines from the centre of enlargement to the vertices of the shape or shapes.

Example 7 Draw an enlargement of this shape, scale factor 2.

> Scale factor 2 means double the lengths of sides. It does not mean double and add the length on, which would be scale factor 3.
>
> The shape must be drawn bigger.
>
> The lengths of all the sides must be twice as long, since this is scale factor 2.
>
> Object and image are similar.

Exercise 11G

Copy the diagrams and enlarge each of the following shapes by the stated scale factor (sf).

1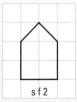
s f 2

2
s f 3

3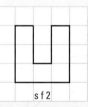
s f 2

4
s f 3

5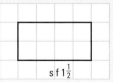
s f $1\frac{1}{2}$

6
s f $2\frac{1}{2}$

7
s f 2

8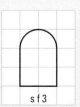
s f 3

9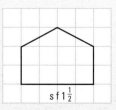
s f $1\frac{1}{2}$

D

Example 8 Draw an enlargement of the triangle, scale factor 2, using point A as the centre of enlargement.

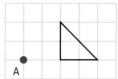

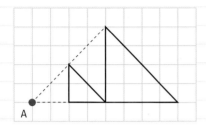

It is useful to draw in additional lines from the centre of enlargement, which will connect the vertices of the triangles. The lengths in the enlargement are twice the lengths of the original shape. The vertices are twice the distance from the centre of enlargement.

Exercise 11H

D

1 Copy each diagram onto squared paper. Enlarge each of these shapes by the stated scale factor (sf), from the given point of enlargement.

a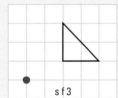

s f 3

b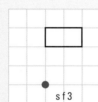

s f 3

c

s f 2

d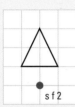

s f 2

e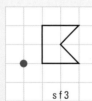

s f 3

f

s f 4

2 Copy each diagram onto squared paper. For each diagram draw two images, one from each of the points of enlargement given.

a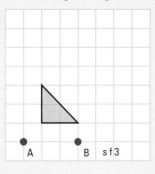

A   B   s f 3

b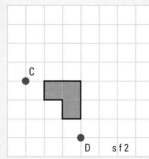

D   s f 2

c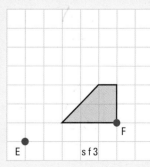

E   s f 3

3 Copy each diagram onto squared paper. For each diagram draw two images, one from each of the points of enlargement given.

a
A (0, 0)
B (3, −1)

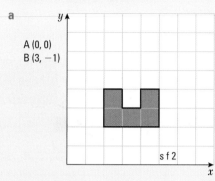

s f 2

b
C (0, 0)
D (−2, 1)

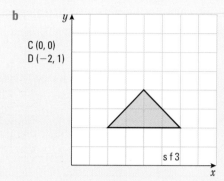

s f 3

c
E (0, 0)
F (−1, 1)

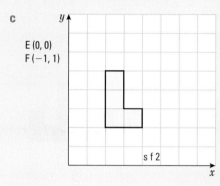

s f 2

🔍 **Example 9**   Describe fully the transformation that maps shape A onto shape B.

This is an enlargement.

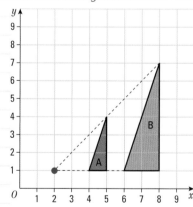

By comparing the lengths of the sides, you can tell that the sides on shape B are twice the lengths of the sides on shape A.

By joining up the vertices (see the dotted lines) you can extend these lines so they meet at the centre of enlargement (2, 1).
So the transformation is
'An enlargement of scale factor 2, centre (2, 1).'

Marks are given for stating three facts:
(1) **transformation is an enlargement**
(2) **the scale factor**
(3) **the centre of enlargement.**

Exercise 11I

C

1 Describe fully the transformation that maps shape A onto shape B.

a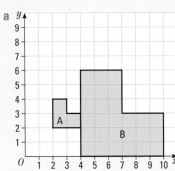

b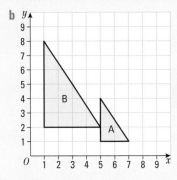

c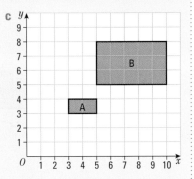

2 Describe fully the transformation that maps shape A onto shape B.

a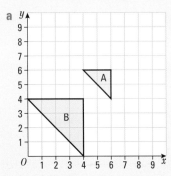

b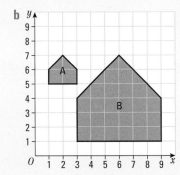

c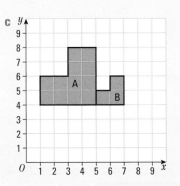

11.6 Combinations of transformations

⊙ Objectives

- You can carry out all four common transformations.
- You can describe all four transformations.

⟐ Why do this?

Graphic designers and fabric printers would use a combination of transformations to produce designs or material for clothes.

⟐ Get Ready

1. Copy this shape.
   Rotate this shape clockwise 90° and draw the image.
   Repeat this twice more.

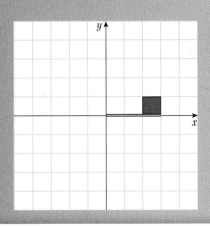

> **Key Point**
> ◉ It is sometimes possible to find a single transformation that has the same effect as a combination of two transformations.

Example 10 Shape A is transformed by a reflection in the y-axis to image B. Image B is reflected in the x-axis to image C.
What single transformation maps shape A onto shape C?

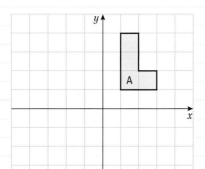

> Make sure you draw all the images carefully, and label them if asked.

> Draw the images B and C on the grid, then compare A with C.
> Describe the transformation that takes A directly onto C.

Shape A is mapped onto shape C by a rotation of 180° about the origin.

Exercise 11J

1 Copy the diagram.
  a Reflect the shape in the x-axis.
  b Reflect the image in the line $y = 2$.
  c Describe the single transformation that is equivalent to **a** followed by **b**.

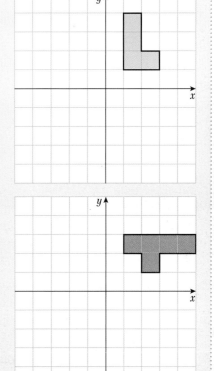

2 Copy the diagram.
  a Reflect the shape in the line $y = x$.
  b Rotate the image 90° anticlockwise about the origin.
  c Describe the single transformation that is equivalent to **a** followed by **b**.

C

3   Copy the diagram.

   a Reflect the shape A in the y-axis.
      Label the image B.

   b Reflect the image B in the x-axis.
      Label this image C.

   c Describe the single transformation that maps A onto C.

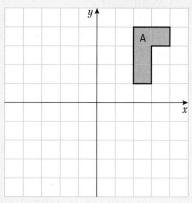

4   Copy the diagram.

   a Rotate the shape A 90° clockwise, centre (3, 3).
      Label the image B.

   b Rotate the image B 180°, centre (6, 3).
      Label this image C.

   c Describe the single transformation that maps A onto C.

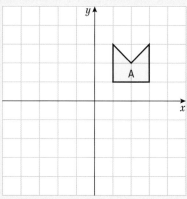

5   Triangle P has been rotated 180° about the point (1, 1) to give triangle Q.

   a Rotate triangle Q 180° about the point (3, −1).
   Label the triangle R.

   b Describe the single transformation that takes triangle P to triangle R.

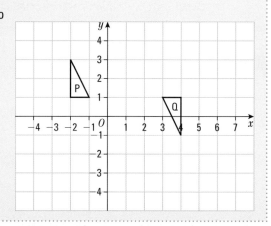

Chapter review

- There are four main **transformations**: translation, rotation, reflection and enlargement.
- A **translation** is a sliding movement made from one or more moves. In a simple translation you need to describe the distance and direction of each move.
- Another way of describing translations is to use a **column vector**, e.g. $\binom{3}{2}$. The top number describes the movement to the right or left, the bottom number the movement up or down.
- In a translation: the lengths of the sides of the shape do not change; the angles of the shape do not change; the shape does not turn.
- A **rotation** can be described as a fraction of a turn, or as an angle of turn.
- The direction of rotation can be **clockwise** or **anticlockwise**.
- The point about which the shape is turned is called the **centre of rotation**.

- It is useful to use tracing paper to assist in rotating a shape.
- The centre of rotation can sometimes be given as coordinates on a coordinate grid.
- In a rotation: the lengths of the sides of the shape do not change; the angles of the shape do not change; the shape turns.
- Images of a shape which are formed by reflecting a given shape about a **line of reflection** (or mirror line) are called **reflections** of the shape.
- In a reflection: the lengths of the sides of the shape do not change; the angles of the shape do not change.
- It is useful to use tracing paper to assist in reflecting a shape.
- The reflection can sometimes be given on a coordinate grid.
- The line of reflection can be given as the equation of a line.
- An **enlargement** changes the size of an object. It changes the lengths of it sides but does not change its shape.
- The **scale factor** of the enlargement is the value that lengths in the original object are multiplied by to get the lengths in the image.
- Shapes can be enlarged from a point called the **centre of enlargement**.
- To find or use the centre of enlargement, draw in additional lines from the centre of enlargement to the vertices of the shape or shapes.
- It is sometimes possible to find a single transformation that has the same effect as a combination of two transformations.

Review exercise

1 **a** Reflect shape **A** in the y-axis.
   b Describe fully the **single** transformation which takes shape **A** to shape **B**.

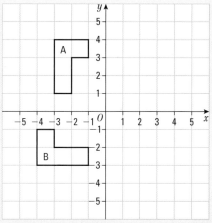

Nov 2008

2 On a copy of the grid, enlarge the shape with a scale factor of 2.

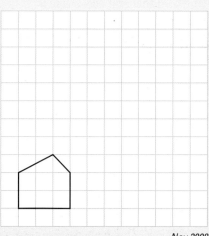

Nov 2008

E

3   Reflect the shaded shape in the mirror line.

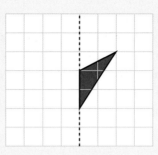

March 2007

4   On a copy of the grid, draw an enlargement
of the shaded shape with a scale factor of 3.

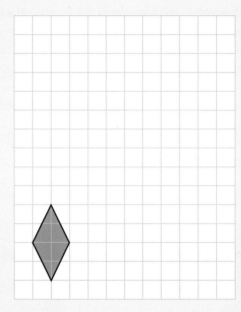

Nov 2006

5   On a copy of the grid, draw an enlargement,
scale factor 2, of the shaded shape.

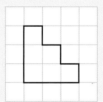

June 2009

D

6   **a**   Reflect Shape **A** in the y-axis.
       Label your new shape **B**.

      b   Translate Shape **A** by
       the vector $\begin{pmatrix} 3 \\ -2 \end{pmatrix}$

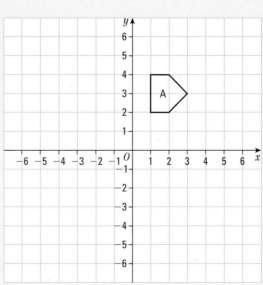

Nov 2007 adapted

D

7 Triangle **T** has been drawn on the grid.
   a On a copy of the grid, reflect triangle **T** in the y-axis. Label the new triangle **A**.
   b On a copy of the grid, rotate triangle **T** by a half turn, centre O. Label the new triangle **B**.
   c Describe fully the single transformation which maps triangle **T** onto triangle **C**.

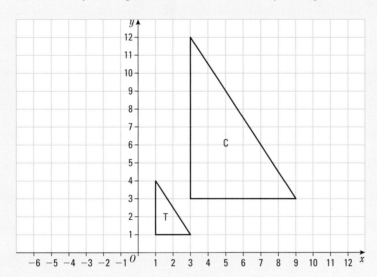

June 2007 adapted

8 On a copy of the grid, rotate the triangle a half turn about the point O.

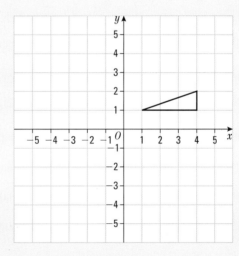

Nov 2006

9 Describe fully the single transformation that maps triangle **A** onto triangle **B**.

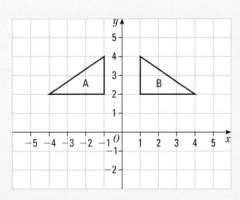

June 2009

10 **a** Rotate triangle **P** 180° about the point (−1, 1). Label the new triangle **A**.

b Translate triangle **P** by the vector $\begin{pmatrix} 6 \\ -1 \end{pmatrix}$. Label the new triangle **B**.

c Reflect triangle **Q** in the line $y = x$. Label the new triangle **C**.

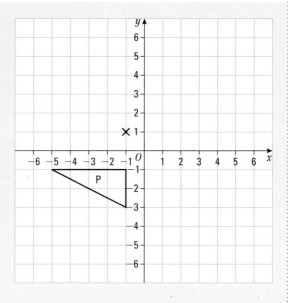

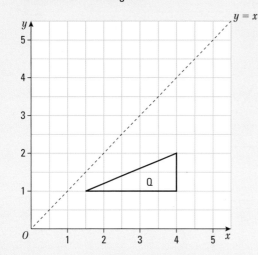

June 2008

11 Describe fully the single transformation that will map shape **P** onto shape **Q**.

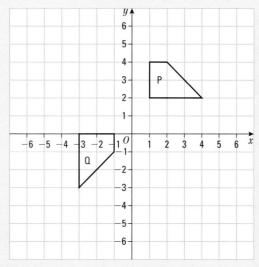

Nov 2007

12 **a** Describe fully the single transformation that maps triangle **A** onto triangle **B**.

b On the grid, rotate triangle **A** 90° anticlockwise about the point (−1, 1). Label your new triangle **C**.

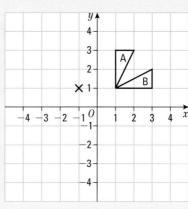

Nov 2006

13 a On a copy of the grid, reflect triangle **P** in the line $x = 2$.

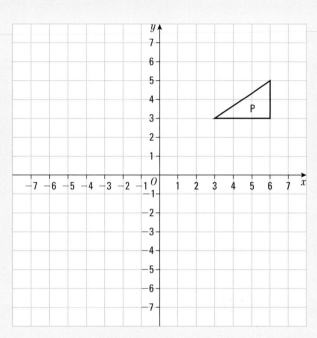

b Describe fully the **single** transformation that takes triangle **Q** to triangle **R**.

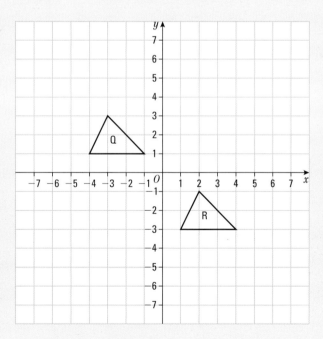

Nov 2006

C

14 Triangle **A** is reflected in the x-axis to give triangle **B**.
Triangle **B** is reflected in the line $x = 1$ to give triangle **C**.
Describe the **single** transformation that takes triangle **A** to triangle **C**.

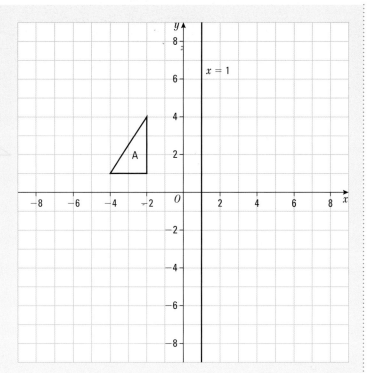

June 2008

12 PYTHAGORAS' THEOREM

The diagram shows the dimensions of the Parthenon Temple in Athens. By using right-angled triangles as the basis for the construction, Pythagoras' Theorem could be used to check that the right angles were accurately constructed. This is an example of maths being used in architecture that dates back to 447 BCE.

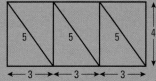

Objective

In this chapter you will:
○ understand and use Pythagoras' Theorem.

Before you start

You need to know:
○ how to square numbers using a calculator
○ how to find the square root of numbers using a calculator
○ how to work out 4^2, 3.5^2, $4^2 + 6^2$
○ how to work out $\sqrt{49}$, $\sqrt{12.25}$.

12.1 Finding the length of the hypotenuse of a right-angled triangle

◎ Objectives

- ○ You understand Pythagoras' Theorem.
- ○ You can use Pythagoras' Theorem to find the hypotenuse.

？ Why do this?

Three thousand years ago the Egyptians and Babylonians used knotted rope to make a 90° angle using a 3, 4, 5 triangle. They used the right angle in the triangle to make their buildings have square corners. These days, builders sometimes use pieces of wood with length 3 feet, 4 feet and 5 feet to do the same thing.

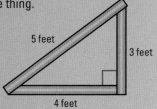

◆ Get Ready

1. Find the value of

   a 4^2 **b** 2.3^2 **c** $7^2 + 24^2$

2. Find the value of

   a $\sqrt{25}$ **b** $\sqrt{169}$ **c** $\sqrt{0.25}$

3. Make a copy of these right-angled triangles and mark the hypotenuse (longest side).

   a    **b**   **c**    **d**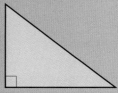

◉ Key Points

- ◉ For a right-angled triangle

  $c^2 = a^2 + b^2$ or $a^2 + b^2 = c^2$

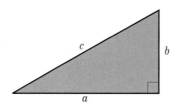

- ◉ To find the length of the **hypotenuse** (c):

  square each of the other sides (a) and (b), add the squares and then square root the sum.

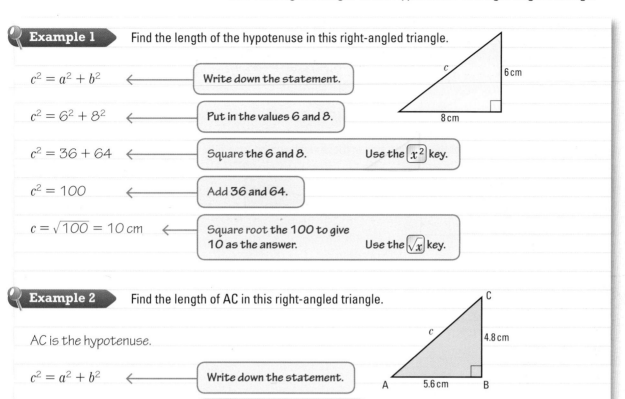

Example 1   Find the length of the hypotenuse in this right-angled triangle.

$c^2 = a^2 + b^2$ ← Write down the statement.

$c^2 = 6^2 + 8^2$ ← Put in the values 6 and 8.

$c^2 = 36 + 64$ ← Square the 6 and 8.   Use the $\boxed{x^2}$ key.

$c^2 = 100$ ← Add 36 and 64.

$c = \sqrt{100} = 10$ cm   ← Square root the 100 to give 10 as the answer.   Use the $\boxed{\sqrt{x}}$ key.

Example 2   Find the length of AC in this right-angled triangle.

AC is the hypotenuse.

$c^2 = a^2 + b^2$ ← Write down the statement.

$c^2 = 5.6^2 + 4.8^2$ ← Put in the values 5.6 and 4.8.

$c^2 = 31.36 + 23.04$ ← Square the 5.6 and 4.8.   Use the $\boxed{x^2}$ key.

$c^2 = 54.4$ ← Add 31.36 and 23.04.

$c = \sqrt{54.4}$
$c = 7.375635566$ cm   ← Square root the 54.4 to give 7.38 as the answer.   Use the $\boxed{\sqrt{x}}$ key.
$c = 7.38$ cm (written to 3 significant figures)

Exercise 12A   Questions in this chapter are targeted at the grades indicated.

1   Calculate the length of the hypotenuse in these right-angled triangles.

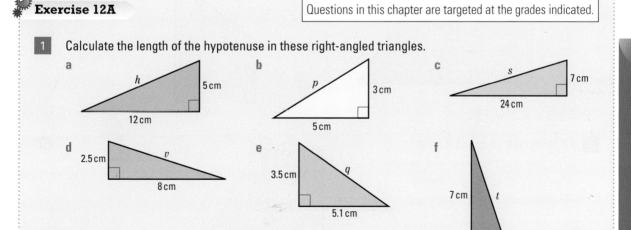

a
h
5 cm
12 cm

b
p
3 cm
5 cm

c
s
7 cm
24 cm

d
2.5 cm
v
8 cm

e
3.5 cm
q
5.1 cm

f
7 cm
t
2.4 cm

C

C

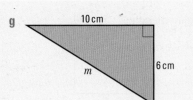

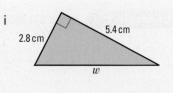

2 Calculate the length of the missing side in these right-angled triangles.

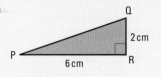

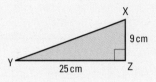

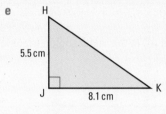

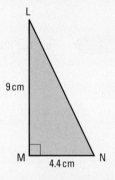

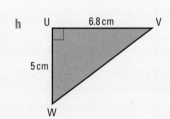

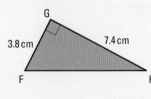

3 Find the perimeter of these trapeziums.
Give your answer correct to 3 significant figures.

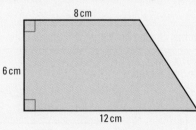

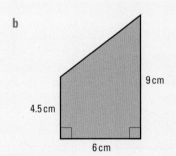

4 A farmer wants to fence a field.
The field is in the shape of a trapezium.
Fencing costs £5.50 per metre.
Find the cost of fencing the field.

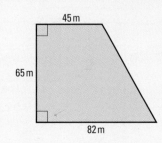

12.2 Finding the length of one of the shorter sides of a right-angled triangle

◎ Objective

◎ You can use Pythagoras' Theorem to find one of the shorter sides of a right-angled triangle.

↻ Get Ready

1. Find the value of
   a $5^2 - 4^2$ b $5^2 - 3^2$ c $5.6^2 - 2.3^2$ d $13^2 - 5^2$ e $25^2 - 7^2$

2. Find the value of
   a $\sqrt{9}$ b $\sqrt{16}$ c $\sqrt{169}$ d $\sqrt{6.25}$ e $\sqrt{576}$

3. Make a copy of these right-angled triangles and mark the two shorter sides.
   a 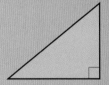   b    c    d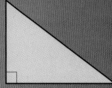

◎ Key Points

● For a right-angled triangle
$$c^2 = a^2 + b^2 \quad \text{or} \quad a^2 + b^2 = c^2$$
so $\quad a^2 = c^2 - b^2 \quad \text{or} \quad b^2 = c^2 - a^2$

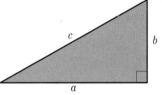

● To find the length of one of the shorter sides (a or b):
square each of the other sides (c) and (a or b), subtract the squares and then square root the sum.

🔍 Example 3

Find the length of BC in this right-angled triangle.

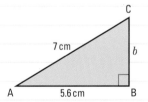

AC is the hypotenuse.
BC is one of the shorter sides.

$c^2 = a^2 + b^2$ ← Write down the statement.

$7^2 = 5.6^2 + b^2$ ← Put in the values 5.6 and 7.

$b^2 = 7^2 - 5.6^2$ ← Square the 5.6 and 7.   Use the $\boxed{x^2}$ key.

$b^2 = 49 - 31.36$ ← Subtract 31.36 from 49.

$b^2 = 17.64$
$b = \sqrt{17.64}$ ← Square root the 17.64 to give 4.2 as the answer.   Use the $\boxed{\sqrt{x}}$ key.
$b = 4.2$ cm

Exercise 12B

1 Calculate the length of the shorter side marked with a letter in these right-angled triangles.

a

b
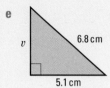

c
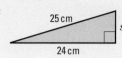

d
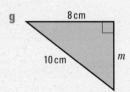

e
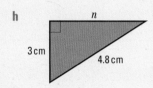

f
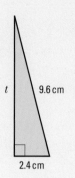

g
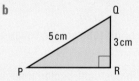

h
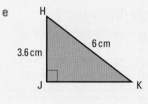

i
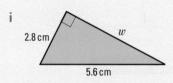

2 Calculate the length of the missing side in these right-angled triangles.

a
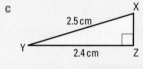

b

c

d
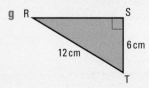

e
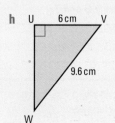

f
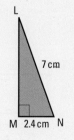

g

h

i
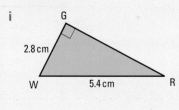

3 A 7.5 metre-long ladder leans against a vertical wall.
The foot of the ladder is 1.5 metres from the base of the wall.
How far up the wall does the ladder reach?

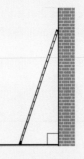

C

4 A farmer has a field in the shape of an equilateral triangle.
Each side of the field is of length 500 metres.
He sells the field at 50p per square metre.
How much money does he sell the field for?

A03

12.3 Checking to see if a triangle is right-angled or not

◎ Objective

○ If you know the lengths of all the sides of a triangle, you can use Pythagoras' Theorem to show whether the triangle is right-angled or not.

◈ Why do this?

In buildings, engineers need to check whether an angle is a right angle or not to ensure that the walls, doors or windows are straight.

◈ Get Ready

Which of these are correct?
1. $5.4^2 + 3.6^2 = 42.12$ 2. $3.5^2 + 3.1^2 = 19.86$ 3. $4.8^2 + 3.2^2 = 33.28$

Key Point

◎ If the length of the longest side of a triangle squared is equal to the sum of the squares of the other two sides then the triangle has a right angle.

Example 4   Prove that the triangle ABC is right-angled.

$6^2 = 36$ ← Square the longest side. $6^2 = 36$

$3.6^2 + 4.8^2$
$= 12.96 + 23.04$
$= 36$ ←

Square the other two sides.
$3.6^2 = 12.96$
$4.8^2 = 23.04$
Add them to get 36.

Since $6^2 = 3.6^2 + 4.8^2$ ABC must be a right-angled triangle.

Both are equal so this proves that the triangle is right-angled because the square of the hypotenuse is equal to the sum of the squares of the other two sides.

Example 5

Josie says that triangle PQR is right-angled because $8^2 = (6 + 2)^2$.
Josie is wrong. Explain why.

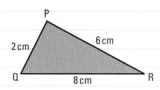

$8^2 = 64$

$6^2 + 2^2$

$\quad = 36 + 4$

$\quad = 40$

> Square the longest side.
> $8^2 = 64$

> Square the other two sides.
> $6^2 = 36$
> $2^2 = 4$

> Since $8^2 \neq 6^2 + 2^2$ ABC is not a right-angled triangle.

64 and 40 are not equal so triangle is not right-angled.

Exercise 12C

C

AO3

1 Check if these triangles have right angles.

    a Triangle ABC where AB = 5 cm, BC = 12 cm and CA = 13 cm

    b Triangle PQR where PQ = 5 cm, QR = 10 cm and RP = 12 cm

    c Triangle XYZ where XY = 4 cm, YZ = 6 cm and ZX = 7 cm

    d Triangle FGH where FG = 3.5 cm, GH = 4.5 cm and HF = 5.5 cm

    e Triangle RST where RS = 6 cm, ST = 8 cm and TR = 10 cm

    f Triangle JKL where JK = 5 cm, KL = 5 cm and LJ = 7 cm

AO3

2 Jenny says that triangle PQR is right-angled because $12^2 = (6 + 6)^2$.
Jenny is wrong. Explain why.

AO3

3 Jason says that triangle PQR is not right-angled because $10^2 \neq (6 + 8)^2$.
Jason is wrong. Explain why.

AO3

4 A acute-angled triangle has three acute angles.
An obtuse-angled triangle has two acute angles and one obtuse angle.
Investigate whether these triangles are right-angled, acute-angled or obtuse-angled.

    a Triangle ABC where AB = 5 cm, BC = 10 cm and CA = 10 cm

    b Triangle PQR where PQ = 5 cm, QR = 8 cm and RP = 12 cm

    c Triangle XYZ where XY = 4 cm, YZ = 6 cm and ZX = 7 cm

    d Triangle FGH where FG = 3.5 cm, GH = 4.5 cm and HF = 6.5 cm

    e Triangle RST where RS = 7.5 cm, ST = 10 cm and TR = 12.5 cm

    f Triangle JKL where JK = 5 cm, KL = 5 cm and LJ = 5 cm

12.4 Finding the length of a line segment

◎ Objective

◉ You can use Pythagoras' Theorem to find the length of the line segment between two coordinates.

❓ Why do this?

Sat navs use Pythagoras' Theorem to calculate the shortest distance between two places.

⬆ Get Ready

Find the lengths of the missing sides in these right-angled triangles, ABC.
1. AC where AB = 3.2 cm and BC = 4.3 cm
2. BC where AC = 7.5 cm and AB = 2.9 cm
3. AB where AC = 9.8 cm and BC = 1.8 cm

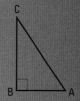

🔍 Key Point

◉ To find the distance between two points on a coordinate grid:
  ◉ subtract the x-coordinates and square
  ◉ subtract the y-coordinates and square
  ◉ add the results
  ◉ square root the answer.

Example 6

A has coordinates (1, 1). B has coordinates (4, 5).
Find the length of the line segment AB.

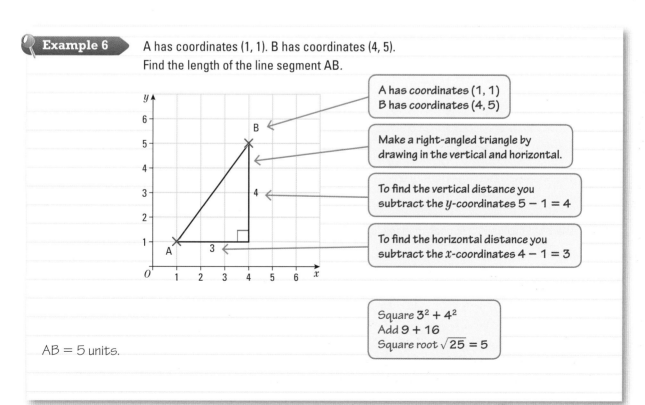

A has coordinates (1, 1)
B has coordinates (4, 5)

Make a right-angled triangle by drawing in the vertical and horizontal.

To find the vertical distance you subtract the y-coordinates $5 - 1 = 4$

To find the horizontal distance you subtract the x-coordinates $4 - 1 = 3$

Square $3^2 + 4^2$
Add $9 + 16$
Square root $\sqrt{25} = 5$

AB = 5 units.

Example 7   Find the length of the line segment ST.

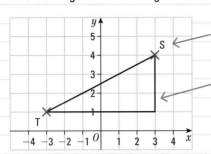

S has coordinates (3, 4)
T has coordinates (−3, 1)

Make a right-angled triangle by
drawing in the vertical and horizontal.

To find the horizontal distance you
subtract the x-coordinates $3 - -3 =$
$3 + 3 = 6$

To find the vertical distance you
subtract the y-coordinates $4 - 1 = 3$

Square $6^2 + 3^2$
Add $36 + 9$
Square root $\sqrt{45} = 6.708$

ST = 6.71 units (to 2 d.p.).

Exercise 12D

C

1   Work out the length of each of the line segments shown on the grid.

 a OA   b BC   c DE   d FG   e HJ

 f KL   g MN   h PQ   i ST   j UV

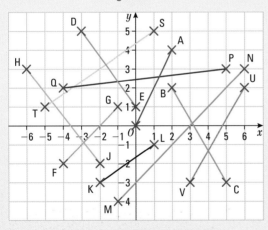

2   Work out the lengths of each of these line segments.

 a   b   c   d

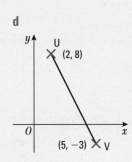

B (4, 3)
A (−1, −2)

Q (7, 4)
(1, −2) P

R (−2, 5)
(5, −3) S

U (2, 8)
(5, −3) V

C

3   Work out the lengths of each of these line segments.
   a   AB when A is $(-1, -1)$ and B is $(9, 9)$
   b   PQ when P is $(2, -4)$ and Q is $(-6, 9)$
   c   ST when S is $(5, -8)$ and T is $(-2, 1)$
   d   CD when C is $(1, 7)$ and D is $(-7, 2)$
   e   UV when U is $(-2, 3)$ and V is $(6, -8)$
   f   GH when G is $(-2, -6)$ and H is $(7, 3)$

Chapter review

- For a right-angled triangle:
  $c^2 = a^2 + b^2$ or $a^2 + b^2 = c^2$

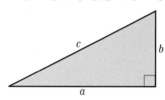

- To find the length of the **hypotenuse** (c):
  square each of the other sides (a) and (b), add the squares and then square root the sum.
- To find the length of one of the shorter sides (a or b):
  square each of the other sides (c) and (a or b), subtract the squares and then square root the sum.
- If the length of the longest side of a triangle squared is equal to the sum of the squares of the other two sides then the triangle has a right angle.
- To find the distance between two points on a coordinate grid:
  - subtract the x-coordinates and square
  - subtract the y-coordinates and square
  - add the results
  - square root the answer.

Review exercise

1   ABC is a right-angled triangle.

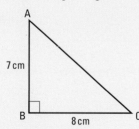

AB = 7 cm,
BC = 8 cm.
Work out the length of AC.
Give your answer correct to 2 decimal places.

ResultsPlus
Exam Question Report

83% of students answered this question poorly. The most common wrong answer was 15, obtained by either adding the two sides (7 + 8) or subtracting ($8^2 - 7^2$).

June 2008

C

C A02
A03

2 **a** Work out the area of the triangle.

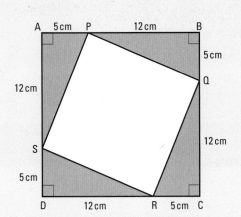

4 copies of the triangle and the quadrilateral PQRS are used to make the square ABCD.

b Work out the area of the quadrilateral PQRS.   *Nov 2007*

3 In the triangle XYZ
XY = 5.6 cm
YZ = 10.5 cm
angle XYZ = 90°
Work out the length of XZ.

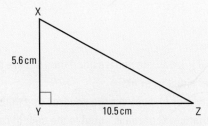

Nov 2007

A02

4

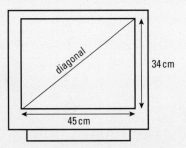

A rectangular television screen has a width of 45 cm and a height of 34 cm.
Work out the length of the diagonal of the screen.
Give your answer correct to the nearest centimetre.   *June 2007*

A02

5 The diagram shows three cities.
Norwich is 168 km due east of Leicester.
York is 157 km due north of Leicester.
Calculate the distance between Norwich and York.
Give your answer correct to the nearest kilometre.

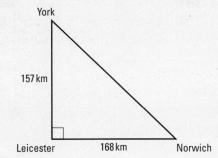

Nov 2006

6

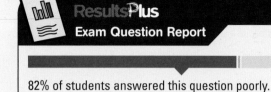

In triangle ABC
angle ABC = 90°
BC = 8 cm
AC = 21 cm
Work out the length of AB.
Give your answer correct to 3 significant figures.

March 2007

7   ABC is a right-angled triangle.
AC = 6 cm
BC = 9 cm
Work out the length of AB.
Give your answer correct to 3 significant figures.

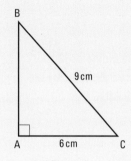

* 8   Prove that triangle ABC is a right-angled triangle.

A03

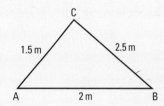

9   A has coordinates (1, 7). B has coordinates (6, 8).
Find the length of the line segment AB.
Give your answer correct to 2 decimal places.

10   P has coordinates (9, 3). Q has coordinates (2, 0).
Find the length of the line segment PQ.
Give your answer correct to 1 decimal place.

June 2006

11   Paul flies his helicopter from Ashwell to Birton.
He flies due west from Ashwell for 4.8 km. He then flies due south for 7.4 km to Birton.
Calculate the shortest distance between Ashwell and Birton.

A03

12   ABC is a right-angled triangle.
Calculate the area of the triangle ABC.

A02

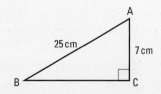

C

A02

13 PQR is an isosceles triangle with PQ = PR.

PQ = PR = 10 cm

QR = 6 cm

Calculate the area of triangle PQR.

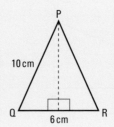

A03

14 A farmer has a field in the shape of an isosceles triangle.

The sides of the field have lengths 500 metres, 500 metres and 600 metres.

He sells the field at 45p per square metre.

For how much money does he sell the field?

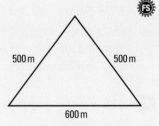

15 A is the point with coordinates (2, 5).

B is the point with coordinates (8, 13).

Calculate the length AB.

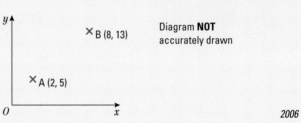

Diagram **NOT** accurately drawn

2006

The following question helps you to develop your ability to select and apply a method (AO2) as there is more than one possible way to raise the fees. The question also tests your ability to analyse a problem and generate a strategy to solve it (AO3).

Example

Fred's Gym charges an annual membership fee of £250, plus an additional weekly fee of £5.

The gym wish to increase the amount paid annually by each member to £600. Work out two different ways they could raise their fees.

Solution

Current amount raised
= £5 × 52 + £250 = £510

> Find the cost of membership for 1 year at the current rate.

Additional amount
= £600 − £510 = £90

> Decide how much more is needed.

Method 1

Increase annual fee to £250 + £90 = £340.
Same weekly fee of £5.

> Experiment with changing the membership fee and the weekly fee to give the new cost.

Method 2

Reduce annual fee to £80 and increase weekly fee to £10.

> There are many other possibilities.

1   I have some 5p coins and some 2p coins.
If I use an even number of 5p coins I cannot make a total of 23p. Explain why not.

 A03   G

2   A group of 5 friends bought 10 items at the Gold Medal Chip Shop.

A02
A03   F

> **Gold Medal Chip Shop**
> Chips 95p
> Fish £2.25
> Sausage £1.80

The total bill came to £15.10.
What did they buy?

3   Gina needs exactly 17 kg of pasta for her restaurant. Pasta can be bought in 3 kg packs for £5.40 each or 5 kg packs for £8.50 each.
How many packs of each size should she buy to get the best value for money?

 A02
A03   E

4   A bar of chocolate costs 50p.
The diagram shows some information on how much of this goes to different people when a bar of chocolate is sold.
What percentage of the cost of a bar of chocolate goes to the growers?

Growers	Retailers	Others
	12.5p	35.5p

5   A cereal company is considering a special deal on its 500 g packets of Tasty Flakes.

 A03   D

Which is the best deal?

6   In a sale all of the items in a shop are reduced by 20%. After the sale the prices are increased by 40%.
What is the overall effect on prices?
Explain your answer.

 A03   C

The following questions help you develop your ability to select and apply a method to get the correct solution (AO2).

Example 1

Susie rides her bike from home to school.

Susie's home is 1.8 km from school.

On her journey from home to school the front wheel on her bike rotates exactly 1000 times.

Work out the diameter of the front wheel on her bike.

Give your answer correct to 3 significant figures.

Solution 1

$1.8 \, \text{km} = 1.8 \times 1000 = 1800 \, \text{m}$

$1800 \times 100 = 180\,000 \, \text{cm}$ ← Change the units to centimetres to get a sensible answer.

$180\,000 \div 1000 = 180 \, \text{cm}$ for 1 rev ← Find the length of one revolution.

$C = \pi d$ so $180 = \pi d$
$d = 180 \div \pi = 57.2958 = 57.3 \, \text{cm}$ ← Use the formula for the circumference of a circle to find the diameter.

Example 2

$PQRS$ is a parallelogram.

PQ is parallel to SR.

PS is parallel to QR.

PQ has a length of $(2a + 3)$ centimetres.

PS has a length of $(a + 2)$ centimetres.

The perimeter of the parallelogram is 25 cm.

Find the length of PQ.

Solution 2

Since opposite sides of a parallelogram are equal, the perimeter can be written as

$$2(2a + 3) + 2(a + 2) = 25$$
$$4a + 6 + 2a + 4 = 25$$
$$6a + 10 = 25$$
$$6a = 15$$
$$a = 2.5$$
$$PQ = 2 \times 2.5 + 3 = 8 \, \text{cm}$$

Now try these

1 The three angles of a triangle are x, $2x$ and $3x$.
Find the value of x.

A02 **D**

2 *BCEF* is a parallelogram. *FAB* is a right-angled triangle.
ECD is an isosceles triangle.
ABC is a straight line. *FED* is a straight line.
Find the value of x.

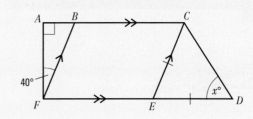

A02

3 James rides his bike to school. His bike wheel has a diameter of 75 cm.
His bike wheel rotates 1500 times on his trip to school.
How far does James live from school?

A02 **C**

4 The diagram shows the design for a window.

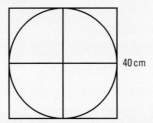

40 cm

The window is square with sides of length 40 cm.
Strips of lead are put round the edge of the window and on the window to make the pattern shown within the square.
Work out the total length of all the strips of lead.

A02
A03

5 The length of a rectangle is $(2x + 3)$ cm. The width of the rectangle is 5 cm.
The area of the rectangle is 35 cm².
Find the perimeter of the rectangle.

A02

MONEY MANAGEMENT

If you are 16, 17 or 18 and you want to continue studying, you might be entitled to Education Maintenance Allowance (EMA).

QUESTION

1. Sarah's household income is £24 000 a year. This entitles her to EMA. She also has a part-time job for which she gets £5.12 an hour, and time and a half on Sundays. As well as studying, she works 12 hours during the week and 8 hours on Sunday. Provided she earns less than £6,475 per year, she pays no tax. How much money per week does Sarah get? Don't forget to include her EMA.

My weekly work schedule

YOUR ENTITLEMENT TO EMA

Your household income	How much EMA you get
up to £20 817 per year	£30 per week
£20 818–£25 521 per year	£20 a week
£25 522–£30 810 per year	£10 a week
more than £30 810 per year	no entitlement to EMA

QUESTION

2. Employees not contributing to a private pension scheme pay 11% NIC on all earnings above £95 a week. If you get paid £5.50 an hour and you work 78 hours in 3 weeks, how much will you pay in NICs?

NIC

When working in any job you need to pay National Insurance Contributions (NICs). Your payments entitle you to social security benefits, including the State Pension. The amount you pay depends on how much you earn.

INCOME TAX

One of the largest taxes for many employees is income tax. The amount you earn is broken into bands and you pay a fixed percentage for all the money in that band.

0% on earnings less than £6475	
20% on earnings between £6475 and £34 800	
40% on earnings above £34 800	

QUESTION

3. If you earn £37 000 a year, how much income tax and national insurance will you pay?

LINKS

- For **Questions 1 and 3** you need to know how to use a calculator for complex sums. You learnt this in **Chapter 1**.

- You learnt how to use percentages in calculations in **Chapter 2**. You will need to use this for **Question 2**.

KITCHEN DESIGN

Britain has one of the highest rates of home ownership in Europe. Home owners often decorate and redesign their properties to increase their value and suit their own tastes.

QUESTION

1. The Chan family are going to replace their kitchen with a total refit. They intend using standard units which can easily be fitted. These units come in three sizes: 600 mm x 600 mm, 600 mm x 1200 mm and 600 mm x 300 mm.

The cooker, fridge-freezer and washing machine are all 600 mm x 600 mm.
The sink unit is 600 mm x 1200 mm.
Cupboard units can be any of the three sizes.

The cooker and fridge-freezer must not be next to each other or near the sink.
The Chan family's kitchen measures 3 m x 4 m.
Using a scale of 1 m = 5 cm, draw a plan of a suitable design for their kitchen.
The picture may give you some ideas.
Do not forget to show the door and windows.

LINKS

- For **Question 1** you will need to understand scale drawings. You learnt how to do this in **Chapter 7**.

- You learnt how to convert units of measure in **Chapter 9**. You will need to be able to do this in **Question 2**.

- For **Question 3** you will need to be able to use ratio in your calculation. You learnt how to do this in **Unit 2 Chapter 6**.

2. Before anything else is done, the entire floor is to be tiled. There are two sizes of tile available.

305 mm x 305 mm sold in packs of 6 at £6 per pack
330 mm x 330 mm sold in packs of 9 at £10 per pack

Tiles can be cut without waste, but for appearance's sake only two pieces can be cut from any one tile. Decide how this is to be done and work out a costing.

3. They are also going to tile behind the sink unit. The area of this tiling is 1500 mm x 600 mm. Wall tiles come in various sizes, typically 10 cm x 10 cm and 15 cm x 15 cm. The 10 cm square tiles are sold in boxes of 25 and the 15 cm square tiles in boxes of 44.

Cost:
10 cm tiles
White £3.99 a box
Coloured £4.99 a box.
15 cm tiles
White £8.99 a box
Coloured £10.99 a box.
Individual tiles of either size or colour can be bought for 50p.

Floor & Wall tiles

Milano

Floor tiles 1
Size 305 x 305 mm
Pack quantity 6

White £6.00

Floor tiles 2
Size 330 x 330 mm
Pack quantity 9

White £10.00

Roma

Optional colours

Wall tiles
Size 10 x 10 cm
Pack quantity 25

White £3.99
Color £4.99

Lisbon

Optional colours

Wall tiles
Size 15 x 15 cm
Pack quantity 44

White £8.99
Color £10.99

32

Using a design that has white and coloured tiles in the ratio 3 : 2, work out how many tiles are needed and do a costing.

Chapter 1 Answers

1.1 Get ready

1 0.25   **2** 2.5   **3** 0.04

Exercise 1A

1   **a** 0.1   **b** 0.25   **c** 0.125   **d** 0.2
   e $0.\dot{1}$
2   **a** 3   **b** 4   **c** $1\frac{1}{2}$ **d** $1\frac{1}{5}$
   e $3\frac{1}{3}$ **f** $\frac{3}{4}$ **g** $\frac{5}{7}$ **h** $\frac{3}{8}$
   i $\frac{2}{7}$ **j** $\frac{6}{7}$
3   **a** 0.4   **b** 0.02   **c** 0.0625   **d** 0.0125
   e 5   **f** 2   **g** 20   **h** 8
   i 25   **j** 100
4 1000
5   **a** 0.025   **b** 1
6   **a** 0.01   **b** 1

Mixed Exercise 1B

1   **a** 0.625   **b** 0.4375   **c** $0.\dot{5}$
   d $0.6\dot{3}$ **e** $0.08\dot{3}$
2 $\frac{1}{9} = 0.\dot{1}$
3 No, $\frac{1}{3} = 0.\dot{3}$
4 $\frac{1}{25}$ or 0.04
5 1.25

1.2 Get ready

1 £6.68   **2** £75   **3** £4.74

Exercise 1C

1 £8.90   **2** £7.10   **3** £2.30
4 £26.60   **5** £56.70   **6** £44.04
7 14   **8** 9   **9** 8
10 34
11 17 days 12 hours
12 6p
13 Current plan:
September   £25
October   £25
November   £25
New plan:
September $15 + (40 \times 0.20) + (30 \times 0.12) = £26.60$
October $15 + (45 \times 0.20) = £24$
November $15 + (35 \times 0.20) + (60 \times 0.12) = £29.20$
Raja should not switch to the new monthly plan because in September and November he would have spent more per month and in October he would have spent only slightly less.

1.3 Get ready

1 36   **2** 8   **3** 5

Exercise 1D

1   **a** 6.25   **b** 10.24   **c** 2209
   d 3.24   **e** 320.41
2   **a** 216   **b** 10 648   **c** 9.261
   d 39.304   **e** 3.375
3   **a** 32   **b** 14 641   **c** 243
   d 20 736   **e** 15 625
4   **a** 299   **b** 20.76   **c** 39   **d** 12.71
5   **a** 11.221   **b** 12.149   **c** 8.335   **d** 1.2

Exercise 1E

1   **a** 23   **b** 17   **c** 34   **d** 25
2   **a** 1.6   **b** 4.7   **c** 3.7   **d** 9.4
3   **a** 12.2   **b** 8.9   **c** 11.1   **d** 15.5
4   **a** 6   **b** 9   **c** 7   **d** 12
5   **a** 3.4   **b** 5.8   **c** 4.9   **d** 4.4
6   **a** 12   **b** 7.7   **c** 0.2   **d** 3
7 James : boat A
Matthew : boats A and B

1.4 Get ready

1 24   **2** 13.5   **3** 2

Exercise 1F

1   **a** 62.41   **b** 7.2361   **c** 79.507   **d** 2.744
2   **a** 313   **b** 1372   **c** 1199   **d** 1120
3   **a** 5.6   **b** 16   **c** 4   **d** 1.5
4   **a** 4   **b** 5.2   **c** 4.5   **d** 5.2
5   **a** 1.02415(...)   **b** 5.27441(...)
   c 2.85209(...)   **d** 1.55266(...)

Review Exercise

1 £3.80
2 80
3 14
4   **a** £1.90   **b** 27
5   **a** 8.41   **b** 1728   **c** 13.69   **d** 10.648
6   **a** 7.2   **b** 28   **c** 8   **d** 2.5
7   **a** 13.7   **b** 2.2   **c** 16.8   **d** 7.4
8   **a** £2.35   **b** £4.25   **c** 5p
9 31
10 26
11 £268.65
12 24.4
13   **a** 40.1956   **b** 6.5   **c** 28.812
14   **a** 4.05975(...)   **b** 0.10053(...)
   c 1.24531(...)
15   **a** 0.57901(...)   **b** 1.24148(...)
16 Recommended daily calorie intakes:
Sophie $655 + (9.6 \times 68) + (1.8 \times 165) - (4.7 \times 32) = 1454.4$
Chelsea $655 + (9.6 \times 55) + (1.8 \times 175) - (4.7 \times 47) = 1277.1$
Kenny $66 + (13.7 \times 98) + (5 \times 191) - (6.8 \times 27) = 2180$

Hassan $66 + (13.7 \times 117) + (5 \times 182) - (6.8 \times 38) = 2320.5$

Hassan has the greatest daily calorie requirement.
Chelsea has the smallest daily calorie requirement.

17 a $1\frac{3}{5}$ b 0.4 c 4

18 $11.94117(...)$

19 Large costs $380 \div 200 = 1.9$p per gram
   Regular costs $350 \div 175 = 2$p per gram
   So Rob is correct. The regular tub is better value for money.

20 $2.26541(...)$

21 a Single burger and regular fries
   b £6.51

Chapter 2 Answers

2.1 Get ready

1 8   2 16   3 4.5

Exercise 2A

1 a £4.80   b 38.7 kg   c £199.80   d 236.8 km
   e 158.4 m*l*   f $20.70   g £13.60   h 1380 m

2 115

3 £48

4 54

5 £49 440

6 £7.50

7 a £14.70   b £22.75

8 £30

9 Cheaper to pay cash. The credit plan costs £705.50.

10 a 38%   b 95 g

11 £5.60 profit

2.2 Get ready

1 15   2 27   3 14.8

Exercise 2B

1 600 g   2 £27 295   3 £96.57

4 £611.60   5 £56.40   6 £89.30

7 £3726   8 £1560   9 £7200

10 £1.47

11 a £59.50   b £153   c £11.90

12 £108

13 Sample calculation for 2010:

Item	Cost before discount	% discount	Cost after discount
Labour	£120	12.5%	£105
Parts	£84	5%	£79.80
		Total before VAT	£184.80

Riverside Garage	Total before VAT	£184.80
	VAT at $17\frac{1}{2}$%	£32.34
	Total with VAT	£217.14

2.3 Get ready

1 $\frac{7}{10}$ 2 $\frac{2}{3}$ 3 30

Exercise 2C

1 a 70%   b 46%   c 65%
   d 12%   e 60%

2 72%

3 90%

4 80%

5 40%

6 36%

Exercise 2D

1 a 70%   b 7%   c 36%
   d 65%   e 36%

2 40%

3 18.75%

4 18%

5 a 15.5%   b 4.5%

6 55%

7 8 buckets

Review exercise

1 70%

2 30%

3 75%

4 a 62.5%   b $\frac{1}{4}$

5 22.5 g

6 a £249   b £357   c £6600

7 60 480

8 Sheds For U $\frac{75}{100} \times 320 = £240$
   Garden World $17\frac{1}{2}$% of £210 = £36.75
               $210 + 36.75 = £246.75$
   Ed's Sheds $\frac{2}{3} \times 345 = £230$
   Jack should buy his shed at Ed's Sheds.

9 £51.75

10 £17

11 £17.04

12 a 55%   b 60%   c 56.25%

13 After 1 year $= 1 \times 1.1 = 1.1$
   After 2 years $= 1 \times 1.05 = 1.155 = 15.5\%$
   Ziggy is not correct. Rachael had a 15.5% pay rise over the two years.

14 a 45%   b 53.6%

Chapter 3 Answers

3.1 Get ready

1 a 78   b 133   c 105

Exercise 3A

1 $x - 7 = 9$ 2 $x + 3 = 11$

3 $8x = 32$ 4 $9 + x = 20$

5 $7x - 3 = 32$ 6 $3x = 21$

7 $3(x + 1) = 24$ 8 $4x + 5 = 13$

9 $2(5 + x) = 16$ 10 $7 + 5x = 27$

11 a $x + 7 = 11$ b 4

12 a $5x = 45$ b 9

13 a $4(x + 2) = 24$ b 4

14 a $2x - 5 = 13$ b 9

15 a $6x + 7 = 31$ b 4

Answers

3.2 Get ready

1 $3x - 4 = 14$ **2** $6x + 2 = 26$ **3** $7x - 4 = 17$

Exercise 3B

1 $a = 1$ **2** $y = 2$ **3** $h = 7$
4 $p = 9$ **5** $q = 10$ **6** $d = 8$
7 $x = 0$ **8** $t = 4$ **9** $r = 3$
10 $k = 1$ **11** $n = 1$ **12** $x = 5$
13 $m = 5$ **14** $y = 16$ **15** $w = 0$
16 $q = 12$ **17** $p = 2$ **18** $t = 0$
19 $a = 12$ **20** $x = 0$ **21** $p = 38$
20 $a = 4$ **23** $b = 1$ **24** $v = 0$

Exercise 3C

1 $a = 5$ **2** $p = 11$ **3** $q = 8$
4 $x = 8$ **5** $y = 13$ **6** $s = 3$
7 $x = 22$ **8** $y = 21$ **9** $s = 27$
10 $a = 1$ **11** $p = 11$ **12** $c = 4$
13 $a = 1$ **14** $p = 5$ **15** $q = 0$
16 $a = 2$ **17** $b = 2$ **18** $c = 15$
19 $p = 5$ **20** $y = 21$ **21** $t = 5$
22 $p = 0$ **23** $p = 24$ **24** $p = 0$

Exercise 3D

1 $a = 2$ **2** $p = 2$ **3** $p = 3$
4 $s = 3$ **5** $k = 5$ **6** $u = 4$
7 $g = 7$ **8** $l = 7$ **9** $j = 2$
10 $f = 4$ **11** $r = 9$ **12** $v = 9$

Exercise 3E

1 $a = 10$ **2** $b = 20$ **3** $s = 12$
4 $c = 30$ **5** $t = 24$ **6** $s = 72$
7 $h = 72$ **8** $f = 28$ **9** $d = 45$
10 $a = 45$ **11** $b = 40$ **12** $r = 52$
13 $a = 60$ **14** $b = 32$ **15** $k = 48$

Mixed Exercise 3F

1 $a = 1$ **2** $b = 3$ **3** $c = 5$
4 $p = 9$ **5** $q = 4$ **6** $d = 8$
7 $p = 3$ **8** $r = 2$ **9** $s = 2$
10 $r = 3$ **11** $e = 1$ **12** $p = 0$
13 $a = 12$ **14** $b = 60$ **15** $s = 30$

3.3 Get ready

1 $q = 7$ **2** $x = 16$ **3** $r = 6$ **4** $p = 28$

Exercise 3G

1 $a = 2$ **2** $a = 3$ **3** $a = 2$
4 $a = 3$ **5** $p = 0$ **6** $p = 2$
7 $q = 12$ **8** $r = 2$ **9** $t = 5$
10 $f = 3$ **11** $r = 13$ **12** $a = 1$
13 $a = 0$ **14** $d = 3$ **15** $c = 4$
16 $a = 3$ **17** $z = 5$ **18** $r = 18$
19 $s = 12$ **20** $b = 18$ **21** $c = 24$
22 $f = 27$ **23** $h = 4$ **24** $x = 15$

Exercise 3H

1 $a = 1\frac{1}{2}$ **2** $a = 3\frac{1}{2}$ **3** $a = 2\frac{2}{3}$
4 $a = 4\frac{1}{3}$ **5** $p = 1\frac{3}{5}$ **6** $p = 4\frac{2}{5}$
7 $e = 0$ **8** $t = 1\frac{1}{2}$ **9** $j = 1\frac{1}{2}$
10 $c = 1\frac{4}{7}$ **11** $k = \frac{1}{4}$ **12** $d = 3\frac{1}{3}$
13 $u = \frac{2}{9}$ **14** $q = 2\frac{1}{4}$ **15** $y = 1\frac{2}{7}$

Exercise 3I

1 $a = -1$ **2** $a = -2$ **3** $a = -4$
4 $a = -1$ **5** $a = -2$ **6** $p = -2$
7 $s = -5$ **8** $p = -2$ **9** $k = -1$
10 $h = -1$ **11** $y = -5$ **12** $e = -9$
13 $t = 0$ **14** $w = -1$ **15** $c = -2$
16 $a = 0$

Mixed Exercise 3J

1 $s = 3$ **2** $d = 3$ **3** $m = 5$
4 $h = 4$ **5** $k = 9$ **6** $y = 2$
7 $p = 1\frac{2}{5}$ **8** $f = 3\frac{1}{4}$ **9** $s = 3\frac{2}{3}$
10 $g = -2\frac{2}{7}$ **11** $f = 4\frac{1}{4}$ **12** $k = 3\frac{3}{5}$
13 $s = -5\frac{2}{3}$ **14** $j = 3\frac{2}{3}$ **15** $b = -\frac{5}{9}$
16 $r = 3\frac{1}{2}$ **17** $t = -3\frac{2}{5}$ **18** $y = -\frac{6}{7}$
19 $e = -\frac{1}{3}$ **20** $f = -1\frac{1}{4}$ **21** $g = -\frac{2}{5}$
22 $h = -1$ **23** $c = -1\frac{2}{3}$ **24** $s = -\frac{5}{8}$
25 $z = 4$ **26** $x = 25$ **27** $p = 4$
28 $c = -18$ **29** $a = 48$ **30** $e = -24$

3.4 Get ready

1 $x = 9$ **2** $b = 12$ **3** $x = -\frac{1}{2}$

Exercise 3K

1 $a = 19$ **2** $b = 0$ **3** $c = 24$
4 $d = 10$ **5** $e = 6$ **6** $f = 16$
7 $g = 6$ **8** $h = 21$ **9** $m = 7$
10 $p = \frac{1}{3}$ **11** $q = 0$ **12** $v = \frac{4}{5}$
13 $x = -6$ **14** $y = 1\frac{2}{3}$ **15** $c = -1$
16 $b = 4\frac{1}{2}$ **17** $d = 7$ **18** $n = 15$
19 $t = -4$ **20** $c = \frac{2}{3}$

3.5 Get ready

1 $g = 22$ **2** $a = 24$ **3** $b = 6$

Exercise 3L

1 $a = -4$ **2** $c = 5$ **3** $p = 6$
4 $b = 1$ **5** $q = 3$ **6** $x = 3$
7 $d = 5$ **8** $y = 3$ **9** $n = 7$
10 $k = 0$ **11** $u = 2\frac{1}{2}$ **12** $r = 2\frac{2}{5}$
13 $v = 4\frac{2}{3}$ **14** $t = \frac{4}{5}$ **15** $m = 2\frac{1}{2}$
16 $g = \frac{5}{6}$ **17** $b = \frac{1}{2}$ **18** $h = 1\frac{1}{3}$
19 $e = 4\frac{1}{2}$ **20** $f = \frac{2}{3}$

3.6 Get ready

1 $a = 1$ **2** $b = 4$ **3** $c = 3$

Exercise 3M

1 $x = 2$ **2** $x = 4$ **3** $x = 13$
4 $x = 2$ **5** $x = 1$ **6** $x = 3$
7 $x = 1$ **8** $x = 1$ **9** $x = 8$
10 $x = 2$ **11** $x = 1$ **12** $x = 4$
13 $x = -3$ **14** $x = 0$ **15** $x = 2\frac{1}{2}$
16 $x = \frac{3}{5}$ **17** $x = -1$ **18** $x = 1\frac{2}{3}$
19 $x = -2$ **20** $x = -\frac{2}{3}$

3.7 Get ready

1 $20°$ **2** $160°$ **3** $10\,\text{cm}$

Exercise 3N

1 8
2 $a = 40°$, largest angle is $80°$
3 12
4 $130°, 80°, 150°$
5 $8\,\text{cm}, 9\,\text{cm}, 7\,\text{cm}$
6 11
7 $y = 7$
8 52 years
9 $15\,\text{cm}$
10 $x = 6, y = 4$

3.8 Get ready

1 20   **2** 12 years   **3** $9\,\text{cm}$

Exercise 3O

1 $x = 1.83$ **2** $x = 8.73$ **3** $x = 4.4$
4 $x = 7.9$ **5** $x = 3.11$ **6** $x = 2.81$
7 $x = 3.3$

Review Exercise

1 a $a = 5$ **b** $c = 10$ **c** $p = 7$ **d** $d = 12$
  e $x = 3$ **f** $b = 4$ **g** $a = -4$ **h** $b = -6$
  i $c = -1$ **j** $e = 5\frac{1}{2}$ **k** $h = -2$ **l** $m = -\frac{3}{4}$
  m $-2\frac{5}{6}$ **n** $-\frac{2}{3}$
2 a $r = 3$ **b** $x = 5$ **c** $c = 5$ **d** $b = \frac{1}{2}$
  e $d = 1\frac{2}{3}$ **f** $y = \frac{4}{5}$ **g** $t = 2\frac{1}{3}$ **h** $w = 2\frac{1}{2}$
  i $u = -3$ **j** $w = -6\frac{1}{2}$ **k** $y = -2\frac{1}{2}$
3 a $x = 2$ **b** $y = \frac{1}{2}$
4 a $x = 4$ **b** $y = 3\frac{1}{2}$ **c** $2t + 23$
5 $x = -1\frac{1}{2}$
6 a $x = 7$ **b** $y = 1\frac{1}{2}$
7 a $a = 3$ **b** $b = 7$ **c** $c = 5$ **d** $d = 7$
  e $e = 6$ **f** $f = 3\frac{3}{7}$ **g** $m = 1$ **h** $t = 3\frac{1}{4}$
  i $a = 3$ **j** $b = 4$ **k** $d = \frac{1}{2}$ **l** $g = 1\frac{1}{3}$
  m $p = -4\frac{2}{3}$
8 $48\,\text{cm}$
9 a $4x + 10$ **b** $x = 6$
10 a $x = 2.35$ **b** $x = 4.55$ **c** $x = 4.27$
  d $x = 3.76$ **e** $x = 2.41$ **f** $x = 1.77$
11 $x = 1.7$
12 a $55.927\,125$
  b $x = 3.65$ gives an answer that is too small. $x^3 + 2x$ gets bigger as x gets bigger, so the solution must be greater than 3.65. Yousef is correct.

13 a $5x + 60 = 360$ **b** $x = 60$
14 Uzma £18, Hajra £38, Mabintou £76
15 A 2.5 cm, B 7.5 cm, C 30 cm
16 A £8, B £12, C £4
17 a If Emil has x CDs, $4x + 12 = 32$.
   b 18 CDs
18 a $x = 3.6$ **b** $7.6\,\text{cm}$
19 $16\,\text{m}$

Chapter 4 Answers

4.1 Get ready

1 $-19, -15, 1.34, 5, 24$

Exercise 4A

1 a $4 < 6$ **b** $5 > 2$ **c** $12 > 8$
  d $6 = 6$ **e** $15 > 8$ **f** $3 < 24$
  g $10 > 3$ **h** $0 < 0.1$ **i** $6 > 0.7$
  j $4.5 = 4.5$ **k** $0.2 < 0.5$ **l** $4.8 > 4.79$
2 a True   **b** False, $2 < 6$
  c False, $6 = 6$ **d** False, $6 < 8$
  e False, $6 > 5$ **f** False, $8 < 14$
  g False, $7 > 6.99$ **h** False, $6 < 6.01$
  i False $7 > 0$ **j** False, $4 = 4$
  k False, $6 > 4$ **l** True
3 a 5   **b** 4, 5, 6, 7
  c 0, 1, 2, 3   **d** 4, 5
  e 2, 3, 4   **f** 3, 4, 5
  g 4, 5, 6   **h** $-2, -1, 0, 1, 2, 3$
  i 0, 1, 2, 3, 4   **j** $-1, 0, 1, 2, 3, 4, 5, 6$
  k $-3, -2, -1, 0, 1, 2$ **l** $-4, -3, -2, -1, 0, 1, 2$
  m 1, 2, 3, 4   **n** 0, 1, 2, 3, 4
  o $-5, -4, -3, -2, -1$ **p** $-3, -2, -1, 0, 1, 2, 3$

4.2 Get ready

1 $-3, -2, -1, 0, 1, 2, 3, 4$
2 $-5, -4, -3, -2, -1, 0, 1$
3 $-6, -5, -4, -3, -2, -1, 0, 1, 2, 3, 4, 5, 6, 7$

Exercise 4B

1 a

   b

   c

   d

   e

   f

Answers

2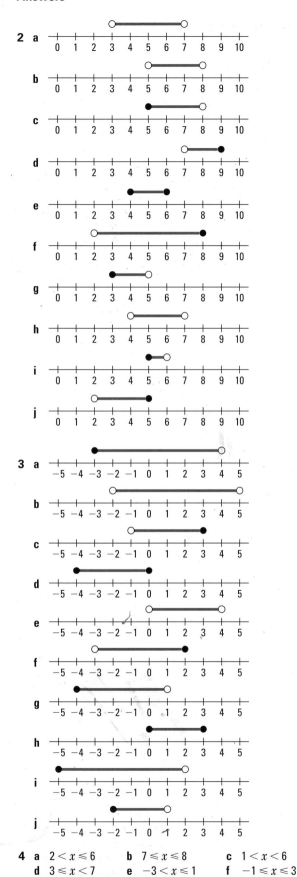

a
b
c
d
e
f
g
h
i
j

3 **a**
b
c
d
e
f
g
h
i
j

4 **a** $2 < x \leqslant 6$ **b** $7 \leqslant x \leqslant 8$ **c** $1 < x < 6$
d $3 \leqslant x < 7$ **e** $-3 < x \leqslant 1$ **f** $-1 \leqslant x \leqslant 3$
g $-4 < x < 1$ **h** $-3 \leqslant x < 4$

4.3 Get ready

1

2

3

Exercise 4C

1 $x < 4$	2 $x \geqslant 6$	3 $x \leqslant 6$
4 $x > 6$	5 $x < 9$	6 $x > 4$
7 $x \geqslant 0$	8 $x \leqslant 5$	9 $x \geqslant 3$
10 $x < 2$	11 $x > 3$	12 $x \geqslant 1$

13 $x > 2\frac{3}{4}$

14 $x \leqslant \frac{1}{2}$

15 $x \geqslant -2$

16 $x > 1\frac{1}{4}$

17 $x < -1\frac{1}{2}$

18 $x \leqslant \frac{3}{4}$

19 $2, 3, 4$	20 $-3, -2, -1, 0, 1$
21 $-2, -1, 0, 1$	22 $0, 1, 2, 3$
23 $-3, -2, -1, 0$	24 $1, 2$
25 $-1, 0, 1, 2, 3$	26 $-2, -1, 0, 1, 2$
27 $-3, -2, -1$	28 $x < 2\frac{1}{2}$
29 $x \geqslant \frac{3}{4}$	30 $x > -3$
31 $x \geqslant -2\frac{2}{3}$	32 $x > -8$
33 $x > 3\frac{1}{2}$	34 $x \geqslant 2\frac{3}{4}$
35 $x \leqslant -\frac{2}{3}$	36 $x > \frac{7}{8}$
37 $x > 1$	38 $x \geqslant 2$
39 $x \leqslant -1$	40 $x > -1\frac{2}{3}$
41 $x < 2\frac{1}{2}$	42 $x \leqslant 3$
43 $x \geqslant 7$	44 $x > 0$
45 $x < 3$	46 $x \geqslant 6$
47 $x < 2$	48 $x > -\frac{4}{5}$
49 $x \leqslant 1$	50 $x \leqslant 3$
51 $x < 2\frac{1}{5}$	52 $x \geqslant 2$
53 $x \geqslant \frac{1}{2}$	54 $x < -3$

55 $x > -4\frac{2}{3}$, smallest integer satisfying inequality is -4

56 $x \leqslant -\frac{3}{5}$, largest integer satisfying inequality is -1

Review Exercise

1 a
```
 -5 -4 -3 -2 -1  0  1  2  3  4  5
```

b
```
 -5 -4 -3 -2 -1  0  1  2  3  4  5
```

c
```
 -5 -4 -3 -2 -1  0  1  2  3  4  5
```

d
```
 -5 -4 -3 -2 -1  0  1  2  3  4  5
```

e
```
 -5 -4 -3 -2 -1  0  1  2  3  4  5
```

f
```
 -5 -4 -3 -2 -1  0  1  2  3  4  5
```

2 a $x \leqslant -1$ **b** $x > 3$ **c** $0 \leqslant x < 2$
   d $-3 < x < 3$ **e** $-2 < x \leqslant 0$ **f** $-1 \leqslant x \leqslant 3$

3 a $-3, -2, -1, 0$ **b** $1, 2, 3$
   c $-2, -1, 0, 1, 2, 3, 4$ **d** $-3, -2$

4 a $x > 10$ **b** $x \leqslant 5$ **c** $x < 4\frac{1}{2}$
   d $x \leqslant -2$ **e** $x \geqslant -1\frac{1}{2}$ **f** $x < 0$
   g $x > -\frac{1}{2}$ **h** $x < 6\frac{1}{2}$ **i** $x \geqslant -2$

5 a $x < 2\frac{1}{2}$
```
  2                          3
```

b $x \geqslant -\frac{1}{2}$
```
 -1                          0
```

c $x > 1\frac{2}{3}$
```
  1                          2
```

d $x \leqslant -1$
```
 -2          -1             0
```

e $x < 2$
```
  1           2             3
```

f $x > 0$
```
 -1           0             1
```

6 $x < 3\frac{1}{2}$

7 a $x = \frac{3}{5}$ **b** $-2, -1, 0, 1, 2, 3$

8 a $x = 3$ **b** $y = 6$

9 a A is x B is $x + 4$ C is $2(x + 4)$
$L = x + x + 4 + 2(x + 4)$
$L = 2x + 4 + 2x + 8$
$L = 4x + 12$
   b $4x + 12 < 50$ **c** $0 < x < 9.5$

10 9.3 kg

11 $0 < x < 4$

Chapter 5 Answers

5.1 Get ready

Graph on the left is pay as you go and graph on the right is contract. To decide which one you would choose you would look at the number of minutes you typically use and see what the cost would be on both types of mobile phone.

Exercise 5A

1 A 1, B 5, C 2, D 4, E 3
2 A 3, B 1, C 4, D 2, E 5
3 A 2, B 4, C 3, D 5, E 1
4 A 4, B 5, C 2, D 1, E 3

5 a 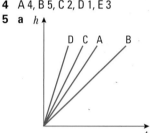   **b**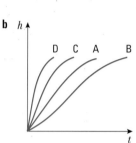

c 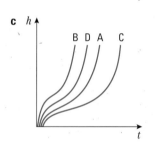   **d**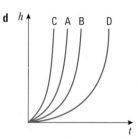

e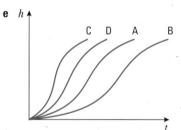

6

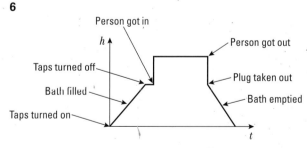

7 The taps were turned on and the bath filled at a constant rate for 2 minutes, to a depth of 20 cm.
The taps were turned on further (e.g. more hot water) for 1 minute, after which the bath was 35 cm deep.
The taps were turned off and the bath left for 1 minute.
The person got into the bath and the depth increased to 50 cm.

Answers

After 3 minutes, more hot water was added for 1 minute, increasing the depth to 54 cm, and the person stayed in a further 0.4 minute.

At 8.4 minutes, the person got out of the bath and the depth decreased to 40 cm.

The plug was taken out and the water drained out of the bath in 2.6 minutes.

8 The balloon climbed rapidly for 2 minutes to a height of 175 m. It then climbed more slowly for 2 minutes to a height of 225 m. It stayed at this height for 2 minutes, before descending slowly for 4 minutes to 175 m.

The burner was used for 2 minutes to make the balloon ascend rapidly to 290 m, where it stayed for 2 minutes. The balloon then descended slowly for 4 minutes to 220 m and then more rapidly for 4 minutes to ground level.

5.2 Get ready

1 a 9
  b 45
  c 15
  d 45
  e −6
  f −12

Exercise 5B

1 a i

x	−3	−2	−1	0	1	2	3
$y = x^2 + 2$	11	6	3	2	3	6	11

ii

x	−3	−2	−1	0	1	2	3
$y = -x^2 - 2$	−11	−6	−3	−2	−3	−6	−11

iii

x	−3	−2	−1	0	1	2	3
$y = -x^2 + 1$	−8	−3	0	1	0	−3	−8

iv

x	−3	−2	−1	0	1	2	3
$y = -x^2 + 4$	−5	0	3	4	3	0	−5

v

x	−3	−2	−1	0	1	2	3
$y = x^2 + 3$	12	7	4	3	4	7	12

b

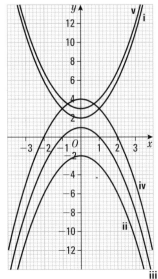

2 a i

x	−3	−2	−1	0	1	2	3
$y = 2x^2 + 1$	19	9	3	1	3	9	19

ii

x	−3	−2	−1	0	1	2	3
$y = -2x^2 + 1$	−17	−7	−1	1	−1	−7	−17

iii

x	−2	−1	0	1	2
$y = -3x^2 + 1$	−11	−2	1	−2	−11

iv

x	−3	−2	−1	0	1	2	3
$y = 2x^2 - 1$	17	7	1	−1	1	7	17

v

x	−3	−2	−1	0	1	2	3
$y = -2x^2 - 1$	−19	−9	−3	−1	−3	−9	−19

b

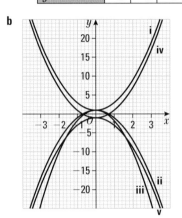

3

b

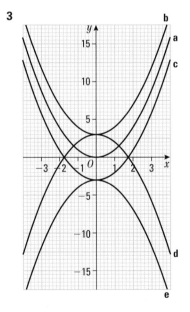

4

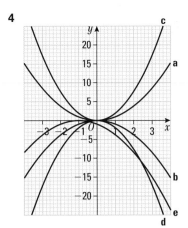

iv	x	-3	-2	-1	0	1	2	3
	x^2	$+9$	$+4$	$+1$	0	$+1$	$+4$	$+9$
	$-2x$	$+6$	$+4$	$+2$	0	-2	-4	-6
	$+3$	$+3$	$+3$	$+3$	$+3$	$+3$	$+3$	$+3$
	$y = x^2 - 2x + 3$	18	11	6	3	2	3	6

v	x	-3	-2	-1	0	1	2	3
	x^2	$+9$	$+4$	$+1$	0	$+1$	$+4$	$+9$
	$-2x$	$+6$	$+4$	$+2$	0	-2	-4	-6
	-3	-3	-3	-3	-3	-3	-3	-3
	$y = x^2 - 2x - 3$	12	5	0	-3	-4	-3	0

5

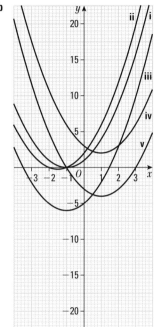

b

Exercise 5C

1 a i

x	-3	-2	-1	0	1	2	3
x^2	$+9$	$+4$	$+1$	0	$+1$	$+4$	$+9$
$2x$	-6	-4	-2	0	$+2$	$+4$	$+6$
$+1$	$+1$	$+1$	$+1$	$+1$	$+1$	$+1$	$+1$
$y = x^2 + 2x + 1$	4	1	0	1	4	9	16

ii

x	-3	-2	-1	0	1	2	3
x^2	$+9$	$+4$	$+1$	0	$+1$	$+4$	$+9$
$3x$	-9	-6	-3	0	$+3$	$+6$	$+9$
$+2$	$+2$	$+2$	$+2$	$+2$	$+2$	$+2$	$+2$
$y = x^2 + 3x + 2$	2	0	0	2	6	12	20

iii

x	-3	-2	-1	0	1	2	3
x^2	$+9$	$+4$	$+1$	0	$+1$	$+4$	$+9$
$2x$	-6	-4	-2	0	$+2$	$+4$	$+6$
-5	-5	-5	-5	-5	-5	-5	-5
$y = x^2 + 2x - 5$	-2	-5	-6	-5	-2	3	10

2

3

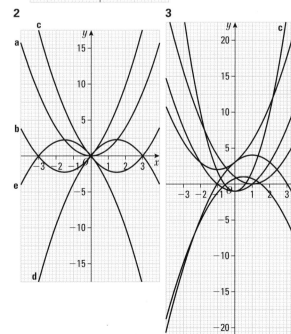

Answers

4

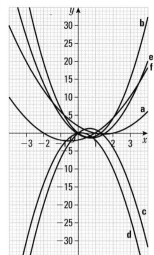

5.3 Get ready

1

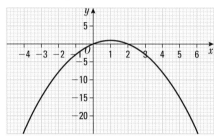

2

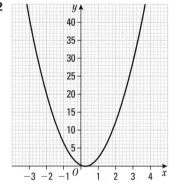

Exercise 5D

1 a

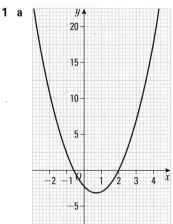

b i $x = -0.5$ and $x = 2$ **ii** $x = -1.8$ and $x = 3.3$

2 a

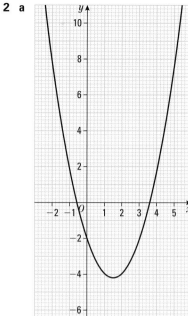

b i $x = -0.6$ and $x = 3.6$ **ii** $x = -1.5$ and $x = 4.5$

3 a

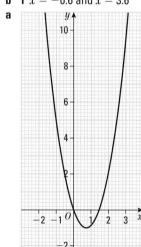

b i $x = 0$ and $x = 1.5$
   ii $x = -0.9$ and $x = 2.4$

4 a

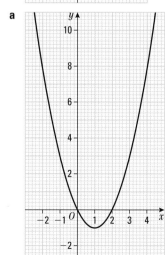

b i $x = 0$ and $x = 2$ **ii** $x = -1$ and $x = 3$

5 a

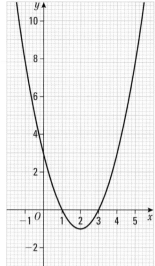

b i $x = 1$ and $x = 3$
  ii $x = 0.3$ and $x = 3.7$

Review exercise

1 A: The temperature remains steady
  B: The temperature is steadily increasing
  C: The temperature steadily increases, then rapidly
    decreases
  D: The temperature is steady to start with then steadily
    decreases
  E: The temperature rises to begin with, then remains
    the steady for a period and finally rises again.
  F: The temperature rises steadily to at the start,
    then remains steady for a period, then falls
    steadily

2 a

x	-1	0	1	2	3	4	5
y	3	-2	-5	-6	-7	-2	3

b

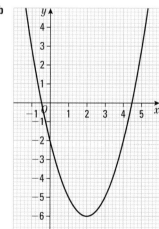

  c $x = -0.4$ and $x = 4.4$
3 a $x = 0$ and $x = 2$
  b $x = -0.7$ and $x = 2.7$
  c $x = 1$
4 $x = 3$

5 a

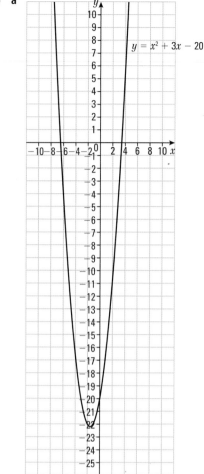

$y = x^2 + 3x - 20$

b $x = 3.2$

Chapter 6 Answers

6.1 Get ready

1 $x = 3$ **2** $x = 16$ **3** $x = 5$

Exercise 6A

1	**a** 4	**b** 9		**c** 23		**d** 5.9		
2	**a** i 9	ii 18		**b** i 5	ii 15			
3	**a** i 6	ii 14		**b** i 7	ii 20			
4	**a** 6	**b** 12		**c** $-6\frac{1}{2}$		**d** -3		
5	**a** i 3	ii 14		**b** i 3	ii $5\frac{1}{2}$			
6	**a** 2	**b** $-6\frac{1}{2}$		**c** 20		**d** $-\frac{1}{4}$		
7	**a** 4	**b** 5		**c** 4				
8	**a** i 5	ii 7		**b** 6		**c** 4		
9	**a** 20	**b** 85		**c** 37		**d** 0		
10	**a** 15	**b** -72		**c** 45		**d** -58.24		

6.2 Get ready

1 $x = -\frac{1}{3}$ **2** $x = 5$ **3** $x = 9$

Answers

Exercise 6B

1 $d = \dfrac{P}{5}$ **2** $I = \dfrac{P}{V}$

3 $w = \dfrac{A}{l}$ **4** $d = \dfrac{C}{\pi}$

5 $h = \dfrac{V}{lw}$ **6** $r = \dfrac{A}{\pi l}$

7 $x = \dfrac{y + 3}{4}$ **8** $n = \dfrac{t - 5}{3}$

9 $y = P - 2x$ **10** $m = \dfrac{y - c}{x}$

11 $u = v + gt$ **12** $t = \dfrac{u - v}{g}$

13 $b = 2\dfrac{A}{h}$ **14** $T = \dfrac{100I}{PR}$

15 $V = \dfrac{D}{T}$ **16** $V = \dfrac{kT}{P}$

17 $T = \dfrac{PV}{k}$ **18** $v = \dfrac{I}{m} + u$

19 $b = \dfrac{2A}{h} - a$ **20** $x = 3(y + 2)$

21 $x = \tfrac{1}{2}y + 1$ **22** $y = \tfrac{1}{3}x - 2$

23 $A = 2(17 - H)$ **24** $x = \dfrac{2y + 6}{3}$

25 $y = \dfrac{3x - 6}{2}$ **26** $q = P + 12$

27 $x = \dfrac{y^2 + 12y}{2}$

Review Exercise

1 a £22   **b** 8 days
2 a £45   **b** £5.50
3 a £2000   **b** £700   **c** 7200 miles
4 a 15   **b** 28
5 9 trees
6 a 6 hours   **b** $P = 35h + 50$
7 a 25°C   **b** 32°F   **c** Fahrenheit, 37.8°
8 a 31   **b** 28
9 a   **i** 68°F
      ii 113°F
      iii 158°F
   b   **i** 100°C
      ii 50°C
      iii 25°C
10 a $P = 4x + 8$ **b** 15.5 cm
11 $P = 5a + 2b$
12 a 262.8 cm³   **b** 769.7 cm³   **c** 203.9 cm³
13 a 7   **b** 5
14 $b = \dfrac{P - 2a}{2}$
15 $x = \tfrac{1}{2}(P - 2y)$
16 $a = 2s - b - c$
17 $D = TV$
18 $h = \dfrac{2A}{a + b}$
19 $x = 5 - 2y$

Chapter 7 Answers

7.1 Get ready

1 Equilateral triangle
2 A square is a quadrilateral with 4 <u>equal</u> sides and 4 <u>equal</u> angles.

Exercise 7A

1 a pentagon   **b** hexagon   **c** octagon
2 a 720°   **b** 1080°   **c** 2340°   **d** 3240°
3 a 7   **b** 11   **c** 22

7.2 Get ready

1 $x = 53°$ **2** $x = 152$ **3** $x = 80$

Exercise 7B

1 $a = 102°$ $b = 55°$ $c = 93°$ $d = 85°$
    $e = 95°$ $f = 138°$ $g = 42°$
2 a 72°   **b** 120°   **c** 18°
3 a 108°   **b** 60°   **c** 162°
4 30 sides
5 36°, 10 sides

7.3 Get ready

1 a and **d**

Exercise 7C

1 **A** and **I**, **B** and **F**, **D** and **G**.
2 a **B** and **D**
   b **A** and **D**
   c **A** and **D**
3

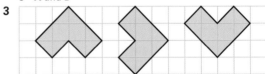

7.4 Get ready

1 a yes   **b** yes   **c** no

Exercise 7D

1 a

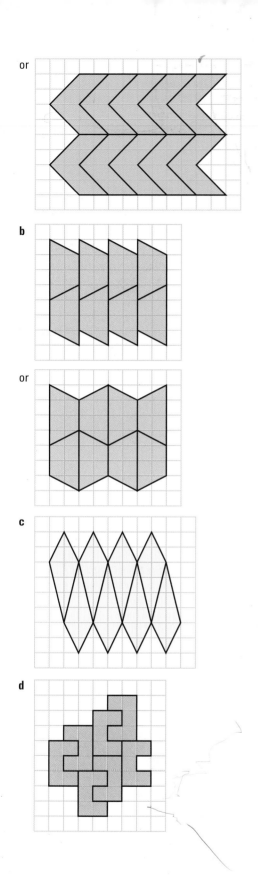

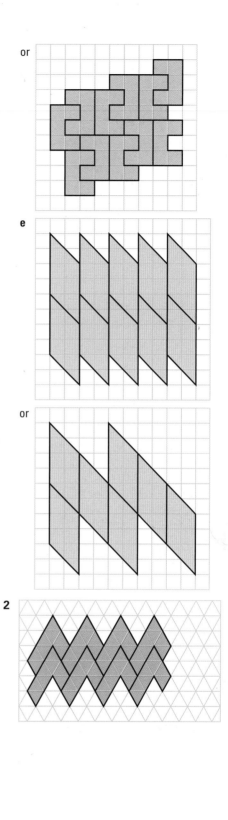

Answers

7.5 Get Ready

1 a
b
c
d
e

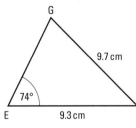

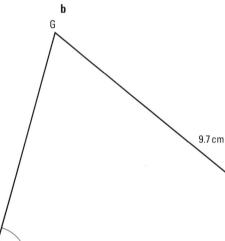

2 a   **b**

c   **d**

e

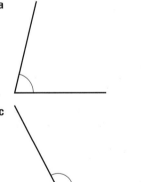

Exercise 7E

1 Students' accurate drawings

Exercise 7F

1 Students' accurate drawings
2 a Students' accurate drawing of quadrilateral
   b 6.2 cm
   c 68°
3 a

G

9.7 cm

74°

E   9.3 cm   *F*

b

G

9.7 cm

74°

E   9.3 cm   *F*

   c 6.3 cm
4 The two sides do not meet as the largest side
   (10.6 cm) is bigger than the sum of the other
   two sides (4.3 cm + 5.1 cm = 9.4 cm)
5 Students' drawings of parallel lines

7.6 Get ready

1

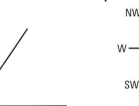

2 $a = 24°$
3 Students' drawings
4 $a = 68°$ $b = 112°$

Exercise 7G

1 a East   **b** North-east   **c** North-west
2 a 072°   **b** 225°   **c** 133°
   d 307°   **e** 220°   **f** 087°
3 a 080°   **b** 111°   **c** 291°

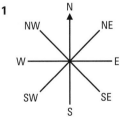

Exercise 7H

1 a 124°   b 320°   c 230°
2 Students' drawings
3 a 293°   b 075°   c 203°
4 a 054°   b 190°   c 263°
5

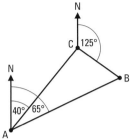

6 235°
7 348°
8 123°
9 295°
10 177°

7.7 Get ready

1 a 5600 cm   b 560 cm
2 a 12 : 24   b 27 : 9   c 12 : 24   d 24 : 12

Exercise 7I

1 11 km
2 a 1.4 km   b 17.4 cm
3

N
60°
10 miles (10 cm)

4

N
120°
2 km
(2 cm)

5 a

N
Milford ✕
2 km
(8 cm)
2.8 km
(11.2 cm)
✕ Hydeside
Whitley ✕

b i 2.3 km   ii 80°
6 19.9 km, 344°
7 108 yards, 017°
8 024°, 124 km
9 Students' accurate drawings

Review exercise

1 a A and C
   b

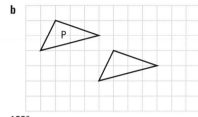

2 122°
3

4 a 078°
   b

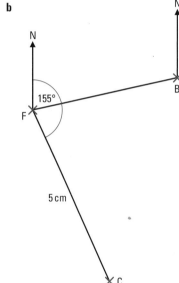

5 2.25 cm
6 1.46 m
7 Students' accurate drawings
8 Students' accurate drawings
9 Students' accurate drawings
10 a Hexagon
   b i 120°
      ii Angles on a straight line add up to 180°.
11 a 330°   b

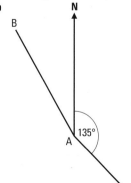

Answers

12 a 60°
  b 120°
13 a 130°
  b 325 km
  c

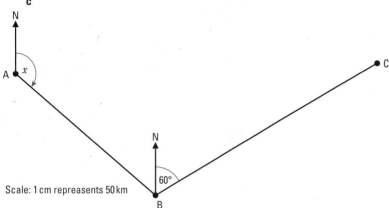

Scale: 1 cm repreasents 50 km

14 144°

Chapter 8 Answers

8.1 Get ready

1 a diameter   **b** radius   **c** circumference
2 a 2   **b** $\frac{1}{2}$

Exercise 8A

1 a 39.6 m   **b** 59.7 cm   **c** 26.4 cm
  d 78.5 mm   **e** 184.7 cm
2 a 21.7 cm   **b** 31.7 mm   **c** 16.7 cm
  d 30.5 cm   **e** 15.7 m
3 11.3 m
4 100.5 cm
5 a 4.49 m   **b** 0.94 m   **c** 4.78

Exercise 8B

1 a 14.5 m   **b** 6.4 cm   **c** 18.5 cm
  d 11.8 mm   **e** 31.8 cm
2 a 4.8 cm   **b** 11.4 mm   **c** 10.2 cm
  d 14.8 cm   **e** 7.9 m
3 59.8 cm

8.2 Get ready

1 78.54   **2** 28.27
3 483.61   **4** 799.44

Exercise 8C

1 a 81.7 m²   **b** 28.3 cm²   **c** 238 cm²
  d 726 mm²   **e** 278 cm²
2 a 707 cm²   **b** 468 mm²   **c** 43.0 cm²
  d 119 cm²   **e** 50.3 m²
3 154.6 m²
4 58.1 cm²
5 a 380 cm²   **b** 81 cm²   **c** 299 cm²
6 411 cm²

8.3 Get ready

1 76.97   **2** 48.69
3 123.37   **4** 16.49

Exercise 8D

1 a i 46.3 cm   **ii** 127 cm²
  b i 25.7 m   **ii** 39.3 m²
  c i 30.8 cm   **ii** 56.5 cm²
  d i 14.3 cm   **ii** 12.6 cm²
  e i 22.1 cm   **ii** 30.2 cm²
  f i 57.8 m   **ii** 103 m²
2 a 3.21 m²   **b** £89.96
3 a 28.5 cm²   **b** 35.7 cm

Review exercise

1 30.9 cm²
2 a 2 cm   **b** 175.9 cm²
3 50.27 cm
4 157 cm²
5 314 cm²
6 2.04 m
7 20.57 cm
8 a 7854 cm²   **b** 125.7 cm
9 £134.40
10 £36.80

Chapter 9 Answers

9.1 Get ready

1   **2**   **3**

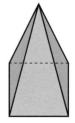

Exercise 9A

1 a 1C, 3A, 4B
b Net of cuboid

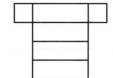

2 a

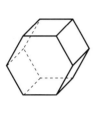 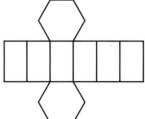

b

 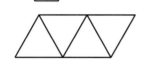

3 a Cuboid but others are possible — most paper is rectangular
Many different possibilities.

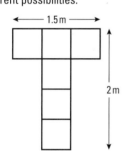

b Cylinder – oil is a liquid and a cylinder will hold more, also less corners for it to get stuck in.

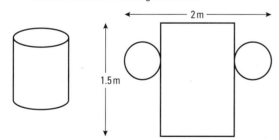

9.2 Get ready

1 A and **T**, **B** and **X**, **C** and **Z**

Exercise 9B

1

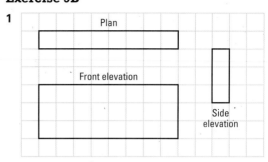

2 a Front elevation   Plan   Side elevation

b Front elevation   Plan   Side elevation

c Front elevation   Plan   Side elevation

3 a   **b**

9.3 Get ready

1 a 45.4 cm^2 **b** 14.5 cm^2

Exercise 9C

1 a 565 cm^3 **b** 188 cm^3 **c** 198 cm^3
2 2.82 cm
3 a 32 **b** 0.696 m^3

Exercise 9D

1 a 15.71 cm **b** 141.37 cm^2 **c** 19.63 cm^2
d 180.63 cm^2
2 a 94.25 cm^2 **b** 226.19 cm^2
3 251.33 cm^2

9.4 Get ready

1 24 cm^2 **2** 8.4 m^2 **3** 28.27 m^2

Exercise 9E

1 a 12   **b** 8
c

d 24   **e** 32

f

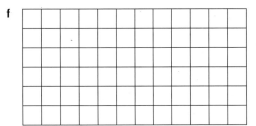

g 36

h 72

i i $\frac{24}{12} = 2$ ii $\frac{36}{12} = 3$ These give the scale factor.

j i $\frac{32}{8} = 4$ ii $\frac{72}{8} = 9$ These are the scale factor squared.

k i 96 ii 512

2 a 16 cm and 20 cm

b 72 cm

c 320 cm^2

3 180 cm^2.

4 a 60 m **b** 2500 m^2.

5 54 cm^2.

6 80 cm and 384 cm^2.

Exercise 9F

1 a 2 **b** 480 cm^3

2 540 cm^3

3 268 cm^3

4 2187 cm^3

5 30 cm $\times$ 24 cm $\times$ 12 cm

9.5 Get ready

1 a 2.5 m **b** 35 cm **c** 630 cm

d 0.35 km **e** 1500 m **f** 36 mm

Exercise 9G

1 a 30 000 cm^2 **b** 45 000 cm^2 **c** 3 cm^2

d 0.34 cm^2

2 a 6 000 000 m^2 **b** 400 000 m^2 **c** 2 m^2

d 0.345 m^2

3 1.45 m^2

4 2.25 m^2

5 a 1.4 m^2 **b** 14 000 cm^2

6 200

7 11.7 m^2

8 1350 cm^2

Exercise 9H

1 a 4 000 000 cm^3 **b** 4.5 cm^3 **c** 0.4 cm^3

d 3000 cm^3

2 a 0.4 litres **b** 5.6 litres

c 1 000 000 ml **d** 0.0035 litres

3 1 000 000

4 a 144 cm^3 **b** 144 000 mm^3

5 42 000 cm^3

6 100

7 675 000 litres

8 2100

9 2.1 cm

10 962

Review exercise

1

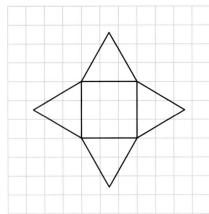

2

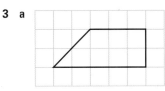

3 a

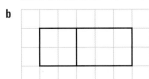

b

4 a 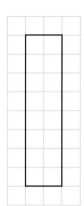   **b**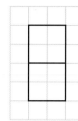

5 5 cm

6 A

7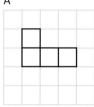

8

9 150

10 a 5 cm

  b i 19   **ii** 8

11 a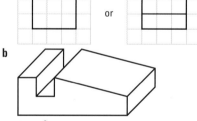

  b

  c 27 cm³

12 503 cm³

13 4.21 m²

14 9.3 cm

15 a 994   **b** 361 cm³

16 Area of floor = 5 × 3 = 15 m²
  Cost of carpet = £18.50 × 15 = £277.50
  Cost of underlay = £3.50 × 15 = £52.50
  Room perimeter = 2(5 + 3) = 16 m
  Height of room = 2.5 m
  Therefore 9 rolls of wallpaper are needed.
  Cost of wallpaper = £25 × 9 = £225
  Total cost = 277.50 + 52.50 + 225 = £555

17 a The cup can hold 159 m*l*

  b 3 bottles, £3.75

18 2430 cm²

19 1250 mm²

20 800 cm³

21 a 250 cm²   **b** 73.49 cm²

22 6540 km³

Chapter 10 Answers

10.1 Get ready

1 ⎯⎯⎯⎯⎯⎯⎯⎯⎯⎯⎯⎯ 5 cm

2

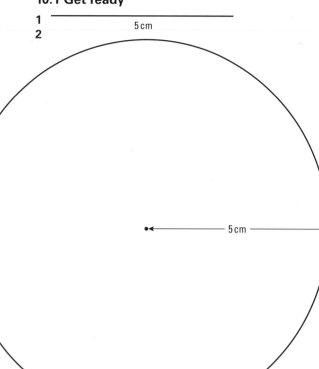

Exercise 10A

1 a 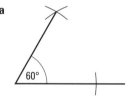   **b**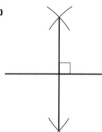

c 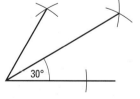   **d**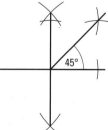

e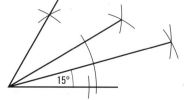

Answers

2 a

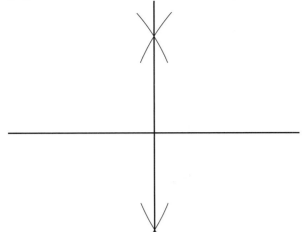

d

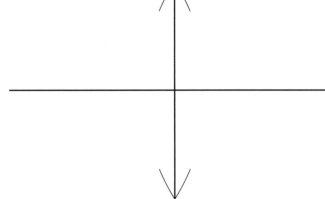

b

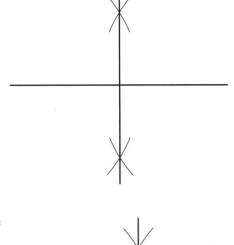

3 a

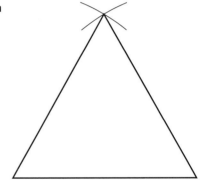

c

b

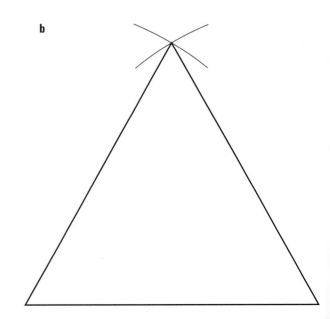

c

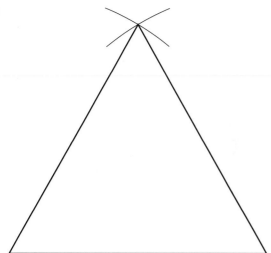

b

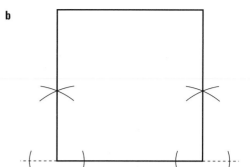

d

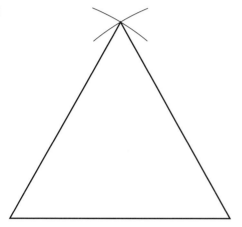

4 a

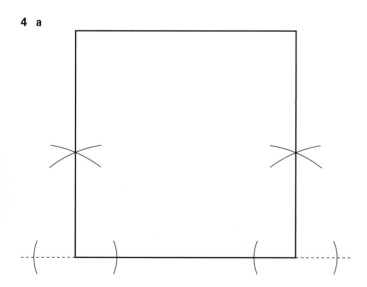

c

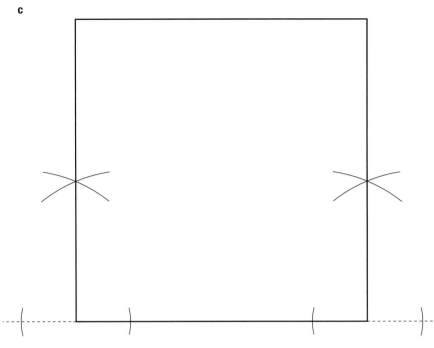

d

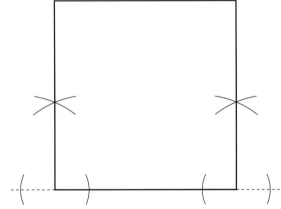

5.

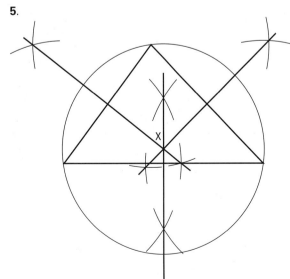

6

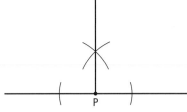

7

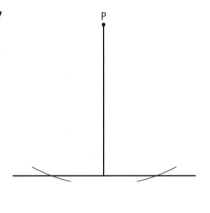

8

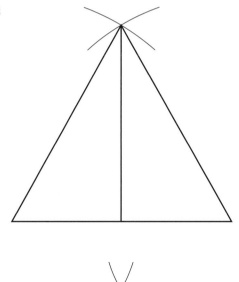

9

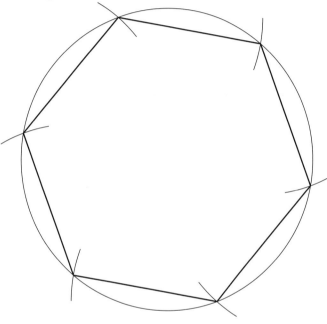

10

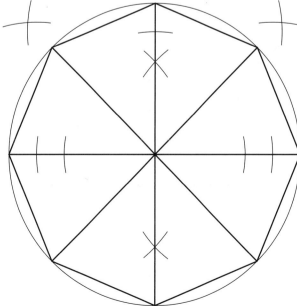

11

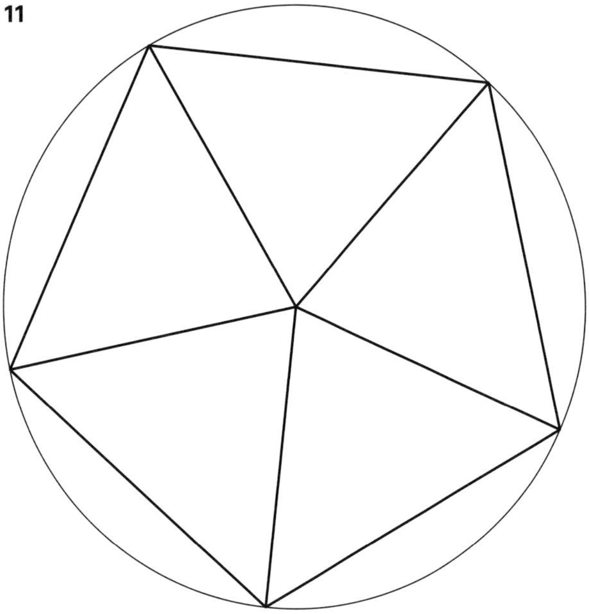

2

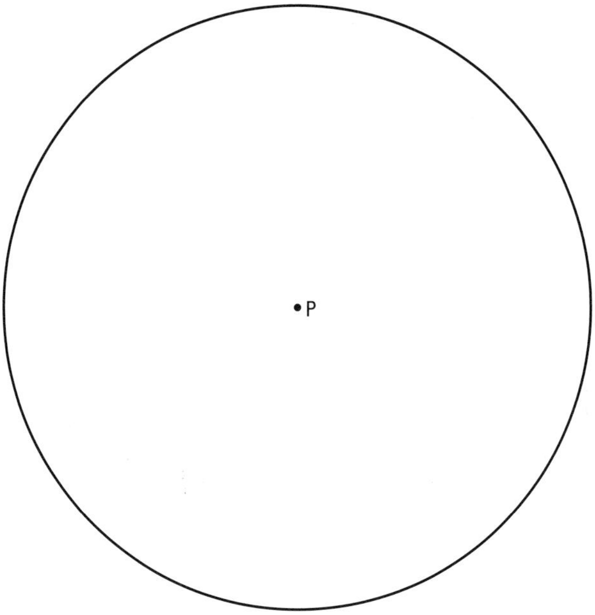

10.2 Get ready

1

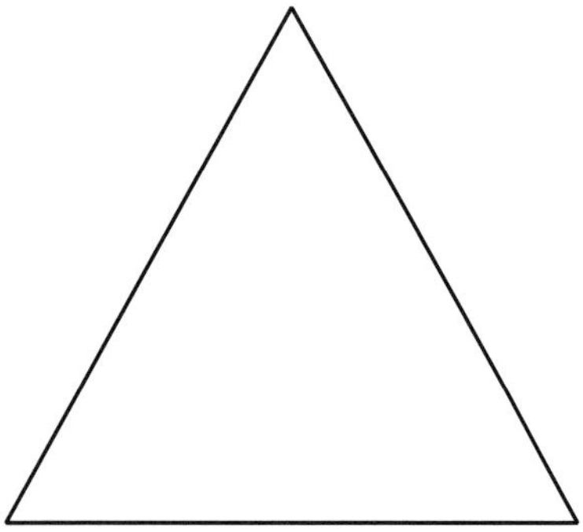

3

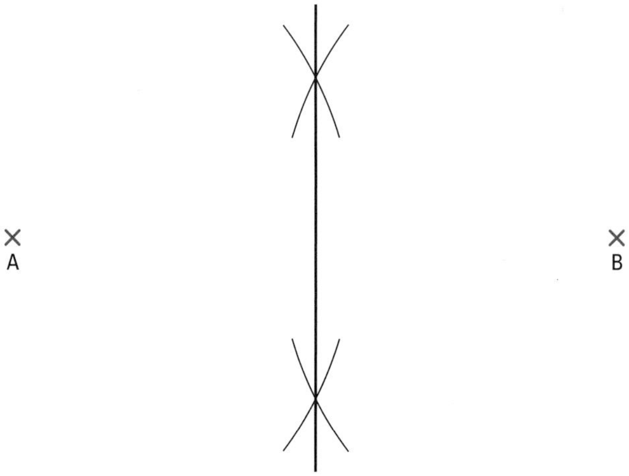

Exercise 10B

1

4

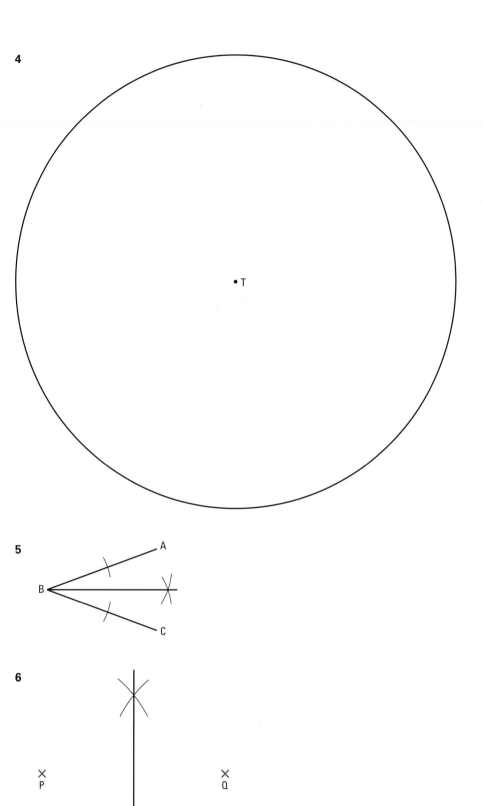

5

6

Answers

7

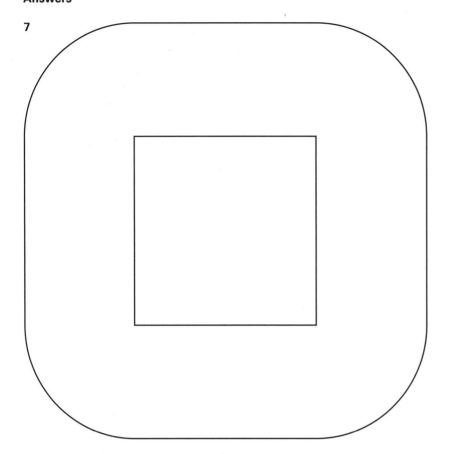

8

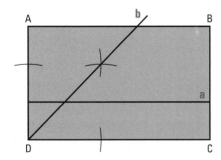

9

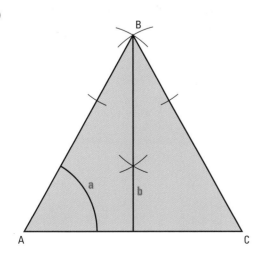

10

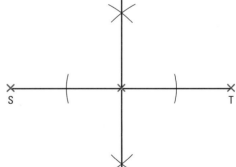

11

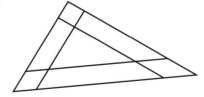

12

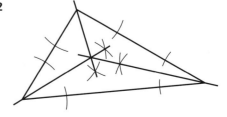

10.3 Get ready

1

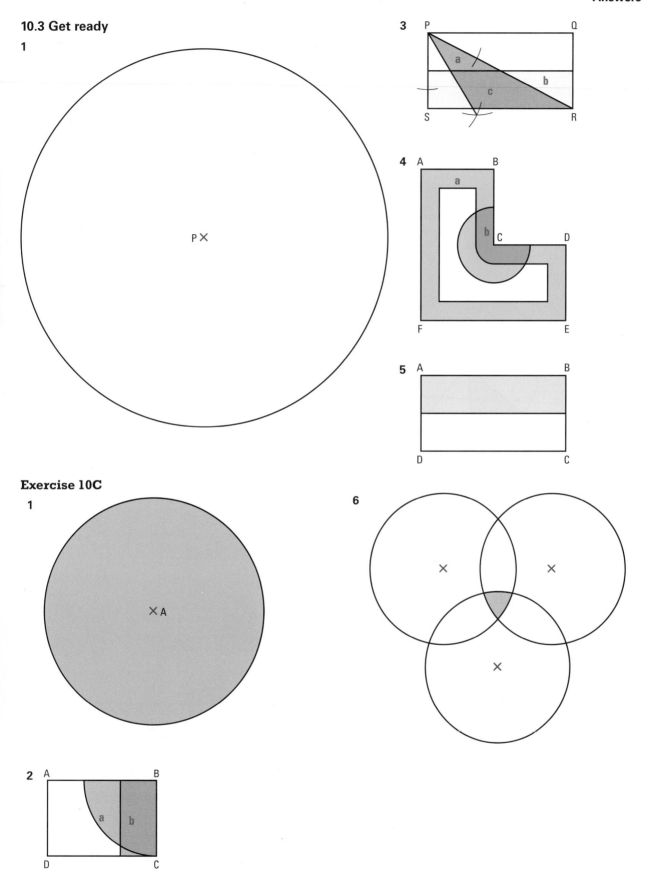

Exercise 10C

1

2

7

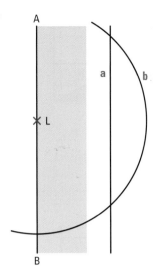

10

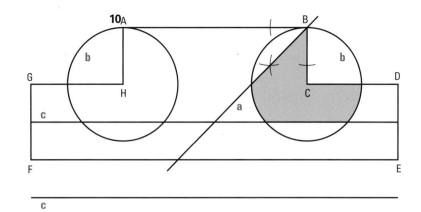

8

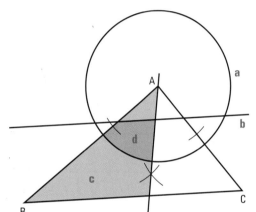

9

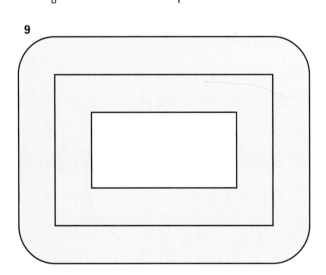

Review exercise

1

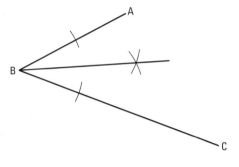

2

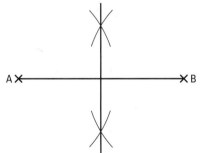

3

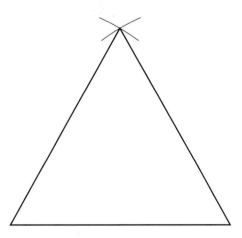

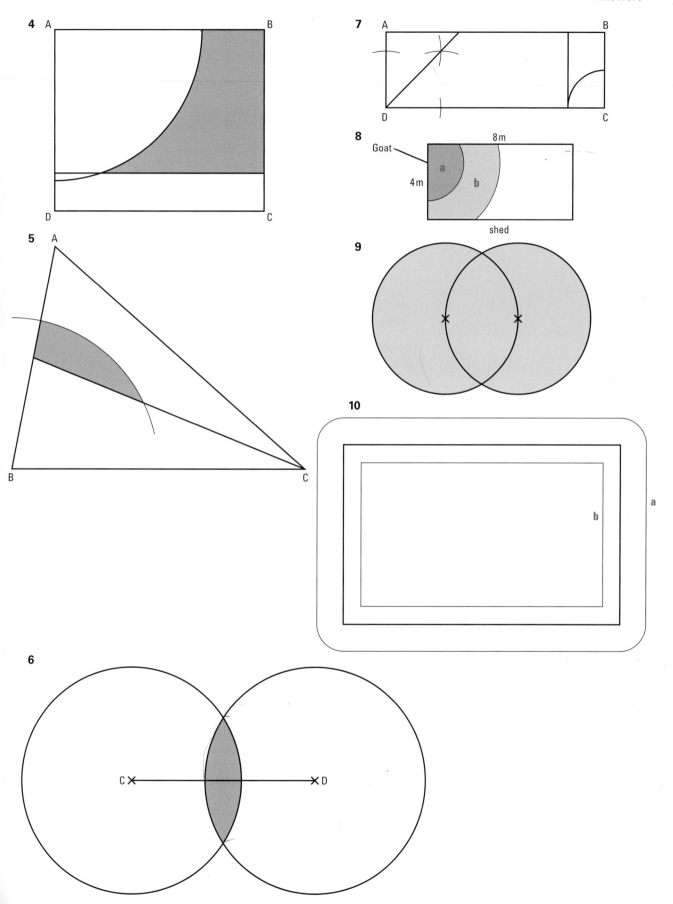

4

5

6

7

8

Goat
8 m
a
4 m
b
shed

9

10
a
b

11

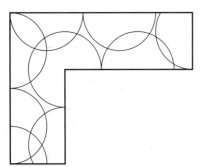

12

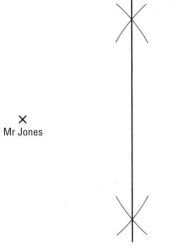

Mr Jones   Mr Parry

13 a

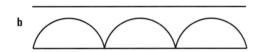

b

Chapter 11 Answers

11.1 Get ready

1 Symmetrical letters:
  A B C D E H I K M N O S T U V W X Y Z

Exercise 11A

1	Rotation	**2**	Translation
3	Enlargement	**4**	Reflection
5	Enlargement	**6**	Reflection
7	Rotation	**8**	Translation
9	Translation	**10**	Rotation
11	Enlargement	**12**	Reflection

11.2 Get ready

1 4 right and 5 up
  2 right, 2 up, 2 right, 3 up
  3 right, 5 up, 1 right

Exercise 11B

1 a

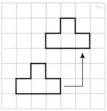

b

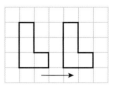

c

d

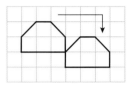

e

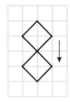

f

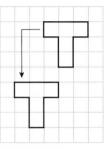

g

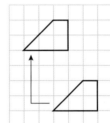

h

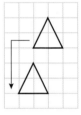

2

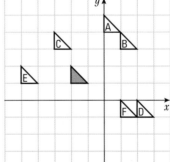

3 a $\begin{pmatrix} 5 \\ -4 \end{pmatrix}$ **b** $\begin{pmatrix} -1 \\ -4 \end{pmatrix}$ **c** $\begin{pmatrix} -4 \\ 3 \end{pmatrix}$ **d** $\begin{pmatrix} 2 \\ 5 \end{pmatrix}$

  e $\begin{pmatrix} 6 \\ -3 \end{pmatrix}$ **f** $\begin{pmatrix} 5 \\ 2 \end{pmatrix}$ **g** $\begin{pmatrix} -2 \\ -3 \end{pmatrix}$ **h** $\begin{pmatrix} 3 \\ 2 \end{pmatrix}$

4 a $\begin{pmatrix} 6 \\ -2 \end{pmatrix}$ **b** $\begin{pmatrix} 1 \\ 5 \end{pmatrix}$ **c** $\begin{pmatrix} -7 \\ -4 \end{pmatrix}$ **d** $\begin{pmatrix} 7 \\ 4 \end{pmatrix}$

  e $\begin{pmatrix} -6 \\ 2 \end{pmatrix}$ **f** $\begin{pmatrix} 5 \\ -7 \end{pmatrix}$

11.3 Get ready

1 a 3 **b** 2 **c** 2 **d** 4

Exercise 11C

1 a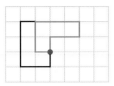

b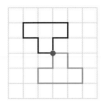

c

d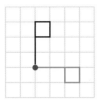

d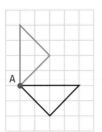

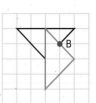

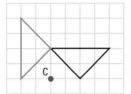

2 a

b

c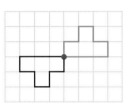

d

4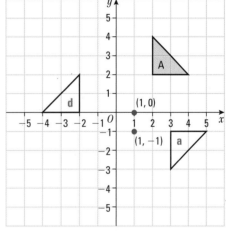

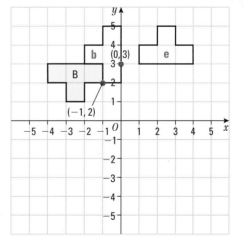

3 a

b

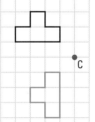

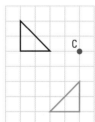

c

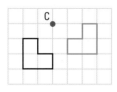

Answers

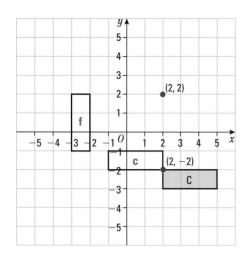

Exercise 11D

1 **a** Rotation of 90° clockwise about $(-1, 0)$
   b Rotation of 90° clockwise about $(0, 0)$
   c Rotation of 180° about $(0, 0)$
   d Rotation of 90° anticlockwise about $(0, 0)$
2 **a** Rotation of 90° anticlockwise about $(-2, 2)$
   b Rotation of 180° about $(2, 1)$
   c Rotation of 90° clockwise about $(0, -1)$
   d Rotation of 180° about $(0, 2)$

11.4 Get ready

1 **a** 1   **b** 0   **c** 1   **d** 6

Exercise 11E

1 **a** **b**

     c **d**

     e **f**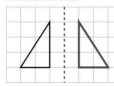

     g 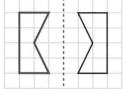 **h**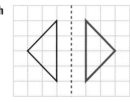

2 **a** 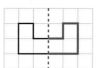 **b**

     c 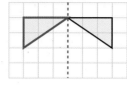 **d**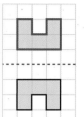

     e 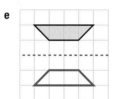 **f**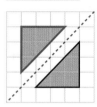

     g 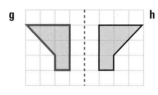 **h**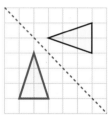

Exercise 11F

1 **a** Reflection in the x-axis
   b Reflection in the y-axis
   c Reflection in the x-axis
   d Reflection in the line $x = 2$
   e Reflection in the line $y = -2$
   f Reflection in the line $x = -1$
2 **a** Reflection in the y-axis
   b Reflection in the line $y = 2$
   c Reflection in the line $x = 3$
   d Reflection in the line $y = x$
   e Reflection in the line $y = 3\frac{1}{2}$
   f Reflection in the line $y = -x$
   g Reflection in the line $y = -1\frac{1}{2}$
3 **a** Reflection in the line $y = 1$
   b Reflection in the line $y = x$
   c Reflection in the line $y = -x$
   d Reflection in the line $x = 1\frac{1}{2}$
   e Reflection in the line $y = -x$
   f Reflection in the line $y = x$

11.5 Get ready

1

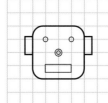

Exercise 11G

1

2

3

4

5

6

7

8

9
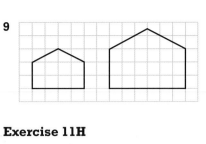

Exercise 11H

1 a
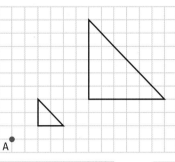

b **c**
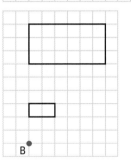 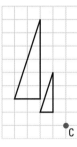

d **e**
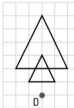

f

2 a
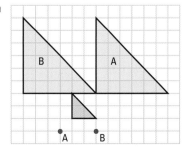

Answers

b

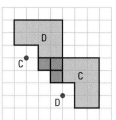

c

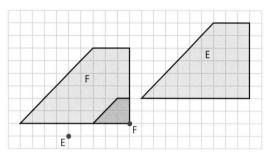

3 a

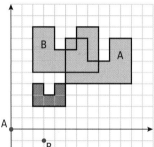

b

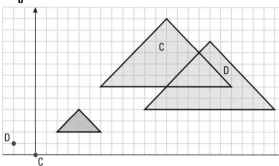

c

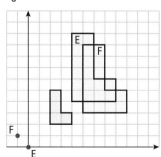

Exercise 11I

1 **a** Enlargement sf 3 centre (1, 3)
  b Enlargement sf 2 centre (9, 0)
  c Enlargement sf 3 centre (2, 2)
2 **a** Enlargement sf 2 centre (8, 8)
  b Enlargement sf 3 centre (0, 7)
  c Enlargement sf 2 centre (9, 4)

11.6 Get ready

1

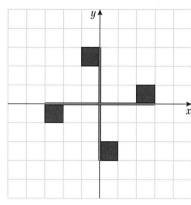

Exercise 11J

1 ab

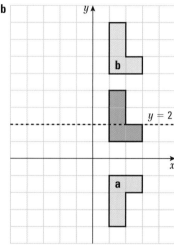

  c Translation by $\begin{pmatrix} 0 \\ 4 \end{pmatrix}$

2 ab

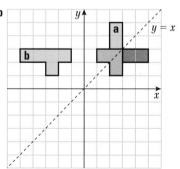

  c Reflection in the y-axis

3 ab

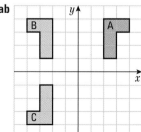

  c Rotation of 180° about point (0, 0)

4 ab

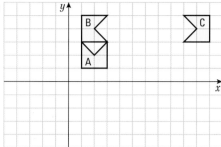

c Rotation of 90° anticlockwise about (6, 6)

5 a

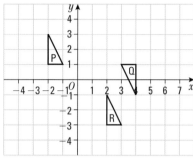

b Translation $\begin{pmatrix} 4 \\ -4 \end{pmatrix}$

Review exercise

1 a

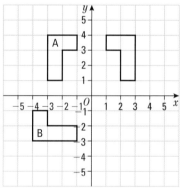

b Rotation 90° anticlockwise about (0, 0)

2

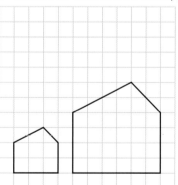

3

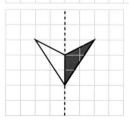

4

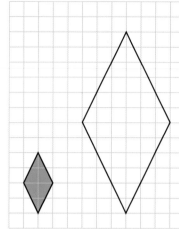

5

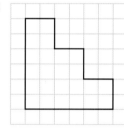

6 a, b

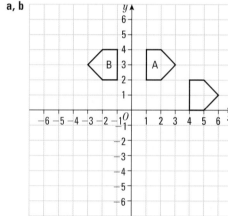

7 a, b

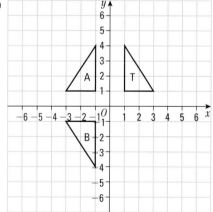

c Enlargement scale factor 3, centre O

Answers

8

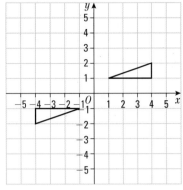

9 Reflection in the y-axis

10 a

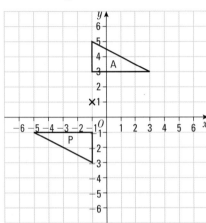

b

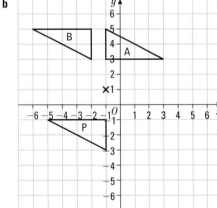

c

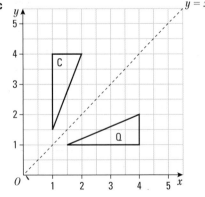

11 Rotation 90° clockwise about $(-2, 3)$

12 a Reflection in the line $y = x$

b

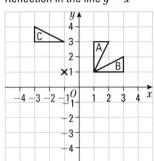

13 a

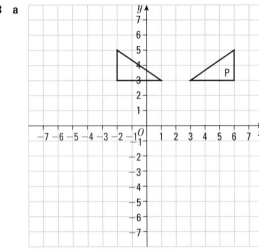

b Translation by $\begin{pmatrix} 5 \\ -4 \end{pmatrix}$

14 Rotation 180° about $(1, 0)$

Chapter 12 Answers

12.1 Get ready

1	**a**	16	**b**	5.29	**c**	625
2	**a**	5	**b**	13	**c**	0.5

3

a

b

c

d

Exercise 12A

1	**a**	$h = 13$ cm	**b**	$p = 5.83$ cm	**c**	$s = 25$ cm
	d	$v = 8.38$ cm	**e**	$q = 6.19$ cm	**f**	$t = 7.4$ cm
	g	$m = 11.7$ cm	**h**	$n = 5.66$ cm	**i**	$w = 6.08$ cm
2	**a**	15.7 cm	**b**	6.32 cm	**c**	26.6 cm
	d	11.0 cm	**e**	9.79 cm	**f**	10.0 cm
	g	13.6 cm	**h**	8.44 cm	**i**	8.32 cm

3 a 33.2 cm
  b 27 cm
4 £1467.50

12.2 Get ready

1 a 9   **b** 16   **c** 26.07
  d 144   **e** 576
2 a 3   **b** 4   **c** 13
  d 2.5   **e** 24
3 a

  b

  c

  d

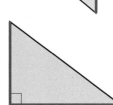

Exercise 12B

1 a $x = 12$ cm   **b** $y = 3$ cm   **c** $s = 7$ cm
  d $r = 11.5$ cm   **e** $v = 4.50$ cm   **f** $t = 9.30$ cm
  g $m = 6$ cm   **h** $n = 3.75$ cm   **i** $w = 4.85$ cm
2 a 5 cm   **b** 4 cm   **c** 0.7 cm
  d 9.60 cm   **e** 4.8 cm   **f** 6.58 cm
  g 10.4 cm   **h** 7.49 cm   **i** 4.62 cm
3 7.35 m
4 £54 127

12.3 Get ready

1 and **3**

Exercise 12C

1 a Yes   **b** No   **c** No
  d No   **e** Yes   **f** No
2 Jenny has squared the sum of the shorter sides. She should
  have squared the shorter sides *then* added.
  $12^2 = 144$; $6^2 + 6^2 = 36 + 36 = 72$
  Since $12^2 \neq 6^2 + 6^2$, PQR is not a right-angled triangle.
3 Jason has squared the sum of the shorter sides. He should
  have squared the shorter sides *then* added.
  $10^2 = 100$; $6^2 + 8^2 = 36 + 64 = 100$
  Since $10^2 = 6^2 + 8^2$, PQR is a right-angled triangle.
4 a Acute-angled   **b** Obtuse-angled
  c Acute-angled   **d** Obtuse-angled
  e Right-angled   **f** Acute-angled

12.4 Get ready

1 5.4 cm   **2** 6.9 cm   **3** 9.6 cm

Exercise 12D

1 a 4.47   **b** 5.83   **c** 5   **d** 4.24
  e 6.40   **f** 3.61   **g** 9.90   **h** 9.06
  i 7.21   **j** 5.83
2 a 7.07   **b** 8.49   **c** 10.6   **d** 11.4
3 a 14.1   **b** 15.3   **c** 11.4   **d** 9.43
  e 13.6   **f** 12.7

Review exercise

1 10.63 cm
2 a 30 cm^2 **b** 169 cm^2
3 11.9 cm
4 56 cm
5 230 km
6 19.4 cm
7 6.71 cm
8 $2.5^2 = 6.25$; $1.5^2 + 2^2 = 2.25 + 4 = 6.25$
  Since $2.5^2 = 1.5^2 + 2^2$, ABC is a right-angled triangle.
9 5.10 cm
10 7.6 cm
11 8.8 km
12 84 cm^2
13 28.6 cm^2
14 £54 000
15 AB is 10

Number

1 An even number of 5p coins will give a even total. The total
  will remain even wen you add 2p coins, so an odd total such
  as 23p cannot be made.
2 3 fish and chips, 2 sausage and chips
3 One 5 kg pack and four 3 kg packs
4 4%
5 20% extra in the pack is the best value for the customer
6 Prices are increased by 12%, as $0.8 \times 1.4 = 1.12$

2D Shapes

1 $x = 30°$ **2** 65°   **3** 3.53 km
4 3.66 m   **5** 24 cm

Money management

1 £142.88
2 £5.28 per week = £15.84 for three weeks
3 £6545 in income tax and £3526.60 in NIC   Total £10,071.60

Kitchen Design

1 No set answer but all conditions must be met for full marks
2 Using 305 mm square £132   Using 330 mm square £160
3

	White	Coloured	Cost
10 × 10	54	36	£7.98 + £2 + £9.98 = £19.96
15 × 15	24	16	£8.99 + £8 = £16.99